C000234830

THE LIVES OF A SHOWMAN

The Lives of a Showman

Mark Lewis

Mark Lewis Entertainment
Toronto

Design by Ariel Frailich

ISBN 978-0-9867329-0-4

To Dennis.
I can't believe he is gone….

Table of Contents

Foreword ix
Acknowledgements xi
A Few Words from My Friends xiii

The Early Years: How I Became a Magician 1
The Later Early Years: Making a Living 23
I Become a Professional Magician 43
No Business Like Show Business 63
On the Road in Showbusiness 79
The University of Evil 93
More Evil at The University 111
The Emerald Isle 135
Auntie Annie 157
How I Became Psychic 179
Canada and the Psychic Fairs 207
The Showman and the Shaman 235
The Showman and the Shaman—Part Two 269
The Final Word 295

Foreword

He's relentless, this Mark Lewis.

Hopefully now, by providing this brief introduction to his memoir, he will kindly remove any reference to me from its pages. I admit that I did work for him some thirty years ago, pitching *Svengali* decks in several department stores in Toronto. I learned a great deal. I learned, in particular, how challenging the life could be. Now you have that opportunity.

Like many others interested in magic and the performing arts, I have acquired thousands of books on the subject. The books that resonate most with me are the ones by performers, those who were out there every day, earning a dollar or two as itinerant showmen. Books like *The Life and Times of Augustus Rapp*, or *Illusion Show* by David Bamberg, self-portraits of magicians that travelled only as far as the public would permit. These books trace triumph and hardship on an ever-shifting terrain. I am pleased that Mark has added to this oeuvre.

The Lives of a Showman is not just a self-portrait of a magician, grafter and seer, but it is also a portrait of a landscape—one spread across several countries and continents. From night clubs in London, to hustling in Blackpool, to upheaval in Ireland during "The Troubles", and the open space of the new world. We are richer for it.

Although he has adopted many names and personae over the years, particularly in the Internet Age, there is only one Mark Lewis. He is a caring, compassionate man—traits not normally associate with a *grafter*. He is also a keen observer of human nature, an excellent storyteller and engaging performer. He knows his audience, and despite his protestations to the contrary, he listens to it.

With this memoir, you now have the chance to listen to him.

David Ben

A rare day off work

Acknowledgements

Special Acknowledgement

The book you are holding in your hands would not have come into existence if it were not for the vision of David Ben. David is the artistic director of Magicana, a non-profit organisation devoted to the promotion of conjuring as an art form.

It was David who first proposed the idea of this work. He seemed to think my adventures would make an interesting story and he cajoled me into putting it all down in writing. It was he who suggested the title and although at first I had a certain reluctance towards it, as time went by it grew on me and subsequently many people have told me that they think the title to be very apt.

I have always considered David to be not only a scholar of magic but a patron of the art. Through Magicana he promotes conjuring through books, lectures and performances. He spends enormous amounts of time on these projects and sometimes I think this activity is not always appreciated as much as it should be.

It is through individuals like David that the ART that is magic will flourish as an art form rather than just a mere entertainment.

This book is not a magic book. But yet magic is always lurking in the background. I hope that after you finish reading it you will be pleased that David persuaded me to write it.

Special Thanks

No author writes a book alone. There all sorts of people who make it happen. First of all I have to acknowledge all the various characters who show up in the book itself. They are all quite real although when I re-read the whole thing even I am tempted to say that I am not sure they exist. Truly the truth is often stranger than fiction.

I have to thank David Ben for starting this book off in the first place. Still, I have given him a special acknowledgement elsewhere all on his own so I expect he will be happy with that. No doubt it will make him feel very grand and important.

I have three other people to acknowledge. First is Ariel Frailich who I have often said is a genius who knows everything. He is the one responsible for laying out this book and for giving invaluable advice about publishing it. He understands books as he understands nearly everything else.

The second person I have to thank is Jeff Pinsky of the Browser's Den of Magic. He is a shrewd shopkeeper as well as a good friend who has given me very good advice on the marketing of this tome. If I make tons of money from this work he will get the credit (but of course no money). If I lose money on the book he will be getting the blame (and definitely no money).

And of course I have to acknowledge Lisa Close and I have absolutely no idea why. I love her dearly even though she has told me repeatedly that this is a dreadful book full of mistakes and she wants nothing to do with it. Still, she has given me a strange sort of guidance, since over the years, whatever she tells me I always do the exact opposite and it always works out well.

You will find Lisa in this book whether she likes it or not. She is after all, part of the life of a showman.

A Few Words from My Friends

I have noticed that most memoirs and autobiographies seem to have a slow start. Mine is no exception. I nearly fell asleep with boredom writing the first chapter. I hope my reader keeps awake while reading it. If he does he will find his reward comes later on.

Anyway I had the idea of spicing up the beginning by asking a few of my friends to write some introductory remarks. Here is the first one by the infamous Jolly Roger, an old friend of mine. Roger is an accomplished children's entertainer, formerly resident in the UK and now an inhabitant of Arizona. But why do I say he is infamous? Oh, never mind. The less said the better....

Instead read his introduction.

It was in the early sixties that I attended the Boy's and Girls exhibition at Bingley Hall in Birmingham, England. I was a teenager, and the prime purpose of the visit was to see a live performance by the pop group "Freddie and the Dreamers". On entering the Hall, I was witness to a large crowd gathering around one of the counters. "Surely this was not Freddie Garrity signing autographs?" I headed towards the crowd to investigate, and came within earshot of a loud rasping Scottish voice saying such things as "Take your time but hurry up". "I like children. I had one for breakfast this morning". "Here's pack number one, here's pack number two, here's pack number three..........which pack shall we use?" "If you move your legs forward, your body will follow automatically.... it's called walking!" On walking closer as instructed, I witnessed a slight gentleman with black hair and glasses, and a devious yet likeable demeanour. He was performing magic tricks and flourishes with a trick pack of playing cards. At the end of the demonstration, many folk in the crowd were reaching for their wallets with intent on purchasing these cards. This was my first encounter with the great Mark Lewis! Who would have known that this was the start of a friendship lasting for over four decades?

It was a few years later after I left drama school in London, and was seeking temporary employment as a resting actor, that our paths crossed again. This time we were working together selling these same trick cards known as the "Svengali Deck" at The Ideal Homes Exhibition at Olympia. We were working for a gentleman called Ron MacMillan, who was, in his younger days, one of the top night club acts in Europe. His dexterity involved the manipulation of billiard balls. We were at opposite ends of the counter, but both managed to draw huge crowds as each of us had extremely loud voices! We teamed up on a number of occasions over the years at Exhibitions like the Festival of Mind, Body and Spirit in London and The Spring show in Dublin. In the early nineties, we both independently decided to leave the UK. Mark immigrated to Canada and me to the USA. Since the advent of the internet, we have been active members of various magicians' forums. Each of us regularly gets banned from some of these for speaking our minds! Isn't it odd how so often others don't like to hear the truth?

Mark is one of the truly interesting characters in the world of showbusiness. He has a brilliant yet wicked sense of humour, and is often misunderstood by his peers. As someone who has known him for much of his life, I consider him to be a man of incredible talent as both a performer and grafter (demonstrator). He is extremely resourceful, and is a walking encyclopedia when it comes to magic and other branches of entertainment. His life is truly one of mystery and intrigue, and he is a wonderful raconteur as will be seen in the pages of this masterpiece. I would consider Mark to be a true showman, and his personality is indeed multi-faceted. I know you will love reading "The Lives of a Showman".

—Roger Blakiston (Jolly Roger)
Arizona 2010

Next we have something from Jeff Pinsky. I mentioned this gentleman in the acknowledgements section. No harm in mentioning him again. As I stated he is the owner of the Browser's Den of Magic in Toronto. This is a very fine magic shop in the Bathurst and Eglinton area of Toronto (at the time of writing anyway) and is well worth a visit. Here is his contribution:

What thoughts enter my mind when I hear the name Mark Lewis? I presume that for many who have met him a collage of images enter their thoughts. Images that include pitchman, hypnotist, close-up magician, children's entertainer, and psychic. Combine those images with his personality and you have the unforgettable Mark Lewis.

I operate a magic shop in Toronto, Canada and I have known this character for about sixteen years. Over those years I have had countless dinners and conversations with him. I have also done business with him. I consider Mark a very good friend and I am very thankful that he asked me to write something for his book.

He is so talented in many areas but at least for me I most enjoy his close-up magic; or perhaps I should write close-up experience?

I have seen him do close-up magic for laymen and magicians hundreds of times. There are very few others who perform close-up magic who would want to follow this master performer. For real people it is more than just watching Mark Lewis—it is an EXPERIENCE! An experience they will not soon forget. And that is Mark's goal. He has told me and others countless times that although he certainly wants his magic to be strong, it is HE, that he wants laymen to walk away remembering—and they do!

For those of us in the magic community and for others with whom he has had more than just fleeting moments, Mark Lewis is a character. And I am certain that I will never meet in my life another Mark Lewis.

I talk with Mark Lewis more than almost anyone else in my life. I do so because whether he likes me writing this or not, I care for him deeply. I know that he is not perfect but deep down he is a wonderful person.

So what thoughts enter my mind when I hear the name Mark Lewis? For me all of the above but predominantly the most unforgettable person I have ever met.

Mark Lewis loves the book Royal Road to Card Magic. *Mark can literally do 95% of the tricks in that book. He would probably correct me and say 100% and he's most likely correct.*

So I hope, dear reader that you enjoy the royal road of Mark's book as he takes you up and down and sideways through his life; most definitely a life worth reading about.

—Jeff Pinsky, *Browser's Den of Magic*
Toronto, Canada
July 21, 2010

And now here are a few words from one of my favourite people. I first met Tony Moore (or Antony as I have always known him) when he was around thirteen years old. He has always known me as Ronnie. He has grown to become highly respected as a musician and songwriter. He recently received a Gold Badge award for his services to the music industry. My chest puffs out with pride every time I hear of any of his achievements and I brag about them incessantly to everyone I know. You would almost think it was me getting the recognition rather than him. Here is what he had to say:

I first met Ronnie McLeod (as I knew him) in the early 70's when I was about twelve or thirteen. I had just stumbled on the ability to spring cards from hand to hand when my parents took me to the Bristol Ideal Homes exhibition, where I saw Ronnie sit at a booth with a big sign saying, "Magic Demonstrations". After seeing him also springing the cards, I precociously went up to him and said, "I can do that!" Thus began a long working relationship with Ronnie, learning magic and selling Svengali decks. I did two summer seasons in Blackpool and even went to Toronto with him for three months when I was nineteen years old.

Those days taught me so much about life AND gave me an income that I used to buy expensive keyboards and equipment, ready to start my life as a professional musician. I always look back fondly on my time spent with him. To many he appeared mean and moody, but to me he was the most generous of souls and a man of honour and passion, a real friend. I eventually stopped working for him to go and play in a band that no one had ever heard of, a band called Iron Maiden... but that's another story.

—Tony Moore
London , 2010

Last but certainly not least is a contribution by Jeff Hinchliffe, a very fine young card magician who is garnering quite a reputation in Toronto for his work. I expect this reputation will become even more widespread in time to come.

Let me tell you a story about this young man. When I first met him he was shy and timid. Then I put him to work selling svengali decks in a Toronto shopping mall. On the first day he was quiet, nervous and very lacking in confidence. By the end of the week he had transformed into an aggressive, animated and quite vocal young showman. It was the most astonishing metamorphosis I have ever seen. A caterpillar changing into a butterfly in the space of one week. Sometimes I think I have created a Frankenstein's monster but that is another story. Anyway read what he has to say:

I've known Mark Lewis for over twelve years now. I first met him as a quiet, shy, fourteen-year-old who'd fallen in love with magic (I'm neither quiet nor shy any more, according to Mark). I'm glad to say we became friends. I've worked for Mark in a variety of environments, from pitching Svengali packs, to working his booth at a Psychic Fair, to assisting him on stage during his hypnosis show. I've gained a lot of confidence and experience working for Mark. His knowledge of magic and things related is immense. I don't know what he saw in me, but I'm glad he saw it. His patience and advice over the years have always been helpful and appreciated.

We all have memories from when we first began taking magic seriously. One of the most vivid memories I have is thanks to Mark. I was fifteen, and I'd just written an essay on magic. It was written in response to various professionals telling me that the most important part of one's performance was for the audience to be entertained. Of course, I noticed this approach was often being espoused by the pros who were somewhat lacking in technical ability (these same pros would often also wholly discount the need for technical wizardry). Being a move-monkey at the time, I was sceptical of this viewpoint and decided to think more about it. My essay ended up suggesting that there wasn't any 'one thing' that was most important. Rather, technical ability, a sense of mystery, and entertainment value were all equally important. You needed to have chops, you needed to fool them, and you needed to entertain them for there to be magic.

I shared my essay with a few people around The Browser's Den of Magic (the local magic shop where I first met Mark) including Mark. After reading the paper, Mark asked me to sit down at the table. He told me he enjoyed the essay. He told me he thought it was good. He pointed out a few grammatical errors I had made (Mark prides himself on his 'British Education'). Then he took out a pen. He turned the essay over, and on the back he wrote something, something which I've never forgotten. He wrote the word TRICKS and then 1% next to it. Underneath the word TRICKS he wrote YOU and then 99% next to it. He explained to me that the most important part of your performance is YOU. Everything else is secondary, and everything else stems from you, who you are. That moment Mark gave me something important, something which has changed the way I approach magic, and something I will have for the rest of my life.

Mark, thank you.

—Jeff Hinchliffe

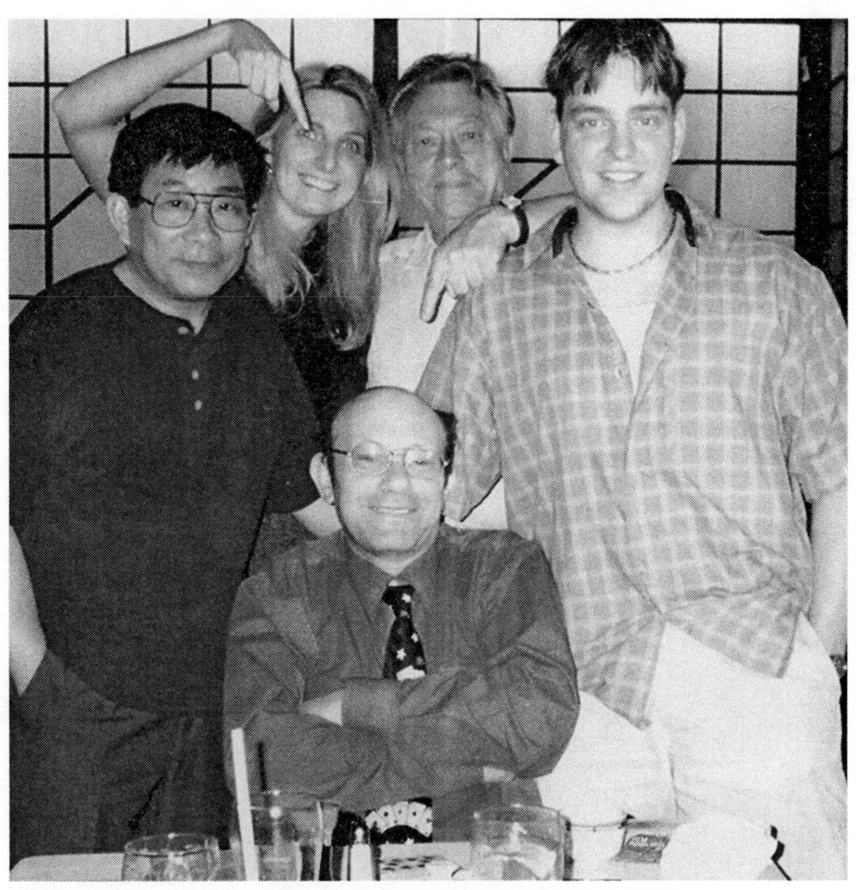

A few more of my friends. Left to right behind me:
Richard Lyn, Lisa Moore, Dennis Adams, Paul Pacific

CHAPTER ONE

The Early Years: How I Became a Magician

I HAVE LIVED A STRANGE life. Actually lives. There have been four lives. One as an entertainer, one as a psychic, one as a grafter and now, one as a writer. My reader will know the meaning of all the four "lives" except one. What is a grafter? Later, good reader. Later....

My original publisher informed me that I was not to write an autobiography but a "memoir" whatever on earth that is. Since I have only a vague notion of the meaning of the word let us hope this tome will be an approximation of what he is talking about.

I am glad I do not have to write an autobiography. If I did I suppose I would have to write about my childhood which was so horrendous that I would rather have a root canal than have to go through the trauma and pain of having to describe it. It was indescribable therefore I shall let it remain undescribed. And if the editor of this literary opus finds my overuse of the word "describe" indescribable then think how the reader feels.

I have just looked at the above paragraph and find it beyond description so perhaps I had better move on.

Let me simply say that as a result of painful family upheaval I was put on a train alone at the age of twelve to undertake an eight hour journey from Glasgow, Scotland to London, England. Within two weeks of this journey I ended up in a children's home where I remained for five years.

When I was nearly thirteen years old I wandered into a public library and saw a book on a shelf. That book started another journey which at this time of writing has lasted fifty years. It was entitled *Magic as a Hobby* by

Bruce Elliot. I borrowed this book from the library but in truth apart from starting me on the journey I am not sure it did me much good otherwise. I couldn't do a single trick in the book since they were all too advanced for me or they required special props that I didn't have access to at the time.

I had shown a little interest in magic in Glasgow and had purchased little magic tricks from Woolworths and I can remember them to this day. I had never really read, however, a book on the subject. This library book was my first introduction to the written word of magic instruction but regrettably not a terribly useful one. I persisted and read all sorts of other more practical works on conjuring. I was making no real progress, however, until I came across a book that dealt with card tricks exclusively. This was more like it for me. I soon discovered that a simple deck of cards could produce enough tricks to last a lifetime. In fact I think it would be safe to say that there are more card tricks in existence than all tricks with other items combined. Now I was making far more progress in my studies. The book was called *Card Tricks* by Wilfrid Jonson and I soon mastered most of the contents.

Around the same time I procured a book that explained other tricks besides cards called *Scarne's Magic Tricks* by John Scarne. This book was far more useful to me than the aforementioned Bruce Elliot book since the props used were for the most part ordinary everyday items to be found around the house. I fumbled through these tricks and sometimes had good success with them and sometimes didn't. These tricks formed the basis of my magical knowledge and built the foundations for future study. Now although I was making modest progress with the Scarne book my real forte were the card tricks learned from the Jonson book. I seemed to take to card tricks like a duck to water and even now fifty years later I am still a card magician at heart.

I have mastered the art of close up sleight of hand with other objects besides cards such as coins, dice, thimbles etc; I have also mastered the art of children's entertainment with more colourful props; I have mastered the art of mind reading tricks (known in the trade as mentalism) and I have mastered the art of stage hypnotism. After all that, however, when it all boils down to it, I am still a card trickster at the very soul of my being.

Every day of my life with very few exceptions I have carried a deck of cards with me. I don't suppose since I took up magic at the age of nearly thirteen years old I have ventured forth without a deck of cards on my person more than twenty times at the most. On the odd occasion that I have forgotten them I feel very uncomfortable and will even go home to get a deck if I am not too far away. If I am too far, then I will possibly end up going into a shop to purchase one. Obsessive I know. And somewhat hard to believe even for me that for fifty years I have carried a deck of cards with me virtually every day. And yet I don't think I am the only magician that has this habit. I haven't checked with my colleagues but I strongly suspect this ritual is endemic among card magicians the world over.

Playing cards fascinate me since there are so many uses for them. You can tell fortunes with them, you can do card tricks with them and, wonder of wonders, you can actually do with them what they were invented for—actually play cards with them!

There is something uncanny about playing cards. It can almost be a calendar. Did you know that if you count the pips on a deck of cards, you will find three hundred and sixty-five? There are three hundred and sixty-five days in the year. There are fifty-two cards in the deck representing fifty-two weeks in the year. There are four suits representing the four seasons. But things get really interesting when you count the deck to see if all fifty-two cards are there. Instead of counting in the usual way, as you deal each card spell one card for each letter thus:

A-C-E, T-W-O, T-H-R-E-E, and so on up to king. Spell the court cards, J-A-C-K, Q-U-E-E-N, K-I-N-G.

You will be amazed to see that the very last card spells out on the G of king. It works out exactly.

Here is the amazing part. Not only does this spelling enigma work in English it also applies in French, Dutch, Swedish and German. For those of you who wish to amuse yourselves with this nonsense please remember that "ch" counts as one letter in German.

I have gone off on a tangent albeit an interesting one at least to me if nobody else. Let me drag myself and the unfortunate reader back to the main story.

Around this time two major milestones occurred which propelled me to major progress in my studies. The first was when I was given a book on card tricks as a present entitled *The Royal Road to Card Magic* and the magic it taught eventually formed the core of my repertoire which has lasted to the present day. Although naturally I learned all sorts of card tricks from other places fully 50% of the card tricks I do nowadays I learned nearly fifty years ago from that one book. It was first published in 1949 and has gone through many editions since then. It was co-authored by Jean Hugard and Frederick Braue and remains to my mind the finest primer on card magic ever written. It is still selling to this day, sixty years later at the time of writing.

The second milestone was another book by the same authors. One day I ventured into a public library and came across a book called "*Expert Card Technique*". This was a more substantial tome than the *Royal Road* book and as it was also written by Hugard and Braue I decided that I had to take it out on loan.

It was no book for beginners and the techniques and tricks therein were very difficult indeed and far too advanced for me. I couldn't do a single trick in the book! However, there was a substantial chapter in the back dealing with the details of showmanship and presentation. It had no actual tricks in it but it did describe how to present magic in an entertaining manner.

The most significant idea it put forward was that it was not the trick that was so vital but the illusion the magician created about himself that was the important thing. I took this to heart and to this day know that it is not the trick that makes the magician but rather the magician that makes the trick. I learned that a magician shouldn't present magic so much as present *himself* doing magic. In other words *he* is the magic. He creates a character and hopefully the audience is charmed by that character as much as it is intrigued by the magic.

In the above paragraph I have used the words "he" and "himself". To be politically correct I suppose I should have written "she" and "herself" in there somewhere. However, it is a fact that there are very few women in magic. Probably ninety percent of performers are male. Why this is I have no idea but I expect that if I thought about it enough I would come up with a reason. However, I don't have the energy, inclination or space to deal with it and this is probably a blessing. I shall leave the matter to the psychologists and press on with my story.

Hugard and Braue gave me the foundations of performing card magic and I built on those foundations. They taught me the tricks in one book and they taught me how to present them in another book. In time I developed a performing character which enhanced the illusion of the tricks themselves.

I showed other kids at the children's home my tricks and they would have been my first audiences. I would also perform magic for the other kids at school and would get pretty good reactions as my skills improved. I would show magic everywhere and anywhere and learned that it was just as important to manipulate people as well as manipulate cards.

One of the banes of my life in those early days were hecklers trying to either spoil the trick for malicious reasons or trying to challenge me and just plain attempting to find out how the tricks were done. These interruptions proved to be a blessing in disguise because they helped me to hone my skills and keep me on my toes. I was showing my card tricks mostly to other young people and of course they would be more prone to heckling and challenging than older spectators might be. By learning to handle the challengers I was able to adapt to any audience.

I was also learning other facets of close quarter magic such as sleight of hand with coins, dice, thimbles etc; but I had not yet ventured on a public stage. All my magic was done in an intimate close up situation for friends and any strangers I could find to amuse. I would perform on the bus, in the park, in the street and even in hotel lobbies. I did not go up to people asking to show them tricks but rather would subtly inveigle them into asking me rather than me asking them.

I would do this by various means but I think my favourite was to read a book on magic in a public place and appear to be learning a trick from said tome. I would have a deck of cards in my hand and start to do fancy shuffles and cuts or do some amazing visual card trick that I seemed to be learning from the book. I would make sure the book had plenty of photos and preferably a garish cover with the word "Magic" plastered all over it. I would flash this cover "accidentally" so that onlookers would know why I had a deck of cards in my hand. Sooner or later someone would ask what I was doing and away I would go. Within minutes I would be doing tricks and an audience would gather around. People would come up out of nowhere. I learned magic by doing it and these early impromptu sessions were very valuable to me in gaining performing experience.

Another major portion of this experience was gathered at school where I would show my fellow students card tricks from the morning I arrived until I went home late afternoon. I neglected my regular school studies because I wasn't particularly interested in them. I was pretty good at English, French and History but the results were more as a result of luck and perhaps natural ability than studious endeavour.

All I wanted to do was magic and I was consumed by it. I would eat, sleep and dream magic. I would find every opportunity to perform it and my enthusiasm was intensive and even perhaps obsessive. I could think of nothing else. One day the headmaster of my school said to me "Lewis, instead of putting 99% of your energy into magic and 1% into school work why can't you put 50% into magic and 50% into school? Wouldn't that be a better balance?" I didn't think it would and continued the study of what I considered obviously more important and I have continued the study to this day albeit with somewhat less intensity.

There was a teacher at my school who was a leader at a Jewish youth club called Brady Boys club in the Whitechapel area of London. If my memory serves me correctly I think the fellow's name was Cyril Kornfeld. He approached me and asked if I wanted to join this club. I said no. He kept on asking me over a period of weeks and I still said no. However, after a campaign of persistent nagging I eventually gave in.

By this time I was around fifteen years old. I was not a particularly sociable type and come to think of it I don't think I have changed much in that regard. I didn't want to go to some youth club and partake in the activities. All I wanted to do was magic and I suppose the only social interaction that I got was from the doing of tricks everywhere and anywhere.

When it dawned upon me, however, that perhaps I could find new audiences at this place I consented to Mr Kornfeld picking me up and taking me there. When I arrived he let me loose to wander around and make myself at home. I did indeed wander but I certainly didn't feel at home. I didn't particularly want to talk to anyone and they didn't particularly want to talk to me. I meandered around watching people play table tennis and other activities but I found nothing to excite my enthusiasm. I resolved not to visit again.

A week later, however, Cyril Kornfeld dragged me there again. This time I brought a book on magic to read because I knew sooner or later I was going to be bored. When I got there, however, I employed my old technique of attracting attention. This is the procedure I used:

I removed the four aces out of the deck and then shuffled them back in making sure that people were watching me while I ostensibly studied the book to apparently learn the trick. After shuffling by various nefarious means known to magicians the world over I controlled one of the aces to the top of the deck, turned it face upwards to display it, then laid it aside. I repeated the procedure twice more, each time making onlookers raise their eyebrows and gasp. I appeared to be studiously ignoring the attention I was getting although in reality I was keeping close tabs on it from the corner of my eyes. Finally I seemed to make a mistake when producing the last ace for display. It was a deliberate mistake and part of my plan. I took the indifferent card rubbed it face down on the table and when I turned it face upwards, it had apparently changed by magic to the missing ace!

After a while of doing this sort of thing somebody asked me if I did card tricks. I said "yes" and before I knew it, away I went performing trick after trick. A crowd gathered out of nowhere and suddenly I was a sensation!

I had garnered good audience reaction in the past from my magic but nothing compared to what was happening now. Suddenly I was surrounded by admirers who were gasping and laughing in a way that I had never experienced before. I must have performed for about an hour or so and it was a heady experience to have so much hero worship and astonishment just from a deck of cards.

I resolved that I wanted more of it so I attended the club very regularly after that for night after night. I would get big crowds around me and fantastic reaction from those crowds. I would sit at a table and for hours on end do trick after trick. I remember at one point one of the youth club leaders saying, "You are the most popular boy here!"

The reaction from the magic was quite incredible and I don't think I have achieved that level of astonishment since. I think the reason for it was that I was so young and innocent looking and people didn't expect that level of expertise from a fifteen year old. I would deliberately fumble sometimes and act absent minded and this built up the effect. I still use that psychological technique to this day. It makes people underestimate you and then you go in for the kill while their guard is down.

One advantage of this youth club experience is that I was forced to expand my repertoire since many of the same people would be there every night. Fortunately during that period of my life I was constantly learning new magic because of my obsessive zeal with the subject. Not only did I do card tricks I became expert with coins, dice and other objects. Cards were, however, the mainstay and the reaction I was getting was very gratifying. There was quite a lot of heckling because I was performing for other young people but this helped keep me on my toes and get better and better at my work.

After a year or so of this the club moved to new premises that were quite a bit more salubrious. I preferred the old place because that was where I got the great reactions from my work. However, progress beckoned and we had to move.

The new premises were in Hanbury Street, Whitechapel where Jack the Ripper roamed in the late nineteenth century. In fact Jack actually murdered a lady there by the name of Annie Chapman. Most unethical of him if I may say so.

The club somehow managed to get Prince Phillip the Duke of Edinburgh and spouse of Her Majesty the Queen to open the new premises. He was going to walk around the club and we were all supposed to be going about our activities in the normal way. It was a bit contrived but we all went along with it. I was sitting at a table doing some card tricks knowing that the Duke would be along soon and I would get a chance to show him something. I had a teenage vision of fame and fortune awaiting me once I performed for royalty. I thought that I would end up getting invited to Buckingham Palace to have tea with the Queen and show her card tricks to distract her from the affairs of state. Needless to say it didn't quite work out that way but Prince Phillip did happen along and I did happen to show him a trick.

Just when he came into the room I remember overhearing someone say to him, "This young man is fantastic with card tricks". This caught his attention and he came over to me. I showed him the trick and awaited the invitation to Buckingham Palace. To my great surprise it didn't come and my royal spectator smiled and then skedaddled out of the room as fast as he could. I was somewhat disappointed since I expected that he was going to exclaim that on returning home he was going to ask his wife to grant me a knighthood.

Alas it didn't happen but suddenly the press descended upon me grinning away. One reporter jovially remarked, "That's one trick the Duke didn't know!" I found out from the reporter that Prince Phillip loved card tricks and did a few himself. Actually quite a few members of the British royal family are interested in magic and in fact Prince Charles the future heir to the throne is a member of the Magic Circle club in London.

As a result of my royal command performance I received a write up in a famous Jewish newspaper of the time that went all over Britain. The Jewish Chronicle had a rather large circulation and for all I know may still be in existence although I confess that I am not going to go to the trouble of checking it out. It was a small paragraph in the paper but it was my first press article and I kept it in my wallet for years. I have since lost it but I remember what it said word for word. Here it is in all its glory:

"The boy the Duke may well remember best was the one who flummoxed him with some particularly baffling card tricks including one called 'Poker Player's Fancy'. A friendly battle ensued from which sixteen-year-old Ronald Lewis who has made an intensive study of card tricks emerged flushed with victory".

Not only was it my first write up it was also my first experience of press inaccuracy. I only showed Prince Phillip one trick rather than "some" tricks. The name of the trick wasn't "Poker Player's Fancy" but "Poker Player's Picnic". The reporter did ask me the name of the trick but perhaps he didn't like it and made up his own. I have no idea. I will take the article's word that I was "flushed with victory" but my memory of the event is that I was irritated that I hadn't been offered a knighthood or invited to the palace.

The newspaper did, however, get my name right. And that brings me to a tedious explanation which I can't be bothered writing about but I suppose I had better get it out of the way.

I am of Russian descent and my family name on my mother's side is Sackov which is Russian and Shackleovitz on my father's side which is equally Russian.

To distract me from this boring explanation about names I am going to go off on a temporary tangent which is far more interesting for me.

I understand that my grandfather on my mother's side was a Russian horse thief and army deserter. It seems that he was a member of the Russian army and got rather bored with it. Instead of resigning his position, which may have presented some difficulties he decided to do the next best thing which of course was to steal an army horse and disappear as far as he possibly could from wherever he was soldiering.

Somehow he ended up in Scotland although I am not sure that was where he originally intended to go. I understand that a lot of Russian Jews en route by boat to America ended up in Glasgow, Scotland by mistake. It seems that they actually thought they were in New York since everyone was speaking English. I am not sure of the actual root of the story but it has something to do with Russian con men depriving them of the surplus portion of their tickets and selling them off and making a profit on it. In order to do so they somehow conned the would-be emigrants that they were in New York instead of Glasgow. I am sure I have got the story all wrong but I believe it was something along those lines and at least it has distracted me from writing this boring section about names which I suppose I had better continue with.

My surname is Lewis and this is how it came about. It seems that my grandfather on my father's side decided that Shackleovitz was a rather cumbersome name in a society where MacDonald, MacTavish and other Scottish names were the norm. It seems that he also came from Russia to Scotland and, for all I know, got off at the wrong stop too. He changed the family name to Lewis which is actually a Welsh name although I have no connection to that particular country except that my brother Howard lived there as a child and to this day has a Welsh accent. He ended up there for reasons that I won't get into. I do wish to be terribly mysterious and get you wondering. I am supposed to be a man of mystery after all. My only other connection with Wales is that I can count up to eight in the

Welsh language which I suppose can be said to be one of my more useless accomplishments in life.

I know rather more about my Sackov grandfather than I do about my Shackleovitz one since he was actually alive at the time of my youth. He owned the Calton Cap shop in Glasgow which was a very famous shop that sold "bunnets". For those of you who do not speak the Scottish language I should explain that "bunnets" are cloth caps that were common wear in Glasgow but have now gone out of fashion although I believe golfers sometimes wear them. My grandfather actually had a small factory in the back of his shop where he manufactured the caps himself. I spent hours there as a youngster.

However, to get on with this monotonous name explanation I was born Ronald Lewis. Later when I got into magic I decided that I wanted a stage name and furthermore I wanted a Scottish one since I was very nationalistic at the time. Scots people living in a heathen environment called England often rebel against the fact. I therefore decided to call myself Ronnie Mcleod which stuck for years and years. Old friends from years ago still know me as Ronnie McLeod. Then one day in a fit of silliness that I regret to this day I decided to call myself Mark Lewis. I have no idea why but I wish I hadn't. Nevertheless, the name has stuck and there is nothing I can do about it. Close friends call me Ronnie. Most people call me Mark. Only members of my family and the government call me Ronald. People that don't like me call me something else.

There. I am glad that I have got that explanation out of the way. It has bored me stiff and knowing I had to do it has postponed the writing of this book for several months. Procrastination afflicts me terribly when writing and if this tome ever sees completion I want the reader to know that it will be the greatest magic feat I have ever performed.

But to continue with this saga of my youth. One day I happened to be doing some card tricks at the Brady club and a youth club leader happened along and watched for a while. He said, "Ronnie, I would like you to join my group". I replied, "What group is that?" The response was, "The

Brady Ramblers". I asked, "Who are the Brady Ramblers?" The man explained to me that the Brady Ramblers were a group of youth club members the same age as myself who sang Israeli folk songs and performed at various charity shows. The name of the youth club leader who made the offer was Greville Janner who later became Lord Janner and he sits in the British House of Lords to this day. I suppose you could say he gave me my first showbusiness break even though it wasn't a paying gig.

I retorted that I couldn't sing and he said that I wouldn't have to. He wanted me to perform my own segment of magic during the performances that the Ramblers attended. I had never performed on a stage before, or in front of a large group of people. All my demonstrations of magic occurred in a close up impromptu environment. I had never done anything on a formal basis for larger audiences.

Not only did I consent to the offer I thrived on it. For a couple of years or so I accompanied the Brady Ramblers to the charity shows and performed my act in between the songs. It was a way of gaining stage experience and I made the most of it. We went to old age homes, community centers and even borstals and approved schools. I should explain to North American readers that the latter two venues mentioned are actually in the UK names for prisons and schools for juvenile offenders. With regard to the borstals and approved schools I remember on one occasion Greville admonishing us, "Don't look down on the people in here. They are the same age as you. The only difference between them and you is that they got caught and you didn't".

Of course Greville was a barrister and I think he took on criminal cases. I base this supposition on the fact that one famous magician told me that Greville got him off a charge of either drunk driving or some equally heinous offence. My memory fails me regarding the actual offence but it was somewhat wicked and involved driving anyway.

I remember Greville advising one young criminal member of the Brady Ramblers. At least I assume he was a criminal who hadn't yet been convicted because of the tone of the conversation. He was advising him in the street outside the premises of the Brady club. I was being very nosey and overheard the conversation although it was none of my business. It seemed that the poor chap was about to go on trial for some wickedness or other. Greville was advising him to go for a jury trial rather than before a judge alone. I heard Greville say, "You have ten times as much chance of being acquitted by a jury than by a judge".

It seems that the logic behind the advice is that judges are very sharp and juries aren't. Judges know things that juries don't. Greville explained, for example that if a character witness does not show up for the defence, a jury will be none the wiser whereas a judge will wonder why no character witness is present. He will assume the fellow has a bad character if his lawyer can't produce a character witness. He knows full well that any lawyer worth his salt will produce such a witness if there is one available. Of course another argument for a jury trial is that judges tend to be pro prosecution and in fact many of them have been prosecutors themselves.

Of course I am not sure what this tangent has to do with my story except to say that I have always remembered Greville's advice but fortunately have not had to use it yet. For some reader, however, it may be worth more than the price of the book since it could save them several years in the clink. I do get a psychic vibe that this book will attract lots of wicked people who will be quite grateful that I have gone off on this tangent. I always like to please my readership.

But to get back on track the experience in performing in all sorts of venues was very useful to me. I was never quite as good on stage as I was doing the close up impromptu magic since different skills were involved. However, I wasn't bad and my expertise was developing.

I performed mostly magic where I spoke to the audience but one day Greville wanted me to perform some trick or other to music. I had seen many magicians perform without speech using pantomime and music. I therefore agreed to do it but was disconcerted when Greville announced that he expected me to do it not to the music normally associated with such performances but to the singing voices of the Brady Ramblers. I protested that having the choir behind me was a distraction and that I didn't think Israeli folk songs were suitable accompaniment to mysterious magic. Greville retorted, "Ronnie, you've got no imagination!" I went ahead with what I considered to be an extremely daft idea but to my surprise it worked out quite well.

We occasionally performed in front of various dignitaries. I well remember doing a mindreading trick for Sir Bernard Whaley-Cohen who was the Lord Mayor of London at the time. I also remember that he didn't seem very impressed with it. I don't think he liked having his mind read by a seventeen year old kid somehow. It was as if it affronted his dignity as Lord Mayor. In fact he tried to tell me how the trick was done in the middle of the show. He was quite wrong but it made no difference. It fell flat with him at any rate even though the rest of the audience loved it.

One day Greville informed me that, although my tricks were good, I needed to work on my presentation of them. He suggested that he would call David Berglas who was a very famous magician of the time and ask him if he would mind helping out a young magician to develop his art. I asked if Greville knew Berglas and he said no. That didn't seem to deter him, however, and he did indeed call David who did indeed consent to advising me on the art of magic.

I find it very interesting to relate that this was the start of a close friendship between David Berglas and Lord Janner which has lasted for around forty-seven years at the time of writing. And all because of me. Truly I am a wondrous influence on the world.

As a matter of fact Greville Janner eventually took up magic himself as a hobby possibly as a result of his association with David Berglas and me.

I was a little in awe that David Berglas had consented to help me out since he was terribly famous at the time and indeed performed quite frequently on British television. I certainly looked forward to meeting him since he was somewhat of an icon among magicians and known as a brilliant performer. Accordingly, one evening I trotted along to the home of Greville Janner to be advised on the art of magic by David who agreed that Greville's house would be a good venue to proceed with this endeavor.

When I arrived I was introduced to David who said that he wasn't going to show me anything but instead he wanted to see what I could do and he would comment upon it. Before he started he did one or two tricks himself and they were fairly amazing. One thing I remember is that he would throw a deck of cards behind his back and catch it in the other hand. Of course this was more a feat of juggling than it was of magic but it was impressive nevertheless.

The most amazing thing he did occurred on the offbeat. In fact, I didn't realise at first he was doing a trick. The house light flickered and suddenly went out. I assumed a fuse had blown or perhaps the bulb had gone dead. Berglas went up to the wall and started feeling various parts of it saying, "I think the problem is about here—or perhaps here!" Suddenly he slammed the wall quite hard and the light went back on again! I was taken by surprise and it took me a moment to realise it was some trick or other. To this day I am not quite sure how it was done although I have heard theories on the matter which may or may not have some validity. At any rate the effect was quite astonishing.

Now it was my turn. But first there was a little conversation which still embarrasses me to this day. Present with me and David were Greville Janner and his wife Myra. Greville remarked that magicians never tell how tricks are done. Myra then wondered aloud if she and Greville should leave the room while Berglas was giving me instruction. At the time Greville wasn't involved with magic although as I have previously mentioned took it up later as a hobby.

She looked at David Berglas quizzically asking if she should remain in the room and Berglas turned the tables and put me on the spot by saying, "It is up to this young man if he wishes you to stay". I spluttered that it would be perhaps best if she and Greville left the room. Both of them did so but Myra did not look very pleased to be ordered around in her own home. I thought from her facial expression that she left in a bit of a huff.

Greville got an urgent call of some sort and he had to leave the house on business. His wife was left all alone banished to the kitchen and we never saw her again the whole evening until it was time to leave. I am still cringing all these decades later over the fact that I had evicted her out of the living room of her own house.

Of course at that time I wasn't too well up on social graces and I was quite zealous in those days in my belief that magicians shouldn't reveal secrets. Nowadays I am far less obsessive over the matter. I won't go out of my way to reveal secrets but I won't have a nervous breakdown over it either.

Berglas then watched me do various magic tricks and gave his useful suggestions on how to improve their performance. I was impressed with what he told me but even more impressed at a later date when I ruminated over the fact that he had taken the time and trouble to help some young magician that he did not know. It was very classy and kind of him to do so.

I can truly say that the evening was the only time I ever received any personal instruction on magic and I am proud to say that apart from that one occasion I am completely self taught in this art. All my knowledge comes from books. The evening with David Berglas, however, was very constructive and certainly memorable.

One day Greville decided to disband the Ramblers probably because his other commitments took up too much of his time. It was a very sad moment and I remember the final performance was at the Victoria Palace theatre. I remember that it was a charity affair and David Berglas was invited to perform as was David Kossoff who was a famous television actor and coincidentally happened to be my cousin although I didn't know him very well.

I saw David Berglas perform at this event and it was very impressive indeed and I can remember a lot of detail even though the show was around forty-five years or so ago. He did a wonderful trick with cigarettes and some pickpocketing along with other marvellous conjuring. One of the best exhibitions of magic I have ever seen.

During this period I discovered that there were such things as magic shops and magic clubs. I used to wander down to Ellisdons magic shop in Holborn during my school lunch hour to watch demonstrations of magic by a fellow called Jon Tremaine who later became a leading professional magician and writer on magic and other subjects. He told me that there was a magic club for young people which was run by a fellow called Huw Parrish.This was the junior section of the London Society of Magicians and was open to young people between the ages of fourteen and eighteen years of age. Mr Parrish was a member of the senior section of this old established magic society which had formed this junior section so that younger magicians could learn about the art without having to associate with the old fuddy-duddies. The meetings would take place in the Conway Hall in Red Lion Square.

I was beginning to get immersed in the community of magicians some of whom impressed me and most of whom didn't. I was very grateful that I had never met a magician for the first two years of my study of the art. I think I would have picked up all their bad habits as performers and it would have affected my progress. I learned things my own way and I was much better off for it.

It was during this formative period that I came across something known as a Svengali deck. This was a trick deck of cards that did some amazing magic. It has had a great influence on my life.

In the opening words of this chapter I explained that I had a life as a "grafter". Now it is time to tell you what a "grafter" actually is. In North America the equivalent word is "pitchman". It describes someone who demonstrates products such as kitchen gadgets, home hardware, toys and other items at fairs, exhibitions, markets, and carnivals. These people gather crowds and demonstrate the products and with fast talk and slick patter persuade the multitude to part with their money. In Britain the expression used to describe these salesman/demonstrators is "grafter" and the activity itself is known as "grafting".

In addition to all the household goods such as paint pads, and non-stick frying pans that were grafting products, there was one magic trick sold as a demonstration item. That was the Svengali deck just described. It was a trick deck of cards first invented by Burling Hull in the early twentieth century. A magic shop owner by the name of W.D. Leroy actually gave the deck its name. Although the trick was invented for the magical fraternity it came into the hands of carnival and street pitchmen and thousands of the decks have been sold to the public over the years most notably by an entrepreneur named Marshall Brodien who sold them on television by means of television commercials. It should be mentioned that not every grafter that sold Svengali decks was a magician. Many were simply expert salesmen who discovered that the Svengali deck would make an excellent product to demonstrate and sell. Apart from this one trick they knew no other magic whatsoever.

However, one exception was a fellow named Joe Stuthard. He was a very fine magician indeed. He was a Canadian who sold these decks all over the world. I shall relate now how I first came across both Stuthard and the Svengali deck.

My first contact with the deck was when I was about thirteen years old. No, I hadn't bought a deck from a pitchman or a magic shop. I simply came across an abandoned one. It was lying all alone on the ground in a public park. How it got there I'll never know and where it is now I will also never know. I picked it up and couldn't understand why there were so many nine of clubs in the deck. And then I fooled myself! I flipped the cards one way and couldn't see any nine of clubs! I couldn't understand it and spread through the cards face upwards. I counted twenty-four nine of clubs. I couldn't understand why they didn't show up when I flipped the end of the deck! And then I got another shock. When I flipped the deck the other way *all* I saw were nine of clubs! No other cards at all, just the nine of clubs! I remember playing with the cards for an hour trying to figure it out. I eventually gave up, and only much later did I discover that the nines were shorter than the other cards and that is what made the trick work.

A year later I went on a school trip to the *Schoolboys and Girls Exhibition*. This was sponsored by the Daily Mail newspaper and took place at the Earls Court Exhibition Centre in London. There must have been more than a hundred different booths displaying and selling all sorts of items that would be of interest to younger people.

I was interested in magic at the time; in fact I had just started learning it. I was also interested in languages. I distinctly remember carrying a book on Esperanto (of all things) around the exhibition. I gave up the study of Esperanto, but I regret to say that I am still doing magic over fifty years later.

One of the first displays that caught my eye was a fairly large booth set up by the Thomas De La Rue playing card company. There was a magician there surrounded by a crowd. He was doing card tricks with a regular deck, presumably a Thomas De La Rue deck. I remember thinking, in my youthful arrogance, that he wasn't very good. On reflection, I think he was better than I gave him credit for at the time. Afterwards, I showed him a card trick of my own, and he humoured me with some complimentary remark. He probably thought, "What an awful little brat". To this day I do not know who the magician was. If he is still alive I just hope he doesn't read this.

I continued wandering through the exhibition, turned a corner and lo and behold, there was another magician! There was a big sign saying, "JOE STUTHARD—THE CANADIAN FUNATIC". He had a clock sign with movable hands and another sign saying, "next demonstration at…" He had a very large crowd around him and he was in the middle of a demonstration. And what a demonstration it was! He was absolutely superb. I was stunned watching him and I remember thinking, "I want to be as good as that!" He did the magic mouse trick and it was absolutely unbelievable. It scurried across his hands, and in and out of a glass. I could have sworn it was alive. Then he demonstrated the Svengali deck. It was the greatest performance of card tricks I have ever seen. I have seen many magicians perform card tricks since, including the greatest names in magic, but I have never seen anything to equal what I saw as a fourteen year old kid, standing in a crowd at an exhibition watching a pitchman performing with a trick deck. For two hours I was enthralled.

When there was a lull in the crowd, I plucked up the courage to speak to this (to my mind) master magician. I certainly wasn't going to go up to him, announce that I too was a magician, and offer to show him a trick like I did to the poor Thomas De La Rue man. Still, I desperately wanted the great Joe Stuthard to know that I was a conjurer. I was too shy to tell him directly so I tried to be subtle. "Do you sell fanning powder?" I asked. This is a special powder that magicians use to make a deck of cards slippery and easier to manipulate. Of course, I knew full well that he didn't sell the stuff but I wanted him to know that I was a fellow magician. He smiled and said, "No, we only sell the mouse and the cards". I said, "OK" and walked away having made my point.

I never did buy anything that day, but I knew I had seen a great magician. I never dreamed when I saw him that I would be selling Svengali decks, magic mice, and other magic tricks at exhibitions, stores etc; for over forty years.

I wanted to be like Joe Stuthard. I never realised at the time how much I would get my wish.

CHAPTER TWO

The Later Early Years: Making a Living

EVENTUALLY I LEFT SCHOOL and had to go out in the world to earn a living. I had a vague idea that I wanted to become a professional magician but, apart from that, I really had no idea what I wanted to do. To complicate matters further I had no idea how to become a professional magician in the first place.

Accordingly I drifted from job to job. I worked at all sorts of occupations for very short periods. I worked in a warehouse, a pharmacy, a supermarket, a shoeshop and many other places. I expect if I had applied for a place in the Guinness Book of Records for recognition as someone who had the most jobs in a short period of time I expect I would have been included in the book somewhere.

The longest job I ever had was in a bank. I lasted ten whole months which was quite a record for me. Most places I only lasted a few weeks. I worked for the Banque L'Indochine in the City of London.

The "City" as it is known is actually only a very small part of London occupying just one square mile. Until the 18th Century the City of London was all of London. Nowadays it is the financial center of Europe and it probably was during the days I worked at the bank. I remember the area was full of offices and banks and I am sure it still is today nearly forty-seven years later. It has around six thousand residents and is almost deserted during the weekend but on weekdays it is buzzing with activity.

I worked in the foreign exchange department of the bank. However, I had developed a crippling shyness and consequently hardly spoke a word to anyone there. In fact, I don't suppose I spoke ten words all day to a single person. Outside the bank I was fine but somehow, once I entered the doors of that place, I withdrew into a shell and wouldn't come out of it.

Outside the bank I wore a hat which was slightly flamboyant and I didn't dare wear it to my place of work. So what did I do? Liverpool St railway station was quite near the bank so I went in there before starting work and put the hat in a coin operated left luggage locker and at the end of the day went back to the station and retrieved it.

The above is quite true and I kid you not. However, read on and raise your eyebrows still further.

Every Friday someone would come round and give a pay envelope to each member of the staff and this would contain the week's salary. However, one Friday the envelope didn't come—at least not to me. I did see other people getting paid but somehow I had been left out of the equation, obviously a little mistake which could easily be sorted out. At least by a normal human being who would enquire where his money was. However, I wasn't a normal human being. I was simply a very shy eighteen year old who was too afraid to breathe a word about it. So I didn't. One week later they discovered that they hadn't paid me and were in great wonder as to why I had never said a word about it. I must inform anyone that owes me money nowadays that this was a very long time ago and my reticence in asking for payment has long since faded.

My shyness in those days was so abnormal that it did tend to put a damper on my everyday living. The only time I came alive was when I was doing tricks. However, nobody at the bank knew I was a magician and I think they would have been astonished if they had ever found out.

I realised that I would have to do something about this shyness problem so I forced myself to take a course in public speaking that I saw advertised. This was a great help since once you can speak to a group, speaking to individuals becomes a lot easier.

Of course, performing magic on a stage also forces you to speak to groups of people and I did do a few public shows now and then. Most of the magic I performed, however, were close up impromptu tricks mostly with cards. I did those everywhere and anywhere, just as I described in the previous chapter.

Another job I obtained was selling vacuum cleaners door to door or actually, in my particular case, not selling vacuum cleaners door to door. I say this because in four weeks of door knocking, I only sold one. What happened is that I knocked on one door and a fellow appeared and realised I was a salesman. He said, "Sorry, I can't stop to talk to you. I am going down town to buy a vacuum cleaner". I couldn't believe my luck and told him that I was selling that particular product and I could save him a trip. He paused for a moment to weigh up the situation and said, "All right, come on in and show us what you've got!" Despite my incompetent demonstration where I accidentally sprayed dust and garbage all over the carpet he purchased one anyway.

At one point I was out of work and desperately needed a job since I was running out of money. I phoned up a friend of mind named Michael Vishnick who later became Michael Vine a noted theatrical agent and television producer. There will be more about Michael later on in this book. Michael at that time had a very odd sense of humour. Come to think of it he still has. It is a great wonder to me that he hasn't been locked up over it!

I told him that I was out of work and he said, "That is no problem. You can have my job. I am leaving tomorrow and they need a replacement. I'll give them your name. Just mention me and they will hire you".

I asked him what job he was leaving and he said. "I am a waiter". This amazed me because I had no idea that he was a waiter since he had never mentioned it to me before. However, I had no reason to doubt him especially when he gave me a phone number to ring and the name of a person in charge of hiring staff.

The next day I phoned the number and asked for the person in question. When he came to the phone I told him that a Mr Michael Vishnick had asked to me to call regarding a job as a waiter. I gave him my name as Michael had instructed me to. I was informed, however, that they had never heard of either Michael Vishnick nor me. I spluttered something to the effect that Michael was a waiter who had just left his job and had recommended me. The fellow responded that they did indeed need a waiter but they had no idea who Michael Vishnick was. However, he did invite me in for an interview and lo and behold I got the job.

I had no idea that Michael had never worked as a waiter in his life and that his whole story was fictitious! When I asked for the phone number of his employer he simply grabbed a newspaper that happened to be open at the advertising section. There were several advertisements among the classified ads looking for waiters and he just picked any phone number at random! The contact name he gave me was the one in the advertisement! It was a daft deception but it worked out in the sense that I actually got a job because of it.

The job was at St James's Club in the heart of London. It was a terribly posh place full of dukes and lords. I had heard that the Duke of Edinburgh visited but I never saw him there. If I had I suppose I would have shown him another trick and tried again to have tea at Buckingham Palace.

I was probably the worst waiter in recorded history. The head waiter was a grumpy old Frenchman who was always telling me that some member of the nobility had complained about me for some reason or other. One complained that I had hitched up my trousers in his presence. The trousers were supplied by the club as part of a waiter's uniform and were not a very good fit hence the frequent hitching up. Another noble lord had complained that I was humming a tune as I served him. Tune humming when serving noble lords was verboten it seemed.

One day one of the seated gentry called me over and in an irritated manner exclaimed, "Waiter, this coffee is too strong. Pour me some milk". I did but I am afraid he picked the wrong person for such a request since he got a little more milk than he bargained for. He now protested that the coffee was too weak. I resisted the urge to tell him to make his own bloody coffee and went to get him a fresh cup that I laid before him in all its somewhat dilapidated glory. He then called me over with a strange complaint.

"Waiter. This coffee is moving within itself". I asked what he meant and he responded, "As I say it is moving within itself. You know—like detergent". After a pause he remarked, "Yes, and it tastes like detergent too!"

After a few weeks of this the excitement of being a waiter was beginning to wear off and I was starting to curse Michael Vishnick for scamming me into this awful job for which I was clearly not suited. Then one day I passed a room where all the members played bridge. The door was wide open and the room was empty. However, I saw all the green baize card tables and my urge to do card tricks there became very strong. I decided to see if the club management would approve of the idea of me entertaining the members with card tricks in the bridge room.

I approached the manager of the club who was quite horrified at the suggestion. I swear his face went white and he looked quite shaken at the very idea. He stared at me with a fearful look in his eye as if he had been confronted by a raving maniac.

After he had somewhat recovered he almost shouted at me, "Card tricks! Card tricks! Are you raving mad? This is a gentleman's club! The members would have a heart attack!"

Actually I thought that he was the one going to have the heart attack and I told him that I was quite sure the members would love some entertainment of this kind. He retorted, "I believe you are originally from Glasgow, aren't you?" I answered in the affirmative whereupon he retorted, "Perhaps you should go back there. Scottish people like yourself seem to have no conception of how an English gentleman's club operates. I rather think you should seek alternative employment preferably back in Glasgow".

And so ended my career as a waiter. I didn't go back to Glasgow which of course is very fortunate for Glasgow. Instead I was able to land a job in a magic shop and of course this was quite enjoyable to me. I could indulge my passion and perform to the customers to some extent.

The magic shop sold a book on juggling so I purchased it and went home to practice. Alas my juggling career came to an abrupt end when my landlady complained about it. I used to practice late at night around one o'clock in the morning and the balls would bounce all over the place. The landlady used to sleep in the room below and my inept juggling used to keep her awake at night. She complained to me, "Mr Lewis, what is it that you are doing at one o'clock in the morning in your room? I keep hearing a lot of banging on the floor". I responded "I'm juggling" whereupon she replied in an exasperated manner, "Well I hope you improve!"

I gave up my juggling activities at that point and went back to card tricks which I was far better at anyway. However, to this day I can still juggle badly and a few years ago I was delighted to get a television commercial booking because of it. Every magician in Toronto went down to the audition and the casting director asked me, "Can you juggle?" and I answered, "Very badly" whereupon she astonished me by looking delighted saying, "Wonderful! We want a bad juggler!" And I got the job and was delighted that all the wasted practice of my youth had some use after all.

I enjoyed working at the magic shop and it was good experience. However, as always I didn't stay put for long and even this emporium of fun couldn't hold me.

I continued drifting from job to job until one day I met a fellow named Graham who did some magic but who had a job in Selfridges department store demonstrating a toy product known as "Blo Bloon". This product is still around under some different name or other and it consists of a little tube which contains a substance that you squeeze out into a small blob. You then insert a little plastic tube into this little mass of goo. The plastic tube was a bit like a straw. You would blow into it and the little blob on the end would grow into a balloon. You then make little faces and pictures on this balloon by various means that I have quite forgotten.

I visited Graham in Selfridges and told him that I was out of work and he promptly said to me, "Would you like this job here?" I assumed he meant the very job he was doing and he confirmed it. He wrote a phone number down on a piece of paper and handed it to me. He said, "All you have to do is to phone this number and ask if they have any openings for demonstrators. They will say 'yes' and hire you for this job and fire me".

Needless to say I found this to be a very odd proposition and I mentioned that this was a very unusual way of getting a job. I asked Graham if he was fed up with the job he was doing and he explained that he had recently become a born again Christian and he felt that the job was no longer compatible with his values. To this day I still don't know what on earth he was talking about and I can't really think why the job would have induced this crisis of conscience. Perhaps there is an obscure reference in some holy book about the evils of making balloons out of a gooey little substance which influenced Graham in this regard but I have no idea where and my potential employment benefactor never did enlighten me regarding the matter.

I asked him why he didn't just leave the job if it bothered his conscience so much. He replied that it would be against his new found faith if he simply upped and left leaving his employer without a replacement. I found all this very peculiar but enquired as to why I had to get him fired to get the job and why couldn't he just leave and recommend me as his replacement? He answered, "Oh, it'll be much easier this way and of course I will be able to get unemployment benefit if I get fired. If I leave voluntarily it will be much harder to get any money from the government". I knew this was correct because of the rules regarding employment benefit at the time.

Still, I still found it all very unorthodox and asked, "How do you know that you will get fired if I simply phone up and say I am looking for a job?" Graham amused me greatly by saying, "Oh, I know they want to fire me because my sales are so low. The trouble is that they can't find a replacement but, if you call, it will solve their problem".

I asked, "How can you be 100% percent sure they will hire me? What happens if they don't like me for some reason?" He amazed me by replying, "They *will* hire you. They are absolutely desperate to get rid of me and they will take the first person that comes along no matter what he is like. They will reason that anybody is better than me".

I found all this very unusual but I took the piece of paper and promised Graham that I would make the phone call the very next day. I had no idea at the time that this would lead to my very first grafting job. I was about to enter the world of the grafter and it would prove to be a very interesting and devious world indeed.

The next day I phoned the number and just as Graham predicted was told "yes" and that they did need demonstrators. I was told to come down for an interview which I duly proceeded to. This interview was conducted by a fellow called Billy Levine who owned the biggest demonstration company in the UK at that time. He had made a lot of money pre war on the black market according to sources in the grafting business. He was a shrewd businessman who knew the grafting business inside out.

He astonished me by asking very few questions. Most jobs I had interviewed for in the past has made me fill out application forms and asked all sorts of questions about past experience but Billy didn't seem to care. He really only had one question which was, "Have you ever done any demonstration work before?" I had worked in a magic shop and, of course, I had demonstrated tricks there. I knew, however, that this wasn't quite what he meant by demonstration since the grafters he hired were expected to draw crowds unlike the magic shop activity where I would only be demonstrating to individual customers.

I stammered that I had indeed done demonstration work but not quite the kind that he meant. I tried to explain the difference between what I did and what grafters did but he interrupted and snapped, "You don't have to tell me the difference. I have two hundred and fifty demonstrators working for me". That shut me up but I could see my job hopes going down the drain because I didn't feel I was giving a good impression at the interview. He, however, didn't seem in the least bit concerned and amazed me by saying, "We might have a little job for you in Selfridges. We have a fellow there who isn't very good and we would like to get rid of him. It is demonstrating a toy product that you blow into balloons". He then showed me a tube of Blo-Bloon, not knowing, of course, that I knew all about it.

He continued by saying "I want you to go down to Selfridges today and study this guy and learn the demonstration. Just watch him and see what you can pick up. Just spy on him and don't make yourself too obvious. He might smell a rat but even if he does, it doesn't really matter. We will fire him tomorrow and you can start on Monday". I should mention that the interview took place on a Friday and it didn't look as if they were going to be giving poor old Graham much notice. Of course "poor old Graham" wasn't really poor old Graham since he had planned to get fired all along and used me as his willing accomplice.

Accordingly, I went along to Selfridges as instructed and informed Graham that I had been sent to spy on him and that he was going to be fired tomorrow. I told him the whole story of how I had phoned and obtained the job just as he said I would. Graham was delighted to hear that he was going to be fired the next day but I still felt the whole thing was a bit weird and told him so. However, Graham told me not to worry and he showed me exactly how to sell the Blo-Bloon. The one thing that worried me was drawing a crowd and I was actually terrified by this. Graham assured me that once I started to make the balloons a crowd would gather automatically. I explained to him that this was what I was worried about since I would be too terrified to speak to the crowd. I was beginning to wonder if I was making a mistake. I did, however, show up to work at Selfridges on the Monday and Graham did get fired on the Saturday before as he was supposed to be.

That Monday I stood there in abject fear wondering how I was supposed to sell these little tubes of gooey stuff. I blew up the balloons and waited for people to stop like Graham said they would. Of course they didn't and I soon realised that I would have to say something to get people to stand still for a few moments and watch the demonstration.

I stood there frightened to death and wondering what I should say to passers by. My natural shyness was kicking in again. After a couple of hours of this I finally made an effort to speak to people. There is an old saying that the best way to conquer fear is to do what you fear to do and get a record of successful experiences behind you. I suppose you could say that courage is not the absence of fear but the conquest of it.

Once I started to talk to people I started to sell to them. At the end of the day Billy Levine phoned me at the store to find out how I had done. When I told him he said, "Well, you did better than the other fellow".

The ironic thing is that the staff of Selfridges hated me. They glowered at me as if I was the devil incarnate. It seemed that Graham was very popular with the staff and they blamed me for getting him fired. I didn't bother trying to explain that Graham enticed me to get him fired in the first place.

This was my first introduction to the grafting business. From that point on I worked for various companies demonstrating bar accessories, storage racks, eyeglass cleaners, and flower holders. It seemed to pay much better than all the regular jobs I had in the past. Billy Levine paid me a basic wage plus commission. Later I found out that the normal way of remuneration for most grafters was to be paid by commission only.

At this point I hadn't yet encountered my most enduring product which was the aforementioned Svengali deck. That moment came one evening when I heard a chance remark which influenced my life for decades and started me on a very strange career path which resulted in the Lives of a Showman.

At the time in London there was a well known magic club called the Vampire Club. They held their meetings in a club in Soho and sometimes put on public magic shows there. One night they held one of these shows and I decided to attend. After the show people were milling about in the pub buying drinks and showing each other card tricks.

I spied a prosperous looking man there whom I knew as Ron MacMillan, a very well known dealer in magic supplies. At the time I had no idea that he wasn't quite as prosperous as he looked. It was the early years of his business and he hadn't quite built it up to the extent that it later became. In fact the business is still in operation nearly forty-five years later at the time of writing. It is known as International Magic and is located in Clerkenwell Road, London. What never ceases to amaze me is that it still has the same phone number as it had forty-five years ago! Nowadays the business is run by Martin MacMillan who is Ron's son.

Alas Ron is no longer with us having passed away just a few years ago at the time of this writing.

Ron MacMillan

But back to my saga. I formed the mistaken impression that Ron was wealthy because that evening he was wearing a very expensive looking overcoat which made him look like a millionaire. I knew Ron by sight but had never spoken to him. I saw him in the bar area of the pub and overheard him say to another magician, "Val, I'll see you at the Schoolboys. You work the Svengalis. I'll give you a third".

I knew instantly what this meant. "Val" was Val Andrews who was very well known in the world of magic at the time. The "Schoolboys" was the *Schoolboys and Girls Exhibition* in London and in fact the very same exhibition that I had seen Joe Stuthard demonstrating trick decks in a few years earlier. The "Svengali" referred to the Svengali Deck that was the very same deck that I had seen Stuthard selling. I soon figured out that Ron MacMillan was offering Val Andrews a third of all sales as commission to sell the decks on Ron's booth at this particular exhibition.

With that knowledge in hand I went down to Ron's magic studio in London and asked for a job at the upcoming "Schoolboys". He didn't know who the hell I was but, just like Billy Levine, asked very few questions and simply gave me the job. I was doomed from that day forth. I duly showed up at the *Schoolboys and Girls Exhibition* and arrived at Ron's booth which was massive. He had lined up around twenty demonstrators in a row, and all around the edge of the booth. The sole item that was being demonstrated at the time was the Svengali deck although subsequently and in months to come, Ron introduced other small magic products for sale.

I worked all day and I remember that I took in fifteen pounds. The cards sold for seven shillings and six pence in those pre-decimalisation days. That meant that I had sold forty decks. I received five pounds commission which was quite a reasonable sum of money in those days. However, the next day I took in eighteen pounds and earned six pounds. Ron had a bonus system that if you took in at least twenty-five pounds he would pay another pound on top of the regular commission. On a couple of days or so I was able to earn this bonus as well.

The money was more than I had ever earned before and I was in a state of great astonishment and elation over it. I had no idea that this kind of money could be earned selling trick decks of cards. Another thing that I found very odd was that Ron paid the commission every night in cash unlike other companies who would pay once a week after you submitted your sales figures on paper. Ron just took the money, counted it and gave the grafter a third there and then. He was quite generous and if there was a surplus of coinage in change he would simply say, "I don't want all this change. You can keep that as well".

After I worked the Schoolboys I had earned quite a lot of money so I jumped at the chance when Ron asked me to work at another exhibition a few weeks later. This was the *Holiday and Travel Exhibition* at the

Olympia Exhibition Centre in London. Ron had the same set up as he had at the Schoolboys with lots of demonstrators set up in a row competing against each other. The amount of traffic compared to the Schoolboys Exhibition, however, was like chalk and cheese. In other words there was no traffic at all. The exhibition was poorly attended and I found out early on in my career how fickle the grafting business could be. It could be manna from heaven and money pouring out of your ears one day and starvation and desperation for customers the next.

I ended up the whole exhibition just playing cards with other exhibitors, wandering around the show and only doing the occasional demonstration. I was earning very little money from selling the cards. This was compensated for by the fact that I was winning a lot of money playing cards with the other exhibitors. These exhibitors in the main were grafters from other stands selling non-magic products.

I used to play a lot of cards for money in those days but I am very glad I gave it up since I have always believed gambling leads to rack and ruin. I think it is the worst vice of all and can lead to even more harm that drugs, drink and smoking. If you win you still lose because the excitement of winning hooks you to keep playing and in the long run you end up penniless.

However, at this particular Holiday Fair I was winning all the way more from good luck than any particular skill I had. I hardly knew how to play the game I was involved in and kept asking the players what the rules were and what the hands meant. I kept winning and winning, however, and the players were getting very resentful and started to think my innocence of the game was all an act particularly when they found out I was a card magician. It didn't help matters when mischievous exhibitors passing by made remarks like, "You are not playing cards with him are you? You must be crazy". They knew I did card tricks and assumed I would know all the wiles of cheating. The truth of the matter is that most magicians are terrible card players and even card magicians know very little about cheating methods. Or to phrase that a bit better they may know about cheating methods in theory but could never carry them out in practice since they don't plain have the mentality required.

Suffice it to say that I had no idea how to cheat at cards and in those days I was hampered in my life by great honesty that would probably have had me nominated for sainthood. Therefore the game was actually above board and I was winning great gobs of money using no deception whatsoever. I wasn't a particularly good player but I just seemed to be getting good cards dealt to me by sheer force of luck.

My playing companions were getting very suspicious and kept hinting that I was cheating. Eventually one of the heavy losers went up to Ron's Svengali booth and asked one of the demonstrators if I cheated at cards from time to time. The magician in question answered jokingly, "I wouldn't put it past him!" Alas the enquirer didn't take it as a joke and was suitably furious and took the reply as evidence of my great dishonesty.

He wound up the other players about my alleged wickedness and convinced them that I was a card shark with a history of great crookedness. This was very far from the truth but they got very angry and threatened to lynch me. The legend persists to this day (forty-five years later at the time of writing) about the time I played cards with the grafters and cheated them out of all their money. If any of them are still alive and reading this—it ain't true and I didn't do it. Get over it.

Overall the *Holidays and Travel Exhibition* was a disaster but I went on and worked many exhibitions for Ron MacMillan all over the country. Ron took space at exhibitions in Birmingham, Belfast, Edinburgh and Cardiff. He sent me to them but this time I was the only demonstrator there on a much smaller booth and the long line of grafters selling the cards at the London exhibitions was discontinued for the out of town shows. I was making more money than I had ever earned in my life but the trouble was that Ron only did a few select exhibitions during the course of the year and it was hard for me to keep going during the times that he wasn't exhibiting somewhere.

One day he took one of his massive booths at the *Daily Mail Ideal Homes Exhibition* in London. The British Broadcasting Corporation had an even more massive booth than Ron did and actually had a small television studio on the stand. There were TV monitors all around the booth and you could actually see into the studio which had a big window. The theme of the exhibit was colour television which hadn't yet been introduced to the homes of the public at large. In those days everyone watched only black and white television. A television revolution was about to take place and very soon British television would be changed forever by the advent of colour. It hadn't happened yet but was going to take place in the coming months. The BBC decided to make a big fuss about it at the *Ideal Homes Exhibition* and ran daily programmes for internal viewing at the exhibition and these shows would be in full colour. This would be the first time in television history that the public would be able to see colour television programmes in action. Although viewers at home wouldn't be able to see the programmes anyone visiting the IDH (common abbreviation used among grafters to identify the *Ideal Homes Exhibition*) would be able to watch the shows.

I was approached by the Stand Manager of the BBC. and asked if I would like to do card tricks on colour television on a daily basis throughout the exhibition which lasted in those days for a month. I asked if I would get paid since I would have to take time away from my work of selling Svengali decks but was told the answer was no. However, I was told, "You will be part of television history and you will actually be the first magician ever to have appeared on colour television in Britain".

I agreed and I must say it was the best television training I ever received. Every day for about fifteen minutes I would do card tricks on TV and I learned such a lot about television over that very valuable month. I learned how to warn the cameraman if I was going to go out of frame and I learned to keep all the action in a limited area. There were other things I learned about television and probably the most important thing I ever learned was to be relaxed and look as if I owned the place. This stood me in good stead over the years since at various times I performed card tricks on television for wider audiences who watched in the comfort of their homes rather than standing around a stand at the *Ideal Homes Exhibition*.

As I stated earlier all this was good experience and I was earning good money but the problem was that Ron just didn't exhibit at enough venues during the year for me to make regular money and when one exhibition finished I might have to wait several weeks or even months before I could get to work again. Fortunately I was meeting other grafters at the exhibitions and shows. These people were selling non-magic related products such as kitchen gadgets and so forth. I was beginning to learn from them the ins and outs of the business and, most importantly, places to work. I was taught how to make deals with department stores and how to book exhibition stands for myself. Accordingly I made a deal with Ron MacMillan to purchase stock from him and go out on my own during the times I wasn't working for him at his own venues.

I started off doing deals with department stores and giving them a percentage of sales. I tended to give them too much until one day I met an old time grafter on a train who gave me very valuable advice. The stores always wanted a bigger percentage and their buyers were trained to ask for more. They would want a third of sales and sometimes as much as 40%. I have even known companies who would pay 50% or 60% to be allowed to demonstrate their products in particularly good venues with lots of foot traffic.

In addition to this the stores would take ages and ages to pay the grafter. You would have to submit invoices to them and it would sometimes take months to get paid and this would create havoc with cash flow.

This grafter whose name I have quite forgotten with the passage of the years told me, "*Never* give a store more than 25%". I protested that I had no choice since the buyers knew they had me over a barrel and that they had good foot traffic in their store. They knew full well that I wanted to work there and would have to pay them as much as a third of sales. He repeated, "*Never* pay them a third! Look them straight in the eye and tell them all you can afford is 25% and that is all they are going to get!"

I protested that the store wouldn't go for the deal and they would tell me to get lost. He said, "No. That is where you and other people who want to get into stores and good venues are making a big mistake. If you look them straight in the eye and refuse to give them more than 25%, they will *always* give in!"

To my amazement I subsequently found out that he was 100% correct. If the store showed initial interest they would *always* give in at 25%. They would often try to get more and say things like, "We never allow concessionaires in at less than 40%". However, if I stuck to my guns they would always give in at 25%.

Never once in forty years have I found an exception to this. There is often great resistance but in the end they give in.

The other advice that the grafter gave me was to tell me about a directory in the UK which had every exhibition listed that I could book space at. I would phone up the organisers of these shows and ask for space. Again I tried to get in as cheaply as possible. I would either call at the last minute when they were unlikely to have sold the space or argue that my particular products were an attraction because of the entertainment value thus deserving a lower price.

Another ploy that sometimes worked was that I would offer them a free magic show on stage if they would let me have a free booth in exchange.

I soon learned that grafters tended to ignore the official price that was marked on the application form and made individual deals with the promoters. If the exhibition turned out to be poorly attended the grafters would often resist paying the full price and they would work out their own deal with the promoter. This worked particularly well with the smaller organisers of exhibitions but not quite so well with the big promoters.

I would emphasise that it was only the grafters who made these deals. Other exhibitors who sold non-demonstration related products always paid the full price. However, the grafters were skilled negotiators and very street wise. They also realised that the demonstrations were attractions in themselves and were one of the main reasons the public came to the shows. This gave them strong negotiating power.

The magic tricks I had for sale were a particularly fun product and gave me the power to negotiate good exhibition rentals. In fact one of the main secrets of my success over the years was that I was able to negotiate reasonable prices to exhibit my products. If I hadn't been able to do this I believe I would have failed very badly since the trick cards and the other magic items I sold simply didn't take in anywhere near as much money as other grafting products such as the non stick frying pan, the knife, the paint pad, the glass cutter and the various kitchen gadgets that were sold by demonstration.

There were of course times during my career that I tried my hands at these other products but in the end I always came back to the card tricks. The non magic product I had the most success with was probably the flower holder. However, I only did well if someone from the company was there to make the flower arrangements. When I was left to my own devices the results were disastrous with water all over the place and some pretty dismal flower arrangements!

Another product I did quite well with was eyeglass cleaners and the "huggers". Now of course the question arises, "What are huggers?" They were little rubber rings that you placed onto the hinges of spectacles to stop them slipping down your nose. I found out later that they were actually very bad for your glasses and after a time would actually tend to break them!

The fellow who supplied me with the eyeglass cleaner used to purchase unused lipstick containers from cosmetic companies and fill them with cotton wool immersed in a well-known detergent called Fairy Liquid. These were the eyeglass cleaners that he sold me. My adventures with the eyeglass cleaners came to an abrupt end when someone had the audacity to murder my supplier, chop his body into little pieces and stuff them in a plastic bag. I remember at the time being most disgruntled over the matter since he didn't seem to be in a position to sell me any more merchandise.

After that I went back to selling the Svengali deck and I remained doing so for the next forty years.

CHAPTER THREE

I Become a Professional Magician

MY EARLY YEARS WERE based in London but I travelled all over the country selling Svengali decks, sometimes for Ron MacMillan and sometimes for myself. However, I still had showbusiness aspirations and wanted to perform on stage.

In those days the main venues for entertainers were working men's clubs, cabaret clubs and nightclubs. The main problem with those venues was trying to capture the attention of the audience most of whom would often be in varied degrees of intoxication. The days of the variety theatres were long gone and performers were deprived of the luxury of having audiences pay to see the entertainment in nice straight rows of seats without the distraction of alcohol.

Instead entertainers had to contend with audience members eating, drinking and general inattention. In addition you would sometimes get waiters wandering across the floor creating a distraction. Audiences were vocal and often rowdy. You had to be fairly tough to survive it all.

The only magicians who were able to avoid all this were those who specialised in entertaining children at birthday parties etc; However, it would be many years before I became involved with this branch of magic which had it's own challenges but yet was far more rewarding than attempting to entertain the inattentive at one in the morning in a London night club.

I lived round the corner from a club called the Regency Club. At this stage of my life I had no experience whatever of appearing on stage except for the charity shows that I did for Greville Janner and the Brady

Ramblers. These, however, were a far cry from the tough conditions prevalent in the club scene. A friend brought me in as a guest to the Regency club whereafter I would attend on a regular basis and soon got acquainted with people and did card tricks for fun to anyone that wanted to see them.

One day I was passing by the club on the other side of the road with a friend who pointed out two men across the street. They were walking out of the Regency and in deep conversation. My friend turned to me and said, "Do you see those two fellows over there?" I answered, "Sure, what about them?" The reply was, "They are the Kray twins". I was no wiser and enquired, "Who are the Kray twins?" The answer proved interesting. "Ronnie and Reggie Kray. They own the Regency Club and they are the biggest gangsters in London. They kill people".

I discovered later that they didn't actually own the club but they certainly had a financial interest in it and were a frequent presence there. The second part of the statement was perfectly accurate. They did indeed kill people and used to do so on a reasonably frequent basis.

I wasn't that concerned as long as they didn't kill me but I did enquire as to why, if they were conducting themselves in such a socially inappropriate manner, they were still walking around with impunity and not residing in one of Her Majesty's prisons.

Of course my skepticism was misplaced. It seems that they did indeed go around killing people and were, in fact, at a much later date convicted of doing so and sent to prison for life. The judge remarked, "I think society deserves a rest from your activities". I suppose it could be said that his Lordship struck a somewhat disapproving tone despite the contention made by some that the Krays only killed fellow gangsters and never ordinary members of the public. I suppose this was quite true and a great comfort to us all.

Later on a movie was made about the Kray twins which I went to see. The bit that surprised me most was the way the Regency Club was portrayed. It looked exactly in the movie as I remembered the place all those years ago. There must have been some good research done and I was more impressed with that little detail than I was with the rest of the film.

I do remember one time going along to the Regency Club and being denied admission by the doorman on the grounds that "Someone has been shot here tonight so we can't let you in". To this day I don't know who shot whom and perhaps it is just as well. I do hope, however, that they cleaned up the blood on the carpet. This sort of thing does leave rather a mess.

Despite this incident I still frequented the club on a regular basis and got to know the management somewhat. I don't think I ever spoke to Ronnie Kray but I certainly exchanged a word or two with Reggie. However, my main contact was with the owner of the club whose name I have quite forgotten.

One day I happened to find out from the club owner that they were looking for entertainers. I didn't feel at this stage that I was competent enough to appear on their nightclub floor doing a magic act although I quite enjoyed doing impromptu card magic on a casual basis for people visiting the club. I did happen to know of a band that I thought were quite good and I proposed to the owner that they be given an audition and I would act as their agent.

He agreed to this and I duly brought the band in one evening to do a free show as an audition. The terrible twins were there watching with scowls on their faces. Not only were they not impressed with the performance, neither was the audience. From the reception I could see my career as a theatrical agent going down the drain before it had even started. At the end of their act I went up to the club owner and asked what he thought. He uttered one word only. "Crap!"

I returned to the place where the band were tearing down their equipment and relayed the bad news to the lead singer who seemed to be the leader of the group. He took the news badly and got quite indignant over it. He then shocked me by saying, "Well, we wasted a lot of time coming out here to do this gig". For those of you who are not wise in the ways of the entertainment industry "gig" simply means job or engagement. I replied that this wasn't a "gig" but an audition. The lead singer huffed and puffed and started to demand "expenses" from the club for their time. I attempted to explain that this was an audition and expenses were simply not an issue. He replied that he didn't expect a professional fee but just a nominal sum to cover his expenses.

We argued back and forth and I got somewhat irritated when the prima donna singer had the temerity to suggest that I paid him myself out of my own pocket. I told him that there was more chance of me being struck by lightning than digging in to my own meagre funds to pay him and his unworthy colleagues.

He then demanded that I go and ask the Kray twins for "expenses" on their behalf. They were sitting there at the back of the club with the owner and various other cronies who did not look like respectable citizens. At the time I assumed that the Krays owned the club and thought that they were the ones responsible for any payment.

I instinctively knew that asking for expenses would be a very bad idea indeed and told him so. He became very insistent so in exasperation I told him, "You can go and ask them yourself if you want". He answered, "Yes I think I will". I warned, "Be careful. Do you know who they are?" He informed me with great vehemence that he didn't care who they were and all he wanted was his "expenses".

He then made me cringe by approaching the Kray twins and the club owner on the other side of the room to demand his money. I didn't know where to look while all this was going on. Naturally I couldn't hear the conversation. All I can tell you is that he came back as white as a sheet and started to pack his gear away at a far quicker pace. I asked him if he had managed to get his "expenses" but he wouldn't answer me. I did see him whisper to his colleagues to get the hell out of the club as fast as they could.

I never saw the band again and my activities in discovering musical talent came to an abrupt end. I do know that the Kray twins gave me somewhat unfriendly looks from that day forth. The club owner seemed amused though and I still kept on friendly terms with him.

Some months later after the band debacle I got the strange idea that perhaps I could after all present an act on the nightclub floor. I had put together an act consisting of card tricks only that could be seen from a distance. I had rehearsed it thoroughly and even tried it out a few times at various venues such as parties and other venues. Accordingly I proposed to the club owner that I present my act on the nightclub floor and if it went over well they would allow me to appear on a regular basis. The owner agreed and it was arranged that the next evening I would perform my act.

I wasn't sure whether I was going to be paid a fee or not but found the courage to timidly ask him if any money would be forthcoming and if so how much? His eyes glazed over and he looked everywhere but directly at me and muttered, "Well yes, you'll be on wages like". I found this rather ungrammatical sentence to be a bit vague but mindful of the band audition debacle of a few months before I decided not to push the matter further. I suppose you could say this was my first professional engagement even though I had no idea how much I was going to be paid or even if payment was an option considering the evasive reaction and body language of the club owner.

The next evening with high hopes I presented my new nightclub act. I remember the Kray twins were in attendance. Things did not get off to a good start. The club was full of inebriated customers who did not show the slightest inclination that they were interested in my stupid card tricks. Not only were they chattering throughout the performance, many of them had their backs to me and were just plain not watching.

To compound the problem waiters were constantly crossing the floor right in front of my performing area. To add to the hassle there was the noise of glasses clinking all over the club as the waiters were serving. There was even the odd heckler for which I was actually grateful since at least they were paying attention.

The real trouble started when I tried to get an audience member up to help me. Nobody would volunteer and they studiously ignored me.

I then took the bull by the horns and directly asked someone at a nearby table to come up and help. He refused so I asked someone else. He refused too. I then saw a woman who seemed to be vaguely interested in the show and asked her to help. She said, "No thanks". In desperation—and I cringe inwardly as I write this—I asked a passing waiter if he would help me. His reply was "Sorry mate, I'm too busy" and he glided straight by me without missing a beat. Somehow I got through the act by approaching tables directly and requesting people to choose cards etc; and participate without having to come up in front of everyone in the performing area. Of course this made the visibility of the act sink into oblivion and the performance deteriorated even further.

All in all, my debut was an unmitigated disaster. I finished my act and skedaddled from the club as fast as I possibly could. I didn't dare look at the club owner or the Kray twins. Instead, I looked at the floor which I thought was going to swallow me up whole. All thought of going to ask the club owner for my rather vague fee had disappeared from my thoughts. Indeed I was so embarrassed that I never set foot in the Regency Club again.

That was not the end of my misery. Around that time I was frequenting various pubs in the East End of London and, for some reason I always seemed to go into the same pubs that the Krays were visiting with their various cronies, including the owner of the Regency Club. As soon as they would see me they would burst out laughing and point me out saying, "There's the magician!" At least I suppose it could be said that, in the end, I did provide good entertainment for them. I felt very uncomfortable every time I bumped into them though and it did happen several times.

The reason I was frequenting the pubs was that, in those days, some of them would actually book entertainers to perform on their very small stages. I got quite a few of these engagements and they provided very valuable experience. Unfortunately I still wasn't any good and one memory comes to me quite vividly. I had approached a pub landlord and asked if I could perform my magic act. I showed him some little pocket tricks which impressed him and he asked, "Do you have an actual act besides these little tricks?" I said "Sure" and he booked me for the magnificent sum of three pounds which even in those days wasn't a great deal of money. However, it wasn't bad and I was happy to get it.

Naturally the act died a death nearly as bad as it did at the Regency Club. However, this time I was determined to get paid. I approached the landlord who was not pleased at all. He snarled at me, "You expect to be paid for that load of rubbish?" I answered, "Well I did perform and I do expect to be paid".

The publican angrily slammed the cash register open and, with great ill grace, thrust three pound notes into my hand. I grabbed the money, turned around to exit the pub and to this day I can hear him snarling to my back, "You told me you had an act! You told me you had an act! You *don't* have an act and you never will!" His statement was only partially true. I didn't have an act at the time of his snarling but I eventually went on to develop a good one but it was a long way off yet.

Mind you most of the pubs I worked I got a reasonable reception although I was far from a polished performer. Although I could still get the fantastic reactions doing the close up magic with cards, coins and other small props somehow I couldn't hack it on the stage. It was a different world entirely and it required a different approach which I had not yet mastered.

One day I happened to read an interesting piece of news in a magazine for magicians. It seemed that a British card magician named Mick Chardo had been creating quite a bit of a stir by appearing in restaurants doing close up magic . He would be paid a fee by the restaurant and would approach tables and ask to show the diners some magic. Once he got their attention he would sit down at the table and perform for ten minutes or so. Nowadays this kind of restaurant magic is very common on both sides of the Atlantic. However, in those days it was unheard of in Britain although the practice was still prevalent in North America. Mick Chardo was a trail blazer in his own way since he was the first one who introduced the idea of close up magic in restaurants to the UK.

He was not a timid type and somehow was able to persuade restaurant owners to use this kind of entertainment even though it was hitherto unknown. I read in the magazine that he had been working at a restaurant in Soho called Ley-on's. This was a well-known Chinese restaurant and was fairly high class.

A few months later I heard through the grapevine that Chardo was no longer working at Ley-on's so I decided that perhaps I should approach them myself. I knew that my close up magic was very strong indeed and that this job would be quite suitable for my talents. Accordingly one day I went in and asked for the manager. I was shown into an office and seated there was an attractive young Chinese woman who from her air of authority was obviously the boss. Also in the office were two businessmen who I assume were suppliers to the restaurant. To this day I am still not quite sure who they were but I know they were not connected with the restaurant itself.

I told her my business and that I had heard that she had used a magician in the past. She had a very skeptical look on her face and wasn't over friendly. She said, "Why is it that people come to me with these crazy ideas?" I asked her how the idea went over in the past with the previous magician. She said, "It was interesting. I suppose it was OK but he told too many dirty stories at the table". Of course I hadn't read this in the magic magazine! I replied truthfully that I didn't know any dirty stories. Still, she looked more skeptical than ever.

Of course I knew what I had to do. I had to perform! I said, "Let me give you an idea of what I can do". I produced a deck of cards and went to work. Her expression didn't change and she didn't smile or show any reaction to the tricks. The two businessmen reacted with great laughter and astonishment and I thanked my lucky stars that they were there.

At one point I did a trick that needed "an invisible hair". This was purely an imaginary hair that I pulled from my head and was purely a part of the presentation of the trick that I was doing. She immediately reacted negatively saying, "We can't have hairs on the table when you are performing. People are eating. This is a restaurant!" I tried to explain that it was not a real hair being used but an imaginary one but she would have none of it. I shrugged and said, "Well, I don't have to do that particular trick. I have plenty of others".

She continued to look unimpressed while the businessmen looked more bedazzled and bewildered. Finally I finished and she said, "Well, I admit that you are better than the other fellow but I don't really think this is suitable for a Chinese restaurant. I have no idea how the other magician talked me into it".

I could see the interview not going very well but suddenly to my great surprise the two businessmen spoke up for me saying how great I was and of course she should have me performing there. One of these men was particularly enthusiastic and said, "I have seen this done in America at restaurants and bars. It is a fantastic idea and you will be the only restaurant in London that is doing it".

He obviously had a lot of influence with her and she finally gave in. She said, "OK. You are hired. My mother will kill me when she finds out". I found out later that her mother actually owned the restaurant but had been in hospital for several months and consequently had left her daughter in charge while she was incapacitated. The daughter was actually a film actress so perhaps this is why she had some sympathy for other theatrical types.

Accordingly I started to perform at Ley-on's and I was quite successful. I hardly ever saw the manageress for which I was quite grateful since she wasn't that friendly or approachable and quite frankly she put the fear of God into me. Still, she gave me the chance to perform for which I was grateful. In fact, now that I think about it there is a bit of historical significance to this story since I was only the second magician in the UK to perform close up magic professionally in restaurants. Mick Chardo was the first and was the original trail blazer for professional close up magic in Britain. Ironically he later gave up magic and became a traffic warden instead.

I remember the aforementioned Michael Vishnick visited the restaurant in the company of another magician. He asked the waiter if I was, "As good as the other fellow" and I was gratified to hear later that the waiter answered, "Oh, he is better—he does more". In other words I had a bigger repertoire.

Now the major difference between performing in UK restaurants and North American ones was the tipping factor. Restaurant magicians in the USA and Canada get tips all the time. In the UK, however, tipping is not quite so prevalent and in those days receiving tips from customers was unheard of especially as the only two restaurant magicians in Britain were myself and Mick Chardo.

This didn't bother me particularly since I was being paid a reasonable sum by the restaurant anyway. One day, however, I was slightly disconcerted when I approached a table and the diner said, "I don't mind you showing me card tricks as long as you don't expect me to tip you!" I told him that I certainly didn't expect tips and that I was well taken care of by the management.

In fact nobody at the restaurant ever tipped me even though I had been performing there for a few weeks every night on a daily basis. It just wasn't the done thing in Britain to tip a magician. In fact, sometimes even the waiters didn't get tipped either!

One night, however, all that changed. Not only did I get a large tip I went over so well that paradoxically it nearly led to my undoing. An American family and their friends came in one evening and I entertained them at the table. They raved and raved about how good I was and in fact they had been the best audience I had ever experienced in the restaurant. They were quite vocal in their admiration and I did notice some frosty looks from the waiters because of the rather loud reactions. This was after all a high class restaurant and rowdy behaviour was frowned upon.

I was given the one and only tip I ever received and it was rather a large one. Of course, Americans tip as part of their culture and it comes quite naturally to them. The father of the family said to me, "You are the greatest magician I have ever seen". I tried to capitalise on this compliment by saying, "Perhaps you could tell that to the management on the way out". The man replied, "I sure will".

And alas he did. I say alas since it turned out to be somewhat disastrous. On the way out he asked to see the manager. He was informed frostily by the head waiter that the manageress was unavailable. He was asked why he wanted to see the manager. He replied that he wanted to tell her how good the magician was. The head waiter said that he would convey his thoughts to the management but the American wasn't satisfied with this. He felt that he was being stonewalled and demanded loudly to see the manageress. The more he demanded to see the management the more he was rebuffed. Regrettably this escalated into an unseemly argument with raised voices and when I overheard all this I wanted to crawl under one of the tables.

The next day the manageress told me that she had heard about the fuss and she did not seem pleased. I told her that it was nothing to do with me and that I couldn't help the over enthusiastic reactions of customers. She didn't seem to be convinced and I ended up in her bad books because of it.

Generally speaking, however, she seemed pleased overall with my performances and I worked there for a month. It was quite a steady booking for me and I liked it very much. One day, however, the manageress's mother came out of hospital. And just as her daughter had predicted she did not approve of the frivolity caused by magicians performing at the tables for patrons.

She told me, "My daughter gets these silly ideas. We are a high class restaurant not a circus. We won't be needing you any more". And so my restaurant magic career came to an abrupt end.

I was, however, quite ambitious and determined to break into showbusiness. Most of my income was derived from the sale of Svengali decks but I didn't find it fulfilling. I wanted to be on the stage. I therefore haunted the offices of theatrical agents and asked them to come and see my show. In those days this was the standard way of operating. Nowadays you submit promotional materials and a video or DVD to an agent but in the old days you would try your utmost to get them to come and view your work at a live performance. Most of the time they wouldn't show up but if you could somehow sell them on the fact that you had talent then the odd time they would come out and see you with a view to possibly booking you in the future.

Accordingly, I haunted the agents' offices and asked them to come and see me. However, when they asked where I was working I would mention some pub or other where I had a booking. Pub engagements weren't very prestigious venues and agents weren't terribly impressed by them so I got nowhere.

One day I wandered into the offices of a noted agency known as the Blackburn Agency and told them about my act. I remember there was a fellow there named Andy Wood and an older lady named Eva. They listened to my story with the usual skepticism but I noticed that Eva seemed to be slightly less lukewarm. Anyhow they promised to come out and see my show if they possibly could and of course they didn't.

I continued, however, to go in and pester them but they only showed slight interest although they did humour me a little. I do remember Eva in some sort of motherly way advising me to do children's shows and saying that there was good money in them. At the time I had no ambitions in that direction but in later years I did indeed become a children's entertainer and found it very rewarding.

At the time there was a weekly theatrical newspaper called *The Stage* and it is still in existence to this day. It had all sorts of advertisements in a category called "Entertainers wanted". The depressing thing was that you would often see the ads worded something like this, "Variety acts of all kinds required. (No magicians)". It amuses me now to think about it but at the time it wasn't amusing in the slightest.

Eventually, I happened to see an advertisement requesting entertainers to audition and this time it didn't say a word about not wanting magicians so I thought it might be worth a try. Accordingly I phoned the number in the paper and was told to report for an interview prior to an audition being set up. I was told to bring any photographs I had of the act. In those days photos were the most important part of your promotional material and they were more important than any literature you had.

I took down the address and prepared to be on my way the next afternoon. However, my sense of navigation became somewhat askew and I got lost. I came to a tiny street called Swallow Street where there were two nightclubs side by side. One was called the L'Hirondelle and the other was named the Stork Room. For some reason which I can no longer recall I was convinced that the L'Hirondelle was the place that the auditions were being held so I wandered in with great anticipation.

There was a small hallway and nobody seemed to be around. It was beginning to dawn on me that perhaps I had come to the wrong address. Just then a small dark important looking man appeared out of nowhere. I was to find out that he was the owner of the nightclub. So many years have passed that I have quite forgotten his name so for the purpose of this story I will call him Mr Mustapha. He was of Turkish origin. I have no idea if Mustapha is a Turkish name or not but it will have to do for the moment.

He looked at me and said, "We are closed until the evening. Did you want something?" I replied, "I have come about the auditions advertised in the paper". His puzzled response was "What auditions? What paper?" I said, "*The Stage* newspaper. It said you were having auditions and I phoned up about it".

He answered, "I don't know anything about auditions. You must have come to the wrong place. Are you an entertainer?" I replied "I am indeed" whereupon he enquired, "What kind of entertainer are you?" I told him that I was a magician. He pondered for a moment and said "I need entertainers. I don't know if a magician would be suitable here though". I told him that my act was a little different from most magicians since it consisted of nothing but card tricks. I told him that the card tricks in question could be seen from a distance and appreciated before large audiences. He didn't seem convinced.

My salvation had always been the close up magic so I immediately pulled out a little pocket trick and showed it to him. His eyes widened and I could see that he was impressed. I then did a card trick and I could see he was sold. He said, "I'll tell you what. We have an early show at 10.00 p.m. and a later show at 1.00 a.m. Do your act here tonight at the earlier show and I'll see how well it goes over. If it works out I will hire you". He explained that I would not be paid for the evening and my performance would act as an audition.

I agreed to this and was quite pleased with myself. I left the club deciding not to bother locating the place where I was supposed to do the audition that was advertised in *The Stage* newspaper.

I duly showed up ready to do the 10.00 p.m. show and Mr Mustapha was there as expected. There were only about five people in the audience and they were at fairly close quarters to the performing area which was not on a stage but on the night club floor itself. There were tables all around the room and I remember a little balcony area with even more tables and chairs.

Because of the sparse number of audience members I decided not to use the microphone. I did a fifteen minute act and it seemed to go reasonably well considering the fact that there were few spectators some of whom were eating and one of whom I inveigled on to the night club floor to help me.

I approached Mr Mustapha for his verdict and he looked undecided. He asked me why I hadn't used the microphone and I replied that I didn't think I needed it because there were so few people in the audience. He said, "Next time use the microphone". I seized on this and said, "Is there going to be a next time?" He answered, "I'm not sure. There were too few people in the audience for me to judge. I would like you to come back at one a.m and do another show for the later crowd. There will be many more people by then and I will be able to see your act and judge it under more normal conditions. If you do this I will pay you a fee of five pounds". In those days five pounds wasn't bad money so I naturally accepted.

I let the club and wandered the streets of the West End of London and came back in time for the 1.00 a.m. show. I was in, however, for an unpleasant surprise. The club was full and the audience was indeed more plentiful. However, they were also extremely intoxicated. I could see this was going to be a difficult show.

I remember the compere (MC to North American readers) was a singer named Johnny Lee. He was at the club on a semi permanent basis and had signed a long contract with them. He introduced me and I went on to inattentive indifference. I tried to gain the attention of the audience to no avail and had to put up with quite a lot of heckling. Somehow I got someone up to help me with the card tricks and he proved to be quite obnoxious. All in all, the act died a complete and utter death.

I walked off stage knowing that I would have to face Mr Mustapha and I was in fear and dread of it. I waited in the dressing room for him but he was nowhere to be seen. I then ventured forth into the club to find him but he seemed to have vanished into thin air. Just then the head waiter approached me and said, "I have a message for you from Mr Mustapha. He had to leave early and wasn't able to watch your act. He wants you to come in tomorrow night and do the 10.00 p.m. show and the 1.00 a.m. show. He will pay you five pounds for the two performances".

I was quite relieved that he hadn't seen my awful show and resolved that I would do better the next time. I duly showed up the next evening ready to do battle again. I performed at the first show to a reasonable size crowd. The act went over quite well and everyone was relatively sober. However, I could see no sign of Mr Mustapha.

The later show died an even bigger death than it had done the night before and the audience was even more intoxicated. I was beginning to learn that doing an act consisting of card tricks at one o'clock in the morning to an audience of drunks was not an effective proposition. Of course the later the hour the more time the audience had to get inebriated.

I came off stage resigned to be told by Mr Mustapha not to come back. However, it didn't happen since there was no Mr Mustapha to be found.

In fact, I had not seen him all evening. Lo and behold the head waiter approached me and repeated essentially the same story as the night before. He told me that Mr Mustapha had not been able to get to the club that night but had left a message that I was to appear again the next evening and again do two shows. Again I would be paid five pounds. I did notice that so far there had been no attempt to pay me the ten pounds already owed to me for this evening's performances plus that of the night before. I broached the subject only to be told to ask Mr Mustapha about it.

I then said, "I will be happy to perform tomorrow night but will Mr Mustapha definitely be in attendance this time?" I was told that he had to audition another act the next night and he would do so at the 1.00 a.m. show. For this reason he would definitely be there.

I duly presented myself at the night club the next evening and did indeed see Mr Mustapha in attendance. I did the first show and went over tolerably well as usual. It was always the second later show that caused the difficulties because by then the alcohol was flowing and the club was busier. However, I saw no sign of the act from Poland who was to be auditioned. I reasoned that he would probably show up at the second show and I was correct.

In the dressing room before the 1.00 a.m. show I found that I was in the presence of a rather egotistical acrobat from Poland. He told me that he had travelled all over the world with his wife and that he was one of the top acts in the business. He also informed me that Mr Mustapha needed a novelty act for the club and was going to decide between him and me.

I had a sinking feeling that I had no chance competing against an obviously seasoned professional especially since so far I had done so badly at the later shows. My negative vibes were confirmed when I went on and died the usual death. He and his wife on the other hand performed with great aplomb and left the nightclub floor to a rousing ovation.

The acrobat, however, didn't come straight back to the dressing room. I noticed that he and his wife had gone to sit at Mr Mustapha's table and were entering into deep discussion with him. I figured that he was probably going to get the job and my showbusiness career was going to come to an abrupt end before it had even had a chance to begin.

My suspicions were confirmed when he came back into the dressing room bragging away to me how he had been booked for a month with an option for another month. He was going to start on the Monday of the following week. It was obvious that I was out for the count but I still had to hear it officially.

I therefore left the dressing room to find Mr Mustapha who had done his usual disappearing act. I then decided to do the next best thing and speak to the head waiter whom I had now found out was actually his brother. As a matter of fact I discovered that many of the waiters and other staff were related to Mr Mustapha and virtually everyone who worked there, apart from the entertainers, happened to be from Turkey.

After locating him I was informed that Mr Mustapha would call me if he needed me but of course I knew quite well that it was perfectly obvious that he didn't. There was, however, the little matter of payment for the three nights I had already worked. I was told to call Mr Mustapha in a few days when he would be returning from some business trip or other.

I remember that all this happened in the Summer of 1966. The reason I remember the year is that at the time I was selling Svengali decks outside Wembley Stadium when the World Cup Soccer Games were in full swing. The main thing I remember is that Mexico was playing some team or other because I was selling the trick decks in droves and mostly to Mexican football fans. On reflection despite my statement above I think they were probably playing England since that was the country we were in.

After a few days selling the decks I decided that it was about time I got paid from the L'Hirondelle and I assumed that Mr Mustapha must have returned from his business trip by now. I found a payphone near the stadium and phoned the club and asked for Mr Mustapha only to be greeted by a secretary who on hearing my name got very excited and said, "I am so glad you phoned. We have been trying to reach you for the last couple of days but we've lost your phone number. Mr Mustapha would like you to work at the club for one week starting on Monday".

I was astonished at this turn of events but naturally quite pleased about it. I did go down to the club on Monday and lo and behold they had my money ready for me for the three days I had already worked. The act died a death virtually every night as usual but the earlier shows were always a little easier than the later ones, although still not spectacular.

I did not see Mr Mustapha all week in the club which was in some ways a relief since he wouldn't witness my act flopping every night. However, one day I went to the washroom and suddenly became aware of a small Turkish man using the next urinal. I quickly realised this was Mr Mustapha. He recognized me and said. "How are you?" I said "Fine. Thanks for the booking". He responded, "You are welcome. I want you to work for another month. Can you do this?"

I agreed in a flash. From being booked for one week I had now had my engagement extended for a whole month. As a matter of fact the month eventually stretched into several more months. I must say, however, that this is the only time in my career I have ever been booked while urinating in a public washroom. I wonder if this event is of great historical significance.

One thing did puzzle me though. I wondered what had happened to the Polish acrobat who was no longer to be seen. I reasoned quite accurately as it turned out, that he had been replaced by me but I couldn't figure out why since he was obviously a sizzling professional act whereas I was simply an incompetent card magician who couldn't handle drunks and died a death every night.

After making some enquiries I found out what had happened. It seemed that the gentleman from Poland used to get highly irritated when the waiters would cross the floor to serve customers and to do so would have to cross the performing area. He felt no doubt quite rightly that it interfered with his act. He remonstrated with them and with Mr Mustapha but to no avail. One night he was fuming mad and threatened the waiters thus, "If you dare to cross the floor again while I am performing you will pay for it".

Of course the waiters simply did what they always did and that was to cross the floor. This time the acrobat lost his temper and ejected his wife from his shoulders into a wandering waiter who went sprawling over the night club floor and the tray of food and drinks went sprawling with him. There were then great screams of Turkish from the waiter and Polish from the acrobat, followed by punches and mayhem. I am quite sure the audience were entertained more by this than any of the acts that were performing that night.

As a result of the uproar the acrobat was deemed to be surplus to requirements and was given the boot. They were then short of an act and the result was that I was given the job and the start of a showbusiness career which has lasted to this day along with my various other shenanigans. My act was somewhat on the mediocre side but at least I never sent any of the waiters sprawling.

With regard to the above-mentioned mediocrity I can only plead in my belated defence that I was raw and inexperienced at the time and had been thrown in at the deep end. Even grizzled veteran entertainers would have had trouble with those intoxicated inattentive audiences. It wasn't just one person that became inebriated—I could have handled that. No. It was the whole darned audience.

Of course upon reflection the act itself probably wasn't that exciting. I do remember the head waiter once approaching me and saying, "Young man, why don't you do something about your act?" I replied, "Why? Is there something wrong with it?" The rather devastating reply came, "Well, let me put it this way. We have a regular customer that comes in every night. As soon as you come on he goes out of the club for a breath of fresh air. As soon as you have finished he comes back!"

I managed to develop a very thick skin as the months went by. I would die a death every night and expected to do so. I would never get nervous before going on stage. The reason for nervousness on the part of an entertainer is that he or she is worried deep down that the act will not go over well. I *knew* my act was going to go over badly so I figured that there was nothing to get nervous about since I knew the outcome anyway!

Still, I was gathering valuable experience at the L'Hirondelle and it stood me in good stead when I later worked easier venues. Over the years my show improved and now I feel that I can work just about anywhere. In fact I often hanker to go back in time and work the L'Hirondelle again but with one difference. I would want to know then what I know now. Alas the time machine that would enable me to do that hasn't been invented yet.

However, the L'Hirondelle was the real start of my career in entertainment and it was to lead to much, much more....

CHAPTER FOUR

No Business Like Show Business

RIGHT NEXT DOOR TO L'Hirondelle was another nightclub called the Stork Room. It was owned by Al Burnett, a noted comedian of the time. It occurred to me that this might be a place to get work. However, it also occurred to me that the management of the L'Hirondelle might not take kindly to me working right next door since I assumed that the Stork Room was a competitor. It turned out ultimately that this was not an issue but it concerned me at the time.

One night I was told that Al Burnett was in the audience and he was looking for acts. The other entertainers on the show were quite excited about this and viewed his presence to be an opportunity to audition.

In my act I picked out a member of the audience to help me on stage—or at least on the nightclub floor which acted as a stage. I saw Al Burnett and the temptation was too great. I figured that if he saw the tricks close up he could not help but be impressed. Accordingly, I invited him up to help in the act. He rose unsteadily to his feet and I could see that he was more than a little bit tipsy.

Of course this wasn't an unusual state of affairs in my audience volunteers and I often had trouble controlling inebriated "helpers" in my early days. Of course the idea may occur to my readers that I shouldn't have picked intoxicated people up to help in the first place. However, at many of the nightclub shows I worked it was pretty difficult to find anyone in the audience who was actually sober. However, with experience I figured out how to avoid the problem. I would scan the audience before the show and select people in my mind that looked relatively sober. When I went on stage I would pick those audience members to help. Of course once in a while even this precaution didn't work and I would end up with the wrong person. However, I will relate later how a veteran magician named Jerry Bergmann solved the problem for me.

Now back to the Al Burnett story. I did my act as usual but he looked too tipsy to take it all in properly. I don't think he understood a single trick even though he cooperated quite well as an assistant. He didn't try to ruin the tricks as some drunks did. He just stood there quietly and did as I asked him.

The act went over quite well for a change and later in the evening Burnett called me over to his table. I thought he was going to book me for his club but that wasn't the purpose of his summons. With slurred speech he told me that he knew my father. I was a little puzzled by this but thought fleetingly that it might be true since my father had been a night club photographer and conceivably Al might have met him at some point. But then he said, "Your father was a great magician" which quite confused me since my dad had never done a magic trick in his life. I managed to splutter, "My father was a magician?" whereupon Burnett exclaimed, "Yes, the great McLeod. He was your father and he was a fantastic magician". To this day I still have no idea who the "great McLeod" was. I have never heard of him. Perhaps I should do some research on the matter.

Since I had been introduced on stage as Ronnie McLeod, Al had put two and two together and came up with five. Of course he wasn't thinking properly because of all the drink he had consumed. I decided not to disillusion him and figured it would be good for business for him to think that he knew my father. After all he owned the nightclub next door and I wanted to work there.

It didn't look, however, as if it were going to be an easy thing to get the job. At the end of the night, after the cabaret was over, I found out that Burnett had booked *all* of the acts on the bill to appear at the Stork Room with one notable omission. Me! It seemed that my wonderful card tricks seen at close range and his supposed friendship with my "father" had not impressed him sufficiently enough to book me. My confidence was a trifle shaken to find that he had hired every entertainer in the L'Hirondelle except me! I was so peeved with this that the next day I decided to take some action.

I phoned the Stork Room and asked to speak to Al Burnett concerning my act. I was told that he wasn't available but that if I wanted to work at the Stork Room I had to go through an agent that they dealt with exclusively. I was a trifle irritated to find that I would have to go through an agent and pay him commission since Burnett had booked everyone directly and in person the night before.

However, I could see no other option so asked for the name and phone number of the agent. His name was Barry Burnett. I thought the surname was an odd coincidence but I shrugged it off. I then phoned Barry Burnett and got through to him straight away. He suggested that I go down to see him which I did.

When I got there I was quite surprised to see a young man who was around the same age as myself sitting behind a desk looking very important. I showed him my photographs and promotional material and told him that I worked at the L'Hirondelle and that Al Burnett had come in and helped me do my act. He said that he would talk to Al and see if he would offer me a booking.

I casually remarked that it was a bit of a coincidence that he and Al had the same surname and he astonished me by saying "Oh, he's my dad!" I found it somewhat ironic that he was the sole agent for the nightclub owned by his dad and that I would have to pay commission to him for an engagement that in theory I didn't really need him for! But of course, I did need him since I couldn't get through to Al Burnett directly and the great man didn't seem to want to book me when he had the chance the night before.

A few days later Barry phoned me and lo and behold he offered me a booking to work at the Stork Room. I was quite pleased to hear this because it meant that all I had to do was walk next door from the L'Hirondelle to fill the booking. My show time was arranged not to clash with my cabaret time at the L'Hirondelle and I had to do two shows a night. This was quite a coup for me since I would now be paid for four shows a night instead of just the two at the L'Hirondelle.

When I went in the first night the head waiter asked me, "Do you get anyone up in your act to help?" I said "Yes". He replied, "Well don't get anybody from that table, that table, or that table" pointing to three tables which were adjoining each other. I said "Why?" but got no reply.

Then the compere came along and asked, "Do you get anyone up to help in your act?" Again I said "yes". He said "Don't get anyone up from those tables down there" pointing to the exact same tables the headwaiter had indicated. I replied, "I know. But why?" He answered, "They are the boys". I had no idea what he was talking about and enquired what he meant. He told me that "the boys" were top criminals of the London underworld. He also pointed out a far corner of the club where he told me officers from Scotland Yard were seated. It seemed they came in every night to keep a tab on the gangsters.

I was introduced and went on stage to do my act. The audiences at the Stork Room were far less rowdy than at the L'Hirondelle but there was still a buzz of inattention and talking. However, it wasn't too bad in comparison and there was only one heckler who was bothering me rather than the several I would have to put with at the club next door. He was, nevertheless, becoming very annoying and was beginning to irritate me. Suddenly there was a shout from the darkness exclaiming, "Be quiet, sonny!"

At first I thought that the shout was directed at me but it wasn't. It had come from the table of the gangsters and was meant for the heckler. There was a sudden deathly hush all round the club as the heckler froze in fear. Everyone in the club went as quiet as a mouse and you could hear a pin drop. It seemed that everyone in the club knew who "the boys" were!

All the inattention and talking died down and I was able to get on with my act in peace. The club was dark as hell and I couldn't see into the audience to pick anyone to help. The only table I could see was the one that the headwaiter and the compere had told me to avoid. It was, however, the table with the friendly gangster and the occupants did look interested in the show. I therefore became brave and picked out one of them to assist. He came up on stage very shyly and indeed looked quite out of place and very embarrassed. Nevertheless, he was good as gold on stage albeit a little self conscious. His pals in the audience loved the show and it went over very well.

In those days the London nightclubs were filled with big time criminals of every description. They were always well behaved and treated the entertainers with courtesy which was more than a lot of the supposedly more "respectable" patrons would do.

By way of illustration regarding the above, during this period I had managed to obtain a booking on odd nights at a small London night club named the Negresco. It was owned by a former entertainer named Ronnie Ross. I was hired to do mainly close up magic at the tables but would occasionally do my cabaret act as well.

A lot of gangsters habituated the place and loved for me to perform for them. They would invite me to their table and insist on seeing card tricks. I always did this with mixed feelings. They were a fantastic audience but I would feel very uncomfortable when they would talk business. I was amazed that they would openly discuss which bank they had robbed and who they had shot that week. There were two reasons I resolved to avoid them the next time they came in. One, I didn't really want to know who their next murder victim was; and two, they kept offering me large sums of money to cheat for them. I was a naïve innocent kid and much more honest than I am now. Besides, I didn't really know how to cheat at cards anyway, so I always refused their offers. They couldn't understand why I wouldn't want to make vast amounts of money for myself. I tried to explain the concepts of honesty to them, but I wasn't very successful. They kept trying to convince me and I kept refusing, so I got quite uncomfortable when they would come in.

Actually the main reason I didn't want to perform for them was that I was running out of material. I had, and still have, a large repertoire of close up magic but the gangsters just dried me up. I really had nothing left to show them. I resolved that the next time they arrived I would make an excuse and not join them at their table. Unfortunately, when they did come in they beckoned to me and said, "Son, we've got a present for you". Then they presented me with a beautiful set of cufflinks with playing cards on them. After that came the usual request to perform and this time, because of the gift I couldn't say no. I tried to though. "You've seen all my tricks," I said, "I've got nothing left to show you". However, they demanded, "Come on, just one!" I was about to try and get out of it when I realised that I had a Svengali deck with me that night. I had been to see a department store buyer and I just happened to have the deck with me. I never performed it as part of a close up magic show, I only demonstrated Svengali decks at venues where I could sell them. But that night I was desperate for material so I decided to show them the Svengali deck.

All I can say is the reaction from those gangsters was unbelievable! They told me it was the best card trick I had ever shown them. The laughter and shouting was so loud it attracted attention from the other tables. I had garnered great audience reaction from these nefarious characters in the past when I worked with regular cards, but this was nothing compared to the excitement generated from the Svengali deck.

Later the owner of the club informed me that the gangsters told him that the trick where the deck all changed to the three of diamonds was the greatest thing they had ever seen.

OK. The above tangent is over and now back to my Stork Room adventures. One night I performed a card trick at the club that had always been my signature trick and in fact it still is all these years later. I would bring one person up on stage to help. The idea was that he would count out seventeen cards on a table and I would send three cards across to him invisibly through the airwaves by magic. He would have twenty cards instead of the seventeen he had previously. Something went wrong (I know not what, to this day) and when the guy counted out the cards he still had seventeen! I simply made a big "to do" about the fact and acted as if the trick had worked! I raised my voice to a dramatic climax saying, "Fifteen, sixteen, seventeen cards!" I placed my hands in an applause cue position and the audience actually clapped like mad! They were too drunk to follow the trick anyway, and I think that was why I got away with it. I do remember Al Burnett watching. He turned to a friend looking puzzled and then turned his attention back to me. He shrugged his shoulders and then applauded like everyone else. It is amazing what you can do with a bit of audacity.

Now I was quite pleased to be working at two clubs but I wanted more. I knew there were quite a lot of clubs in the heart of London that I could get to quite easily by the London subway system which is known as the "underground" or "the tube". Accordingly I decided the best thing to do was approach these venues directly. I decided to actually go down to the clubs in person and see what headway I could make.

My first call was at the Gargoyle nightclub in the heart of Soho. This was actually a strip club owned by a fellow named Jimmy Jacobs. When I got there I met a man named Philip Midgely who managed the club for Jimmy. I told him that I was working at the L'Hirondelle and the Stork Room and this impressed him. He told me to come the next afternoon for an audition and show what I could do.

This time Jimmy Jacobs was in attendance and watched the act. There was nobody in the club except messrs Midgely and Jacobs. In the context of the act I had to get someone up to help me and chose Philip Midgely who essentially saw all the card tricks close up and was very impressed. Jimmy Jacobs seemed pleased as well and offered me the job. However, he offered a very low pay rate of fifteen pounds a week that, even in those days, was considered somewhat meagre. I protested and told them I was getting far more at the other two clubs. Jimmy Jacobs countered this by saying, "You have to do two spots at the other clubs. Here you only have to do one spot. It will be very easy work. And we will make you top of the bill".

I was very flattered to think that they would make me top of the bill but later my ego was deflated to find that "the bill" consisted of only me, and two striptease artists. At the other clubs there were always a few variety acts on as well as me but of course no strippers since the L'Hirondelle and the Stork Room were not strip clubs.

Jimmy then stunned me by saying, "You'll have some stiff competition. David Berglas worked here last week!" I was taken aback to discover that my tutor of a few years back had appeared at the Gargoyle the week before. Mind you I am quite sure he wasn't working for fifteen pounds a week. Still, I was somewhat surprised that Berglas would consent to appearing in a strip club. However, I found out later that he was a friend of Jimmy Jacobs and they both belonged to a showbusiness club known as the Grand Order of Water Rats. I expect David did the week as a favour to Jimmy. So I added the Gargoyle to my list of clubs to work. I was now doing five or six shows a night consisting of two each at the L'Hirondelle and the Stork Room and one at the Gargoyle plus the occasional appearance at the Negresco.

The Gargoyle proved to be a much quieter and more civilised venue than the other two clubs. There was no drunkenness and no heckling. In fact the audience was deathly quiet and you could hear a pin drop. The lighting was quite strong on the cabaret floor and I couldn't see the audience very well. It was actually an almost graveyard like atmosphere and the applause was somewhat muted, although loud enough to be heard. It was as if the people in the audience didn't want anyone to know they were there.

And of course they didn't. I realised later that the reason for the quiet atmosphere was that the businessmen and others who frequented the club wanted to simply sit there in the darkness and be titillated by the strippers. It was a sort of sick, dirty old men atmosphere and quite different from the raucous receptions strippers got in the Northern England clubs that I later worked.

Of course I had to get someone up to help in the act and bring that person into the glare of the spotlight. I am sure he felt uncomfortable being brought up onto the cabaret floor but I had to do what I had to do.

The astonishing thing is that one of the strippers was actually a transsexual man who had a sex change operation. The odd thing is that he was far better looking than the woman stripper! And nobody knew (including me) that he was actually a man rather than a woman. Truly I lived in a strange world at that time.

Of course there were no women in the audience and most of the men who attended the show came on their own. No buddies to cheer on the strippers and yell out, "Get em off!" as I was to see frequently in the northern clubs. The strippers performed in complete silence and the applause they got at the end of their acts was even more muted than my own.

I ended up performing at the Gargoyle for several months. I enjoyed working there because it was a wonderful rest from the other two clubs where the audiences were very rowdy indeed particularly the L'Hirondelle. However, the L'Hirondelle proved to be a haven of peace compared to the next club I added to my repertoire. That was the Blue Angel where I was to eventually experience the worst and most badly behaved audiences I have ever come across in my life.

I phoned the Blue Angel and was told that the entertainment was handled by a woman named Beatrice Braham who was a variety agent. I called her and told her that I was appearing at the L'Hirondelle, the Stork Room and the Gargoyle which duly impressed her and on the strength of that she booked me for one week to appear at the Blue Angel.

As mentioned already the audiences were hell on earth. They were in the main what are known as "hooray henries" in England. The nearest way for me to explain the meaning of this term is to say that it describes the idle rich but that wouldn't really convey the meaning either because it was much more than that. To say that it describes upper class twits would be more accurate. In the UK there has always been a bit of a class system and just because you have money does not make you upper class. Upper class represents the hoity-toity types that went to exclusive private schools such as Eton and Harrow and talked with posh accents.

This was the type of audience that frequented the Blue Angel and regrettably they didn't hold their drink very well. It also seemed to be a hobby with them to treat the entertainers with the utmost disrespect and heckle them unmercifully. Virtually 90% of the entire audience was intoxicated and it was a very rough atmosphere. I remember one poor lady singer having to put up with a drunk jumping up on stage uninvited, taking his trousers down and bending over in front of her showing his bare behind. I am not sure what message he was trying to convey to her but whatever it was she didn't seem to appreciate it.

I went through hell on earth every night trying to please these idiots but of course never succeeding. The worst part was trying to find someone relatively sober to come up and help. One night I decided to part with my usual procedure of getting someone up on stage to help me because of the drunkenness and since the audience was very close to the stage I merely approached people in the crowd to assist by selecting cards and suchlike. I had great difficulty finding anyone sober that I could approach except for one particular relatively cooperative person. The audience seemed to pick up on the fact that I was kept using the same person all the time and started to yell out, "stooge!" or "plant" implying that the fellow was a secret confederate of mine in the crowd. I then very foolishly exclaimed, "No, anyone can come up on stage to help me!" That was an invitation to disaster for up bounded some idiot in a tuxedo and a very posh upper class accent smelling of drink and slurring, "I'll help you!"

I very doubtfully asked him to select a card and he showed no willingness to do so. I decided to get rid of him and follow the advice of one of the nightclub hostesses at the L'Hirondelle who had previously advised me "Why do you keep those drunks on stage? You should be like other magicians I have seen and get rid of them". This of course was very good advice but she didn't tell me what to do if they refused to go. And yes—this fellow refused to go! I asked him to go back to his seat and he refused. He then whispered to me, "I'm only kidding, it's all right—I'll behave myself".

Unfortunately, it wasn't all right and he did not behave himself. In fact, he became far worse. Not only did he select a card he picked out three instead of one, threw two of them into the air and tore the third one in two pieces dropping them on the floor. He then grabbed the little table I used on stage and held it high above his head and started to walk around with it. It was now dawning upon me that this fellow was not an ideal assistant to have as a volunteer. The audience started to shout, "Get off the stage!" To this day I don't know if they were shouting "get off" to him or "get off" to me.

Suddenly the stage staff put out the lights on stage as a hint for me to get off. I had read somewhere, however, that the show must go on and didn't take the hint. I just kept on talking like the idiot I was. So what happened? They put the lights back on again!

Then two waiters appeared on stage and tried to remove the man but he refused to go. And what did the waiters do? They gave up and left me with him!

If I had been more experienced I would have simply given up the show and left the stage but of course I had no idea what the hell I was doing so I was stuck with my unwelcome visitor.

Suddenly I heard a woman in the audience shout to me, "Don't worry, magician—I'll get him off the stage for you". So saying she bounded up to the performing area to supposedly help me. However, she was just as drunk as he was. Before I knew where I was the pair of them started dancing together in each other's arms and it finally dawned on me that perhaps it was time to leave them to it. This was the worst night of all but the next night turned out to be the best.

I was told when I came in the next evening that the usual clientele were not going to be allowed in the club because there was a special outside function booked as a private event and I would have an entirely different and higher class audience. I was of course very happy to hear this but when I heard that 100% of the audience were all from Sweden I took fright and said, "I don't speak one word of Swedish!" I was merely told to "Try your best" which didn't make me feel any better.

My fears turned out to be groundless. Every single one of the Swedes present could speak perfect English and, what was even more wonderful they had perfect manners and were a decided contrast to the idiotic British audiences I had to put up with during the rest of the week. The act went very well and I felt a lot better than I had for quite a while. Anyway I finished the week in one piece (just about) and resolved not to work this awful club again.

One year later, however, I read something in the newspaper that prompted me to change my mind. It seemed that the club had changed hands and had been sold. The new owner said that he was going to try and attract a different clientele to what had normally been coming in. I was very pleased to hear this and phoned up and asked about performing there. I refrained from telling them that I had already performed at the club a year before. Even though the new owner would never have seen me perform I felt that since I had died a horrible death at the club night after night it might be better to keep quiet about the fact that I had worked there. I was informed that they would be doing auditions at the club on a particular afternoon and I could come along and do my act and if they liked it they would book it.

I duly showed up and was horrified to realise that the lady who seemed to be in charge of the auditions had a very familiar name. It was Beatrice Braham who had booked me the year before! Although the club had been sold they still kept the same agent. Still I hoped that she would not know who I was since, as far as I was aware she had never been into the club the week I performed or at least I had never seen her there. I had only spoken to her on the phone so reasoned that I might get away with it. Since the act had gone so badly the year before I didn't want her to realise that I had already performed at the club.

However, unbeknown to me she *had* visited the club on one of the nights I had appeared and had indeed seen my act. This all came out when I did my audition and realised she was staring at me with quite an unfriendly glare. When I finished she snorted, "I think I've seen you before!" I lied. "I don't think so". However, there was no fooling Beatrice who snapped, "I *have* seen you before. I booked you in here last year!"

I was greatly embarrassed to be exposed as the incompetent card trickster who died a death nearly every night the year before. Fortunately, despite this she booked me anyway. I expect she knew that it was the norm for entertainers to die a death at the Blue Angel and she probably thought nothing of it. She booked me for a whole week just like the year before and the act went over a bit better this time because the demographics of the audience had indeed changed and I could work in comparative peace.

But of course this story is getting a little ahead of itself. Let us go back to a year before when I was struggling at the Blue Angel. While I was working there I decided to approach a large Chinese restaurant in Soho known as Young's Chinese Restaurant to see if they would like to have a magician perform. I had been in there before and knew they had entertainment from time to time so decided to try my hand at getting work there.

I brought along some photographs of the act to show them and they showed some lukewarm interest. I remember there was a tall Chinese man called Andrew that I spoke to. He has stood out in my memory because he spoke perfect English without a Chinese accent and the fact that he was tall was unusual in itself since most Chinese people are of short stature. He was the manager of the restaurant but not the owner.

Andrew told me that he would show my photographs to his boss but I didn't feel he was particularly interested. A few days later I had heard nothing so decided to phone and find out what the verdict was concerning my act. I spoke to Andrew who told me that they weren't interested in booking my act. This of course was a disappointment but I took it in stride. However, a week later I realised that I had left my photographs at the restaurant and since, in those days photos were expensive I decided that I wanted them back.

Accordingly, I went down to the venue to retrieve them. I saw Andrew and asked for my photographs. He looked very uncomfortable and went to look for them and told me to wait. After what seemed a very long time he came back and said, "I can't find them. Phone me tomorrow and by then I will ask the staff and find out where they are".

I did as I was told but when I phoned him the next day he became very evasive and said he was busy and to call the following week. I have always been persistent so naturally I did so. He never seemed to be available and I was beginning to feel that he was avoiding me. I figured that he had lost the pictures and it eventually turned out that I was correct but somehow I wanted him to tell me that straight and not keep me wondering what was going on.

Eventually I went down in person to the restaurant and confronted him. He looked embarrassed and told me he was going to have a word with the owner about me and my photographs. He told me to wait and about ten minutes later came back and said, "We have looked everywhere for your pictures and we can't find them. They are lost. We are sorry. However, the boss said he would like to hire you to do your act on Sunday night".

I realised that the reason for my booking was the fact that they had felt guilty about losing the photographs. I was happy at this turn of events and realised that losing the pictures had turned out to be a blessing in disguise.

I did the booked engagement on the Sunday night and it turned out to be great. The audiences at the restaurant were far better behaved and more receptive than the drunken hecklers I had to put up with at the other venues. In fact the act went over so well that the owner booked me for the next Sunday night. I cannot fully recall the name of the owner so many years later but I have a feeling it was a Mr Leung. Even if it wasn't it is the name I shall use in this narrative.

Young's Chinese Restaurant only had entertainment once a week and I was not booked for the full week like I was at the other venues. However, it was extra revenue earned and the audiences were very receptive. I was booked very sporadically and not every Sunday although the bookings were not infrequent. However, all that was to change because of my trusty close up magic.

At the end of every show Mr Leung would come up enthusiastically and ask me to show him some card tricks privately. I always did but one day the fellow who played the drums at the venue took me aside and said, "You shouldn't show so many tricks to Mr Leung after your show. Show him one and when he asks to see more tell him you will do so providing he books you for the next Sunday". This turned out to be wonderful advice and it worked like a charm. As soon as Mr Leung asked to see more tricks, as he always did I would say "Do you want me to come next Sunday?" and he always agreed. He knew quite well that I was extorting the booking out of him but he didn't mind because he loved my card tricks so much. I ended up working on Sunday nights at the restaurant for months on end.

I was now very busy indeed and making a lot of money. I remember at one point doing seven shows in one night running from one venue to another. Luckily they were all quite near each other and I was able to fit in all the shows at the time the cabaret was scheduled.

I thought that now I seemed to be established, working quite high status establishments on a regular basis it might be time to approach the agents and try to get them to come and see my act. In the past when I was working pubs the venues weren't very impressive so they weren't tempted to make the time and effort to come and see me work.

Someone advised me to go and see a fellow named Vincent Shaw, a very established agent who managed Harry Corbett and Sooty. In Britain to this day Sooty is an icon and household name. The amazing thing is that he is a mere glove puppet! In those days Harry Corbett was the fellow who operated the puppet. He became quite a TV star. In fact, Sooty had been a celebrity glove puppet even when I was a kid. I well remember when I was around six years old seeing Sooty on television hitting Harry

Corbett over the head with a stick and Harry saying in exasperation with a distinct Northern England accent "Don't do that, Sooty!"

I approached Vincent and told him where I was working and he agreed to come in and see me perform at the L'Hirondelle. He actually showed up too which was a surprise in itself since in those days agents would often promise to show and didn't. After the performance he asked me to visit him the next day. I did so expecting that he was interested enough to offer me work. He didn't do so but at least he took the time to give me advice and constructive criticism concerning my photographs which I appreciated.

I then went to see another agent that I had pestered in my pub days. She was a nice elderly lady who had an office in Charing Cross Rd in the heart of London but I cannot remember her name or much else about her. When she heard that I was now working at more prestigious venues she agreed to come in and see me work. Again after the show she asked me to come in and see her the next day.

When I did so she criticised the entire cabaret and every act in it. However, she didn't say one bad word about my own act but I think she was being tactful. She told me that she didn't have any work for me but suggested that I should take a trip up north to work the working men's clubs which were in great abundance in Northern England. She said that if I ever wanted to do that she had connections up there and would make a few phone calls for me. She was as good as her word a few months later and you can read all about it in the next chapter.

As a matter of fact the next chapter will detail how I eventually went on the road as an entertainer and left the London scene to seek my fortune elsewhere. Turn the page, dear reader and read on, read on....

CHAPTER FIVE

On the Road in Showbusiness

IT WILL BE RECALLED that in Chapter Three of this literary masterpiece I described frequenting a well known agency known as the Blackburn Agency looking for work. As explained, there was a lady there named Eva who was sympathetic to me and a fellow called Andy Wood who was a little more lukewarm.

Since I seemed to be moving in higher performing circles with all the prestigious nightclubs I was now working I decided it was time to revisit this agency. Accordingly, I did so and told them that I was working at the L'Hirondelle, the Stork Room, the Gargoyle, the Blue Angel, the Negresco and Young's Chinese Restaurant. They obviously didn't believe me and questioned me about it with great incredulity. Eventually I persuaded them that I really was performing at these venues and as if in a daze, they said they might just come and watch me work.

One week at the L'Hirondelle a new act joined us. She was a South African singer named Zona who was quite successful in her work and had travelled quite widely as a performer. She never actually watched my act which was fortunate given the fact that it wasn't much good. However, I did show her some card tricks in the dressing room and she raved and raved about them.

I didn't give the matter much thought but one night, about an hour before the cabaret was due to start she remarked to me, "Someone mentioned your name today". I was a bit puzzled by this since I didn't think she would know anyone that would know me. She then related to me the following story. It appeared that she had visited the Blackburn Agency in connection with a tour she was doing for them. She casually mentioned to them that she was working at the L'Hirondelle and it seems that everyone in the office exclaimed simultaneously, "Do you know Ronnie McLeod the magician?" She answered them in the affirmative but was a little taken aback at the sudden unanimous interest in an obscure card magician. She was further surprised when everyone feverishly asked "Is he *really* working at the L'Hirondelle?" Zona confirmed that I was and it seems that Andy Wood asked "Is he really any good?"

Since Zona had been impressed with my close up card magic she not only told Andy that I was good she implied to everyone in the office that I was the greatest magical discovery since Houdini. She raved about how wonderful I was based on the card tricks I had shown her. Of course, she had never seen my awful cabaret act which died a death every night but probably assumed that it was every bit as good as the impromptu card trick demonstrations she had witnessed.

They were quite taken aback by the fact that I really was working at the prestigious L'Hirondelle and even more in awe of the fact that Zona, an artist whom they respected very much was raving that I was the greatest discovery since sliced bread. In fact after the astonishment had sunk in Eva suggested to Andy Wood that he go down and see me work. It would kill two birds with one stone since he could also watch Zona's act and discuss business with her at the club.

Zona related all this to me and, of course, I was very glad to hear it. I asked her if Andy was actually going to come and see me work. She said, "I told him how fantastic you were and he is indeed coming in especially to see you". I asked, "When?" She surprised me greatly by saying, "Tonight!"

I gulped knowing that I could be in a bit of trouble. We had just done the early show and I knew he could only be coming in later to the second show at 1.00 a.m. where everyone would be as drunk as a lord. It did not bode well for my act to be seen under those conditions.

However, there was a bit of luck that was running in my favour that evening. Johnny Lee, the compere, had been taken sick and couldn't come in that night. He was the top of the bill star act of the cabaret and in addition to his duties as compere, also finished the show with his own singing performance. Since I was the only entertainer there who did any kind of talking in his act I was asked for that one night to be the compere and fill in Johnny's spot in the cabaret. That meant that I finished the show with my mediocre card trick act. It had the great advantage of making me look better than I actually was since I seemed to be topping the bill. Of course, it was all an illusion brought on by the absence of Johnny Lee. It was the first time I had ever compered anything but I actually did it reasonably well. I noticed at the first show my cabaret act had gone over better than usual and I think it was because by the time I came on to do my performance the audience was used to my personality since I was the compere. Just introducing the acts and being the last act on the show gave me some extra prestige with the audience and it helped me greatly during the early 10.00 p.m. performance.

I knew I would need more than this, however, since the 1.00 a.m. late show would be the one with all the inebriation to contend with. I mentioned this to Zona and she told me not to worry about it since she would put Andy in the mood to like my act even if he didn't! I also voiced my concerns to the waiters and they smiled conspiratorially and said, "Don't worry—we'll take care of it!" The waiters quite liked me possibly because I did not throw large women from my shoulders and send them flying like my Polish predecessor did. Nevertheless, I was puzzled as to how the waiters "would take care of it" but it certainly became clearer before the night was over.

Andy Wood showed up as expected and sat at a table in the audience in company with Zona and they seemed to have a strong rapport together. I noticed that as the evening wore on he was imbibing rather a lot of drink which I found out later the waiters and Zona were deliberately encouraging him to do. I don't think he paid for the drinks either. It seems that the waiters were aware of my situation and wanted to do all they could to help and they figured that getting Andy a little tipsy would be in my favour.

The only time Zona left Andy was when I, in my capacity as compere introduced her to do her act. As soon as she finished, she went straight back to sit with him and I thought they were overly friendly with each other.

I seemed to be doing quite well as the compere despite the usual intoxicated clientele. I seemed to be building up audience rapport which I knew would help me later when I came to do my own act at the end of the cabaret. The prestige of compering and closing the show made me appear to be top of the bill and it was quite an illusion that proved to be of great benefit for me.

I noticed that Andy was getting tipsier as the night wore on and, by the time I was due to do my act he wasn't really in a fit state to judge whether it was any good or not and in any event he seemed to be more interested in Zona's charms than the cabaret show.

Eventually I closed the show with my wondrous card trick act. Luck was with me all the way and the audience laughed quite a bit at my inane remarks. No doubt this was partly because I had built up a rapport with them when I acted as compere. However, the trump card was that the waiters hid in the darkness and every time I finished a trick they would applaud and cheer like hell and it appeared that I was a superstar. Zona added to this illusion by saying to Andy , "Isn't he fantastic? I told you how wonderful he was!" Since she appeared to be whispering sweet nothings in his ear all night long, he naturally agreed with her assessment.

I well remember that I mentioned somewhere in my act that I was from Scotland and a particularly drunken heckler yelled out, "I'm from Scotland too!" even though he had a Yorkshire accent. He had been heckling all evening so I had plenty of opportunity to hear it. I answered him, "Well it's nothing to be proud of, you know!" and the whole audience erupted in laughter particularly his raucous friends and companions at the table. It wasn't particularly funny but somehow it seemed to hit well at the time and the great reception to the response was heightened by the waiters hiding in the darkness yelling and cheering. The upshot of the evening was that my act went over better than it had ever done and Andy Wood had been conned into thinking I had a great act.

After the show was over I looked for Andy Wood and Zona but they seemed to have disappeared. I needed a breath of fresh air and went outside the club. Just at the entrance I saw Andy and I approached him. He raved about my act and told me to visit the agency tomorrow. He said, "To be honest I didn't expect much from you. I thought when you used to visit the office you didn't show much confidence. But Eva said to me, 'I've got a feeling about that boy' and Zona was giving you rave reviews, so I thought I had better check you out. You do a great act and handle the hecklers very well. Quite honestly I didn't expect to find someone in the Barbara Streisand league".

Odd as it was to be compared with Barbara Streisand who as far as I know has never done much in the way of card tricks, I was flattered nevertheless. It is also interesting to me that she is just as famous now at the time of writing as she was at this conversation with Andy Wood of over forty years ago. Good for her of course.

I duly wandered over to the offices of the Blackburn Agency the next day and saw Andy Wood there who was in a much more sober state than the night before. He congratulated me on my act and offered me a tour of American army bases in Germany. It would be for a period of three weeks. He asked me how much I wanted.

On entering the office I had seen some contracts lying about for this self same tour to Germany and I had spotted one for rather a large sum of money to be paid to some act or other. Therefore I quoted the amount I had seen on this contract. Andy dropped his jaw and spluttered "We can't possibly pay you that!" With the audacity of youth I exclaimed, "Well that is what you are paying so and so". Forgive me for forgetting the name of so and so. It was rather a long time ago. Andy replied, "He is a closing act. You aren't. We can't give you that kind of money". I responded "Well I was a closing act last night. I did close the show after all". Alas, Andy had sobered up by now and wasn't ready to fall for it. He did offer, however, a reasonable sum of money and I accepted.

My nightclub engagements were coming to an end anyway so the tour of Germany was offered at an opportune time.

In February 1967 I embarked on my first foreign tour. In fact it was the first time I had ever been out of the country. I went by train and boat and after an interminably long journey, I finally arrived in Frankfurt and booked into a hotel frequented by theatrical types like myself. The next day I went to see the agent who was my contact in Germany. I was instructed as to my schedule and performing locations. A car would pick me up each evening at the hotel and, in company with other entertainers, I would be taken to a different US base every night. We travelled all over Germany, or at least up to two hours outside Frankfurt, which isn't quite the same thing I suppose.

It was an interesting three weeks and I learned a lot. Sometimes the act would go over well and sometimes it wouldn't. The audiences were a bit better behaved than the crowds I had encountered at the London nightclubs but I still encountered difficulties. My main mistake was panic, and trying to change the act each night to make it work. Of course, the more I changed it, the worse the situation would get. I would take a trick out of the act and put another one in. I would talk fast one night and slow down another. I would use comedy one night and another night become serious.

The result of all this chopping and changing meant that sometimes the act would go over great and sometimes it wouldn't. You could say I was learning my craft.

There was an MC (American term for compere) that I worked with frequently. He was also a magician and would often do his act on the same bill as I was on. His act didn't clash with mine since I only did card tricks and his material was more varied. His name was Jerry Bergmann and he was a very well established professional.

I studied him and learned a lot by watching him. I remember that he could speak several languages, including German. Of course he only had to speak English when performing since the audiences consisted entirely of American soldiers stationed in Germany. One day he gave me some very good advice which would have been useful when I was working the London nightclubs. I told him that I had encountered drunks on stage. He told me that the best thing to do when that happened was to get the culprit to select a card from the deck and to go back to his seat in the audience and sit on his selection.

The procedure now was to simply ignore him and get someone else up to help. From time to time the drunk would call out from the audience, "What about my card?" Jerry instructed me to simply say, "Later" and ignore him completely. I subsequently used this idea on a few occasions in the future although pretty rarely because I was learning to be a bit more selective as to who I got on stage. However, one or two did slip past over the years and I used this technique which worked like a charm. It did cost me a playing card but it was worth it.

During this period I would hear the entertainers in Germany talking in hushed tones and in great admiration about an Irish comedian named Hal Roach. It seemed that he would tell a joke and when nobody laughed he had another joke that would make fun of the audience for not laughing. I suppose you could term it a "cover" joke. In other words it would cover the fact that nobody laughed at the first joke. For example, if he cracked a joke and the response was lukewarm he would tap the microphone saying, "Testing, one, two, three!" and he would then get the laugh he was looking for in the first place.

It seems that Hal would even use the "cover" joke when it wasn't necessary. He would still say it even when the audience laughed wholeheartedly since the cover joke was always funnier than the original joke.

I wondered who this Hal Roach fellow was. On my return to Britain I was to find out and I will show you later on how he fits into this story.

All in all, the German tour was a valuable experience for me. I went over better at the officer's clubs than I did for the enlisted men who were a bit more rough and ready. Overall I did reasonably well but not fantastic. You could say that I got the job done and was learning my craft before live audiences and of course this was the best way to gain experience.

I returned to London and wondered what I would do next since the nightclub bookings had now run their course and come to an end. I made the usual rounds of the agents' offices but didn't really get anywhere. Finally I did wander into some agent's office and regrettably all I remember about him forty years later is that his name was Harry. His secretary asked me to wait for him in the small reception area. He had left a door slightly open and I could hear him talking on the phone to someone. I overheard him say, "One weakness I have is that if someone is talented I feel that I have to give him a chance". This gave me some encouragement and I wondered if I was going to get a good result.

When I eventually got in to see him he was affable enough and was impressed to hear that I had been to Germany and had worked the London night clubs. He asked, "How did you do with the US troops on the bases? Did you go over well?" Naturally I embroidered the truth somewhat and told him that I went over very well at every show. He asked, "Did you know that there is a US army base right here in London?" I was very surprised to hear this and said so. Harry continued, "I'll tell you what. You can do an audition there tomorrow night and I will be there to see what you can do".

I duly showed up the next night at the Army base and it was just like the ones in Germany. I did notice that the audience of US soldiers was somewhat rowdy which didn't make me feel too great. Somebody told me that the famous singing star Englebert Humperdinck was in the audience.

I shared the dressing room with two professional acts who gave me an inferiority complex by ignoring me completely and putting on theatrical makeup. I had no idea how to put on makeup, and come to think of it, still don't. Since the days of music hall and variety theatre (known as vaudeville in North America) had died out, entertainers rarely applied makeup anymore.

One of the entertainers said to the other, "Nobody puts makeup on any more. It just shows how unprofessional show business is getting". This made me feel very uncomfortable since I was one of the "unprofessional" people he was talking about. I tried to hide my embarrassment by pretending to get my props ready which of course didn't take long since the only prop I had was a deck of cards.

The fellow that made the remark about unprofessionalism finally noticed me and saw the deck of cards. He said, "Do you do card tricks?" I told him that my whole act consisted of card tricks. He said, "You must be very good if you can hold the attention of a big audience with just a pack of cards. Can you show me something?"

I complied with his request and showed him and his friend card trick after card trick and they raved and raved with the usual enthusiasm. The fellow who made the request was particularly impressed and was beside himself with amazement. His reaction was so voluble and animated that I promptly forgot my embarrassment over not putting on makeup and started to get my confidence back.

He turned out to be the compere for the evening and promised to give me a big build up when it was time for me to perform. Alas, he kept his word. And I say "alas" because in his enthusiasm for my close up work he went quite overboard when introducing me. He announced me as "one of the world's greatest magicians" (yes, he actually used those words!) and built me up far more than he should have done. When I went out to perform, it was soon apparent to everyone that I was nowhere as good as he had made me out to be.

I had gone on quite late in the show and followed a strong musical act. The crowd was quite inebriated and rowdy and were rougher audiences than the soldiers in Germany. Consequently the act died a most horrible death. As I have already mentioned Englebert Humperdinct was in the audience and I hope I never meet him in person or, if I do, that the night he saw someone do card tricks on stage at a US army base in London has been erased from his memory.

I decided to get out of the base as fast as I could and just as I was leaving I bumped into Harry who had seen the whole debacle. To my surprise he said, "Phone me tomorrow". I did do this the next day and apologized for the awful show. He said "The other acts said you did better tricks in the dressing room than you did on stage". Not surprisingly he never offered me any work and I never heard from him again.

After the debacle I decided to leave for Manchester to see if I could break into the working men's clubs which were booming in the North of England. Of this more anon but let me jump ahead one year just after I returned from working up North.

I got a call out of the blue one day from the Blackburn agency to see if I was interested in doing a show for an American army base in London. My alarm bells went off and I asked a lot of questions to make sure that it wasn't the same base that I had suffered at a year before. After I received the info I decided that it couldn't possibly be the same place because the address seemed different, as were several relevant details. I figured that there was more than one US army base in London.

Accordingly, I went along but when I got there I realised to my utter horror that it was indeed the very same place and the very same room that I had died an utter and complete death in the year before. The audience seemed just as rowdy as they were the previous year and for a moment I contemplated turning around and going back the way I came.

However, there was no escape and I made my way to the dressing room where the various acts were assembled. There was a fellow there who represented the Blackburn agency and he was an old pro entertainer named Charlie Munyard who knew the business inside out. He was the one who was deciding on the order of the bill. He said to me, "I think it is best if you open the show". I had read in some daft magic book or other that the worst position for an entertainer to occupy on a bill is the opening spot. Of course, this was good advice in the old vaudeville or music hall days but it was not valid information for modern performing conditions. I wasn't to know this so I tried to protest Charlie's suggestion saying, "There are two musical acts on. Why don't I go on in between them and split them up a bit so that one music act doesn't follow another?"

Charlie would have none of it responding, "No. That would be a very bad idea. They are both very strong acts and it would kill you to be between them. You should open because audience attention is at its height during the beginning of a show. You see how boisterous they are out there right now? Can you imagine how they are going to be later on when the show is under way and when they have had a few more drinks inside them? They will pay no attention and you will die a horrible death".

I reluctantly agreed and it was the best thing I could have done. When I went out to entertain them with the same act I had died with previously, I did so with great trepidation. However, I was in for a pleasant surprise. The audience *loved* the show! They hooted, hollered, cheered and begged for more. They virtually gave me a standing ovation. I say virtually since only about half of them stood up. The rest were too drunk.

I came off stage in a state of great amazement. I couldn't believe that the self same act that I had died a death with the year before to the self same kind of audience had gone over so astonishingly well. I eventually realised that it was the shrewd judgement of Charlie Munyard that had made it so. If I had gone on later, the audience would have murdered me. I learned a great deal that night and to this day, if I am on a bill with other artists I try very hard to get the opening spot since I know that the audience will be at its most attentive then.

Now let me take one step a year back to where I was in my story. After my first debacle at the US base I decided that it was time to try my luck up north at the working men's clubs which were so prevalent in Northern England in those days.

I went along to the elderly lady agent that promised me months before that she would help me find connections up north and found that she was as good as her word. She told me, "You seem to have worked very hard so I will do this for you". Consequently, right in front of me she phoned a few agents in Manchester and thereabouts to inform them that a young card trickster would be coming to visit them soon and that she recommended that they give me work.

I remember she phoned one established agent of the time named Vic Rawlings who seemed reluctant to get involved with me but she insisted, "Look Vic, use him once and if he's no good then don't use him again. What have you got to lose?"

It was very nice of her to put herself out on my behalf since she was getting no revenue from it. This goes to prove that the attitude often expressed by entertainers, that variety agents are greedy bloodsuckers, isn't always true!

Accordingly, one day I got on a train to Manchester to seek my fortune in the northern clubs. I booked into some dreadful theatrical guest house and made friends with the other entertainers that stayed there. I called up the agents that I had been given the names of by the nice old lady in London along with a few other local agents and clubs that I found out by myself with a little detective work. Eventually I started to get a little work and then a little more. I stayed up north for about a year working here, there and everywhere.

I found that northern audiences were very different from their southern brethren. Less heckling and a lot less drunken behaviour. That is not to say that it was entirely eliminated but it was more muted. They were still, however, tough audiences. They would sit silently, staring at you with their arms folded for one minute. At the end of that minute the verdict would come in. If they liked you they would unfold their arms, relax, laugh and enjoy the show. However, if they didn't like you, then they would simply ignore you and resume their conversations with their friends and even turn their backs to you. If you did not pass their approval you would hear a buzz of conversation around the room and you were done for. It was really like going before a jury. If you were found guilty the sentence would be complete indifference to your act.

There was, however, something fair about it. In London, you were doomed from the moment you went out on stage. Up north they gave you that one minute to impress them before they decided that you were not worth watching. I always thought that was very fair since at least you were in with a chance of gaining rapport with that precious minute you were granted.

I remember the northerners had a quick wit. Once I worked at a venue where they all had to pay at the door in order to see the cabaret. I was being heckled and I retorted, "Well, I've got the last laugh. You have had to pay to see this load of old rubbish!" The retort came quick as a flash, "No lad, we've got the last laugh! You haven't been paid yet for your load of old rubbish and you're probably not going to be!"

However, I was getting better at my work and the experience of working night after night was paying off. A big turning point was shortly after I arrived in Manchester I got a week's work at a large club and was surprised to see on the bill the legendary Irish comedian Hal Roach that I had heard about in Germany. I shared a dressing room with him and other entertainers but didn't talk to him much. I watched him night after night, however, to see what I could learn.

The first night he died an utter and complete death. The second night the same thing happened. However, the third night he went over big and stormed the place. I took careful note that he did exactly the same act word for word as the previous two nights that he died the death. Then the fourth night he got fantastic reaction again and the audience loved him. The fifth night he went over great again. As he did the sixth night. However the last night he died another awful death and nobody was interested in his show.

I observed that he did exactly the same act on the nights he went over well as he did on the nights that he went over badly. It then dawned on me that in Germany, when I was chopping and changing the act in sheer panic to find something that worked, I was doing the wrong thing. I decided from that moment on to keep to the same act whether it went over well or not. I wouldn't panic and keep trying something different out of desperation. That is not to say that I wouldn't gradually bring in little improvements bit by bit over time but my days of wholesale change on a massive basis to my act were over. I had learned a lot from Hal Roach.

Decades later I saw him in the lobby of an Irish hotel where he was working and I felt obliged to approach him and belatedly thank him for what I had learned so many years ago. He had no idea who I was or what I was going to say and rudely brushed me aside. I am afraid he will never know how much he influenced me unless he reads this. Serves him right for being so grumpy!

After a year of the northern scene I returned to London and got a call from Philip Midgely from the Gargoyle club. He told me that he was starting a side business as a variety agent and wanted me to do a gig at the March Cabaret Club which I seem to remember was in East Anglia. At the same time Ron MacMillan called me and wanted me to sell Svengali decks in Cardiff at an exhibition. The exhibition was on for two weeks and the last week would have been the week I was supposed to be at the March Cabaret Club. I hadn't sold Svengali decks for a while and I was itching to do it again. It is a funny thing about that business. When I was doing it I hated it but when I stopped doing it I would get withdrawal pangs and want to do it again. I was torn between doing the March Cabaret Club or going to Cardiff. Eventually I decided to do both and arranged with Ron MacMillan to find someone else to do the last week of Cardiff while I went on to March.

Alas, once the grafting business gets its hooks into you, it doesn't let go easily and I started on the grafting path once again of which more anon....

CHAPTER SIX

The University of Evil

WHEN I WAS IN Cardiff I decided to approach a department store there to see if I could work the six weeks leading up to Christmas. I figured that the Svengali deck would do very well during this period. The store agreed to have the demonstration promotion and in mid-November I opened up. I did very well and made quite a bit of money.

The showbusiness work had dried up by this time possibly because I was too busy promoting the Svengali deck. After Christmas I returned to London and continued to work the trick decks in earnest. I travelled all over the country working at various Ideal Homes Exhibitions that I booked independently of Ron MacMillan and on these occasions he would merely supply me with the merchandise but I wasn't working for him directly.

One day I booked the Preston Ideal Homes Exhibition. When I was there it dawned upon me that Blackpool was only forty minutes away by train. Blackpool, then and now is the biggest and busiest holiday resort town in Britain. A friend of mine was working there and I decided to pay him a visit. This was the aforementioned Michael Vishnick who had organised my employment as a waiter in a very odd manner in years past. His name was now Michael Vine and at the time of writing he is a well known theatrical agent and television producer. However in those days he was selling Svengali decks on Blackpool's Central Pier.

At the end of the Preston exhibition I journeyed to Blackpool to see Michael. I loved the place and could see opportunities to make money there. I therefore decided to move from London and instead live in Blackpool.

It was one of my better decisions. I loved Blackpool and there was quite a lot of showbusiness activity there as well as opportunities to sell Svengali decks.

I worked many seasons there at different venues. There was Lewis's department store (no—I didn't own the store!), Woolworths, T.J. Hughes, Central Pier, Bensims Bazaar, and Ripley's Odditorium. In addition to this I opened up a magic studio for professional magicians and ran a two-bit mail order company selling magic to the trade. The magic studio didn't make much money but it did give me a base from which I operated my various activities. I also did many magic shows in and around Blackpool but this activity was somewhat curtailed since I was so busy selling Svengali decks during the summer season.

Blackpool has the longest summer season in the UK starting in June and ending at the very end of October. The reason for the long season is the famous Blackpool Illuminations, known as "the lights" that occurs during September and October. It consists of a most remarkable display all over the city of coloured lights, particularly on the main promenade. It attracts tourists by the thousands and prolongs the season with day-trippers, as well as the usual holidaymakers who come for the week.

The weekends are packed with people who come to see the illuminations and September and October have the busiest weekends of the entire season. I write this in the present tense because I assume Blackpool still operates in this way today. If it doesn't it will be proof that I need to do more research when I write a book. Quite frankly I can't be bothered so I will simply assume things are as they always have been. It will save me an awful lot of time checking it out which I would find terribly tedious and I feel in a lazy mood.

I titled this chapter "The University of Evil" because that is precisely what Blackpool was in those days. I often used to think that, in modern times, if God were ever to destroy a city in the same way that he destroyed Sodom and Gomorrah in biblical days, Blackpool would be his first choice. The town was full of wicked grafters, fortune tellers, run out workers (I will explain this later on) and other sundry rogues and vagabonds. The whole mentality of the town was to rip off the holiday-makers and transport their money into local pockets. Of course many of the vendors and business owners of Blackpool were perfectly honest but rather a large percentage weren't. My title of "The University of Evil" I believe to be a very apt one but don't tell the Blackpool Tourist Board I said that and I hope to God they don't read this book.

The first venue I worked was Lewis's department store. The Blackpool store was one of a chain of many stores around the country. I had already worked at the Lewis's stores in Glasgow and Birmingham so arranging the Blackpool promotion was comparatively easy. I arranged the scheduled demonstrations for the entire season of twenty weeks.

There were other grafters working in the store and I soon got to know them. There was Jimmy Trainor and Jonathon Whitehead who were working a hair cutter gadget where the customer could cut his own hair and presumably save money on barbers. They were taking in an absolute fortune and would work one hour on and one hour off alternately. They would have a chair in front of them into which they would inveigle some innocent victim to sit down and have a free haircut. They would then build a crowd around the customer demonstrating what a wonderful haircut they could give with this gadget.

One day Jimmy Trainor cut a chap on the back of his neck and sliced a boil open. There was blood pouring from the fellow and no doubt the crowd were horrified. However, Jimmy had a silver tongue as all grafters do and managed to convince the poor unfortunate that the bloody mess was evidence of how effective and sharp the hair cutter was. I don't know exactly what he said but instead of suing him or complaining to the store management the chap actually purchased one! I do know that it took Jimmy quite a while to clear up the mess afterwards.

Jimmy is still around and when he heard I was writing this book he incessantly demanded to be included in it somewhere. Well there you are, Jimmy. You are now in the damn book and destined to become famous for doing bodily harm to your customers. Now shut up and leave me alone.

Jimmy's partner Jonathon was a real character and I liked him very much and even took him to Cardiff to work a store with me after the Blackpool season was finished. I really liked his company. He worked the hair cutter and I worked the trick deck. I often wondered how he sold so much merchandise since nobody could understand a word he said. He talked with a thick northern accent but that wasn't the problem. He would intersperse his demonstration spiel with cockney rhyming slang and I am quite sure that nobody understood a word he said. However, he sold a ton of merchandise because of his amusing personality. I was beginning to learn that these Blackpool grafters were far better showmen than all the rather awful magicians that I hung around with in the London magic clubs, even though none of them knew a single trick.

Grafters have to draw a crowd, hold them with their personality and then the hardest part is yet to come and that is getting the people to part with their money. The greatest asset that grafters have is instinctively timing their words and emphasising certain phrases in their speech to make sales. I learned it as well simply from being around these people and it rubbed off on me automatically.

However, I had yet to meet the greatest character of them all. One day I was chatting to Jimmy and Jonathon when a rather well built fellow with a surly look on his face came over to join us. He looked a bit unkempt and had paint all over his face. He was up on the third floor of Lewis's whereas the haircutter duo and I were based on the ground floor, or as North Americans say—the main floor. The reason I had not yet met him was that he was on the different floor.

I took an instant dislike to this surly intimidating individual with a very rude manner. And of course the paint streaking all down his face didn't help either. The reason for the paint was that he was working a product known as the paint pad, which was some sort of method of applying household paint and I am not sure if the paint got on his face by accident or if it was part of the demonstration.

I had just met Dennis Adams. Little did I know at the time that Dennis would become a lifelong friend who sadly passed away just as I was writing this book. I miss him terribly and have dedicated this work to him.

As Dennis talked—actually growled would be a better description—I noticed that he was very well spoken with an accent that was far removed from the more working class speech patterns of the other demonstrators. The accent was almost what you could call upper class and despite his appearance and surly manner it did show a certain well-bred side to him. This softened my antagonism to him somewhat.

Dennis at work

The little group of grafters decided to go to the pub and dragged me along with them. I have never particularly liked pubs or their atmosphere but would go along with the grafters for their company. The grafters certainly loved pubs and drank more than was good for them. And I was to find out that Dennis loved the pubs more than most and in those days drank more than anyone I knew. Later on in life he sobered up considerably.

As we talked in the pub I performed some tricks which amused the assembled company and then talked about other things. I can't remember what triggered the remark but suddenly, Dennis looked at me with a strange mixture of compassion and curiosity and blurted out, "Ronnie. You seem to be a lost soul". At the time I was and I expect I still am but it was an astute observation and I realised this flamboyant and seemingly obnoxious character had a very shrewd side to him.

I grew to like him more and more as the conversation wore on and he turned out to be a lifetime friend. He was probably the funniest man I ever met in my life and just his normal conversation would have people in stitches. He would say outrageous things and yet escape censure most of the time. Coming from the mouth of anyone else the things he said would give great offence but somehow Dennis would get away with it.

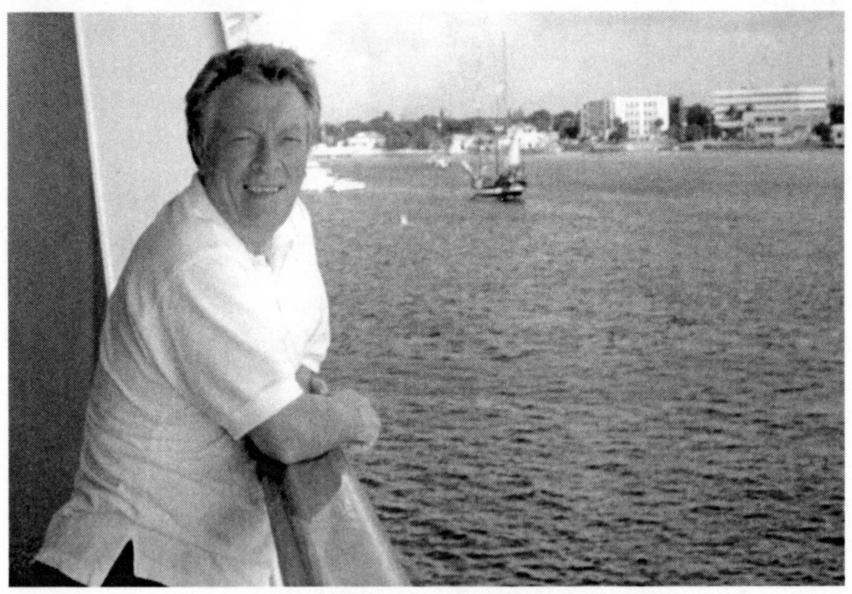

Dennis at sea

His wife Bessie once likened him to me as "a great big harmless bag of wind" and it was a perfect description. Dennis was a most generous individual who would do anything for you if he liked you and he had many friends who loved him right up to the day he died. And they love him still.

One of the stores that I worked at was Woolworths and there seemed to be a very odd business arrangement going on there for such a reputable company to be involved with. However, I was in Blackpool which as I have already explained was a place of great crookedness, and wickedness was the rule rather than the exception.

They had rather a lot of grafters demonstrating in their emporium and indeed far more than their neighbour, Lewis's department store next door. Lewis's did have quite a few but Woolworths easily exceeded the quantity and I found it odd to see such an excessive amount of them working.

However, I was to find that there was more going on that met the eye. The store manager had a lot of autonomy from the head office in London and this allowed him to get up to various unofficial profitable shenanigans which weren't strictly on the up and up. I know the manager's name and I expect he is somewhat dead by now but caution impels me to simply refer to him as Mr B.

It seems that the reason that there were so many grafters in the store was because Mr B encouraged them to be there. He brought in different cash registers which were not official Woolworths cash registers and the money taken in was not part of Woolworths official sales. The store percentage which was supposed to go to Woolworths actually went into Mr B's pockets. Or perhaps only part of it did. I am not sure of the exact details although several scenarios were suggested to me. One was that Mr B would have a few genuine "official" grafters and a few "unofficial" ones. The official ones were declared to head office and the unofficial ones were kept under wraps so to speak. The official percentages went to Woolworths and the unofficial ones went to Mr B.

I first got wind of all this when word went out to all the grafters not to come in for two days since visitors from head office were coming up from London. I couldn't figure out why we were all getting kicked out for a couple of days but it was explained to me by the other grafters. I was very innocent in the ways of the world at the time and I couldn't believe that Mr B was able to get away with such shenanigans. I was told that Woolworths head office had a good idea that their store manager was up to mischief but turned a blind eye to his shenanigans because Blackpool was considered to be a special case among all the hundreds of Woolworths Branches all over the country.

This was because Mr B brought in fantastic revenue to the Blackpool location and was one of their greatest managers. It was said that his location in Blackpool brought in the most revenue of any other Woolworths store in the country except Oxford Street in London. Because of this the big cheeses in London tolerated Mr B's excesses and "under the table" style of working. Blackpool was considered to be almost like outlaw country and different rules applied to that particular Woolworths store.

To aid Mr B in this nefarious operation was a chap called Bert Higgins who was a local Blackpool grafter. Mr B put Bert in charge of the other grafters under the fancy title of "concession manager" which of course, was a load of old cobblers since Bert was just a double-dealing grafter like the rest us. Naturally, head office in London had no idea of Bert's existence or that his "salary" was merely a percentage of Mr B's cut of the action. And of course Bert put his own products into the store as well although he was far too grand to demonstrate them himself. He always hired another grafter to do the work.

Bert was a dapper fellow in his late fifties or early sixties so would be extremely dead by now. After all this was around forty years ago at the time of writing. He always wore a carnation in his buttonhole as he strutted about in a very self-important manner through the store. Power had gone to his head and the money had gone into his pocket so he was a very happy man.

He once said to me, "Ronnie, if I had your personality, I would be the Lord Mayor of Blackpool". I was very flattered by this until I found out that Bert used to say that to virtually every person he ever met.

He and Mr B had a very profitable thing going for years until the store was torn down to make way for an indoor flea market. Woolworths turned out to be "wool worth the money" for them. Excuse me for my bad joke.

Of course corruption in high places is not entirely unknown in the grafting business, even outside Blackpool. I well remember a certain grafter who used to bribe a mall manager in order to obtain certain advantages such as the best locations in the shopping centre and other favours. And this was one of the biggest malls in Birmingham.

Mention of this fellow prompts me to tell a little story about him which has gone down in legend in British grafting circles. I shall call him Harry mainly because that was his name. The incident happened in Glasgow, Scotland. He had a large crowd in front of him at the Scottish Ideal Homes Exhibition and one woman started to walk away. Grafters don't like people in the crowd walking away because they can start an exodus of other people, particularly if the person is near the front of the crowd since they can disrupt the whole audience while they are exiting.

Harry expressed his irritation by issuing a reprimand that took the form of making some remark about Glasgow, England. Any Scot will tell you that this will raise the hackles because Glasgow is not in England—it is in Scotland. Of course Harry knew this and uttered the line in a spirit of great provocation as grafters often do even though they know that it could ruin the whole demonstration. And of course Harry had an English accent that inflamed the situation even more.

The woman was highly displeased and started to call him a few names. He replied thus: "Madam, you are an idiot. Please turn around and show everyone what an idiot looks like".

Harry had not read "How to Win Friends and Influence People" and had neglected to attend seminars in how to promote good customer relations.

The woman was now fuming and retorted, "I don't think that is funny and I have the right to walk away whenever I like".

Harry replied in what he no doubt thought was a reasonable manner, "Madam, two thousand years ago they nailed a man to a cross. He didn't think it was funny either but at least he stayed there and didn't walk away".

For some odd reason a number of customers took umbrage at this and went off to the exhibition management office to complain. Half an hour later Harry was no longer an exhibitor at the Scottish Ideal Homes Exhibition.

Mention of Glasgow reminds me of a particular Scottish grafter and prompts me to go off on another tangent that is nothing to do with Blackpool but would certainly be in the best university of evil tradition. It all happened around forty years ago or so but the details are etched in my mind nevertheless.

I am hesitant to tell the following story since it could be perceived as having a racist tinge to it. I can only say that it merely recounts the facts as they happened at the time. I apologise in advance to anybody from Pakistan who reads it and is offended by it. Pakistanis are hard working and honest people who don't deserve this anecdote but alas it does indicate racist attitudes that were prevalent in Britain forty years ago and I believe are still prevalent today but happily to a lesser extent. Anyway what happened, happened. The incident occurred and wishing it didn't won't make it go away. So here it is.

I had better call the chap Hamish to protect his identity in case he is still alive. Hamish is a good Scottish name and I think it kind of suits him. He had a heart of gold but admittedly had a few rough edges. One of those rough edges consisted of a hot temper which tempted him to assault various members of the public from time to time. I well remember he had a large crowd in front of him but was being heckled by a rather vocal Pakistani gentleman who expressed doubts about the effectiveness of the product. I rather think that this was a little unwise since the product was actually a kitchen knife. On a previous occasion Hamish had expressed his displeasure by inserting said knife into the body of another impertinent person but of course, that is another story for another time.

This time Hamish did not use the knife. Instead he picked up a nearby plank of wood that had a nail sticking out of the end. Now what the said plank was doing in the vicinity I have no idea but I am able to provide details of its destination after Hamish picked it up. He landed it across the face of his tormentor who promptly bled all over the place and made rather a mess. Protruding nails and planks of wood do have that effect on people I have been led to believe.

The crowd did not disperse in horror as one would expect it to. Perhaps they were fascinated by the entertainment value inherent in the proceedings. Hamish decided that since he now had everyone's attention he would give a speech in his defence. He gave a rousing talk about how the bleeding victim deserved everything he got since he was harassing a poor innocent demonstrator merely trying to make a living. Hamish sensed that he was winning the battle for hearts and minds and decided to appeal to good old-fashioned British racism that was prevalent at the time. He spluttered that the fellow had come to Britain from another country and was taking jobs away from good British workers and had shown his great ingratitude to the country that had given him refuge by interfering in the work of one of it's citizens who was merely trying to make a living.

After Hamish gave the speech he received a rousing round of applause from the crowd and had massive sales of his product. However the bleeding Pakistani gentleman didn't quite see it in the same way and went off to find a member of the local constabulary who decided to charge Hamish with assault. Hamish had a previous conviction, the details of which I shall relate shortly. If he were to be found guilty of a second offence the results would have been very serious for him.

On the day of the trial, however, the star witness for the prosecution showed a strange reluctance to testify. He did not show up in court but the police managed to find him in a nearby pub. They tried to persuade him to come to court to testify but he showed great resistance in the matter and claimed to have forgotten all the details of the assault. The case was thrown out as a result and Hamish walked free as an example to all of the great fairness of British justice. Of course, the story that circulated among the grafters that Hamish had found out the chap's address and gone round to the fellow's house to offer him several thousand pounds for his silence may have had something to do with it. It is quite amazing how a little bribery can bring people together in harmony sometimes. I should emphasise that I have no evidence that the above rumour concerning bribery was true. Grafters do spin yarns sometimes. However it does make one wonder....

Hamish wasn't quite so fortunate on another occasion. He was a superb grafter and in fact was one of the best I have ever seen. Unfortunately, he used to blow his considerable earnings in the betting shops of Britain. On every British high street are shops known as bookmakers where gambling on horseracing is perfectly legal. Hamish would lose money hand over fist at one particular betting shop. He was somewhat peeved by this and decided that the best way to recoup the money was to demand it back at the point of a gun.

I don't think he was terribly experienced at armed robbery but grafters are game for anything so he thought he would give it a whirl. Consequently he donned a stocking mask and equipped himself with a firearm to commit the dreaded deed.

He entered the premises to complete the mission and indeed the money was handed over. However, Hamish had a very distinctive voice so this rather gave the game away. He was, after all, a regular customer and the staff recognized who he was straight away. However, since they were looking at a loaded gun they decided that it would be rather sensible to hand over the money anyway.

The most amusing part of the story is that when Hamish made his getaway and exited the shop two female staff members who had been to lunch when the awful deed was done returned just as he was leaving. One of them recognized him immediately since he had quite a distinctive build and exclaimed in great puzzlement, "Hello Hamish, what on earth are you doing with that silly stocking over your head?"

Alas poor Hamish spent a year in jail as a guest in one of Her Majesty's prisons.

Another wicked grafter I knew also went to jail and this is how it came about. He was stopped by the police for speeding but decided to fight the ticket and appeared in court to do so. He informed the magistrate that the reason for his speeding was that he was a member of MI5 (the British Secret Service) and was on urgent government business that was essential for national security. Believe it or not, the magistrate bought into the fantastic story and cancelled the speeding ticket. The police, however, were somewhat peeved over the outcome and chose not to believe the story quite so readily. Consequently they investigated the matter and as a result charged the poor chap with perjury. Alas, the would be secret agent ended up in the clink. He did have the compensation, however, that he didn't have to pay the speeding ticket, which just goes to prove there is always a silver lining to the darkest cloud.

Another story along the same lines concerns yet another wicked grafter who also got stopped in London for speeding. His story was equally as fanciful. He informed the police that he was the royal veterinarian and he was in a hurry because of the urgent ill health of the Queen's corgi dogs. It was vital that he see to them as quickly as possible. The constabulary were very accommodating; in fact too accommodating. They insisted on giving him an escort to Buckingham Palace. So off he went with a police car behind him and one in front of him en route to the royal household despite the fact that it was not his original destination. The poor grafter could not escape since he was boxed in by the two police cars. Of course, when they all arrived at Buckingham Palace gates, the fraud unfolded and the truth emerged. Not only was the grafter charged with speeding he faced another charge of wasting police time!

I suppose I had better return to my tales of wickedness in Blackpool. And there was certainly nothing more wicked than the "run out" which I promised earlier to describe. To help explain what follows, here is a brief definition. A "run out" refers to a high pressure sales technique which relies on confidence and confusion to deceive a group of people into spending unduly large amounts of money for what in fact is inexpensive or even defective merchandise. In part, the technique involves gaining the public's trust through the promise/distribution of "slum" items (usually products such as inexpensive pens or lighters) along with the creation of a sense of fevered urgency and whipping the crowd up to a buying frenzy. A lot of this excitement is generated by the greed of the crowd who think they are getting fantastic bargains.

The run out is related to the grafting business in the sense that a crowd is gathered and sold to but it is also a world of its own. Some of the operators do indeed come from a grafting background but in many ways this is a different kind of operation from the usual demonstrations of kitchen gadgets and other run of the mill products.

Sometimes the "run out" is termed the "ram" and the operators are called "ram workers". "Ram" is a grafter's expression meaning "rip off". If you ram someone you rip him or her off. I am not 100% sure why the operation is known as the "run out" but I speculate that the name comes from the fact that sooner or later the team gets "run out" of town. They always get closed down. However, for some odd reason they reigned in Blackpool for a very long time. Perhaps it was because of the constant turnover of holidaymakers or maybe it was simply the shady mentality of the town. That is not to say, however, that they were not harassed by trading standards officers and the police of which more anon.

There is a most excellent book entitled *The Hard Sell* authored by Colin Clark and Trevor Pinch. The best description of the mechanics of the "Run Out" is detailed in this work. The authors state that the reason it is known as the "Run Out" is simply because the customers "run out" of money!

In North America there is a somewhat diluted version known as the "Jam Auction" which although unethical is a tad less ruthless.

I can tell you quite a bit about the UK version even though I have never worked it myself. This is because I have been around dubious behaviour rather a long time. It was very prevalent in Blackpool when I was there with several locations along the promenade. I don't know everything about it but I can tell you what I do know.

Interestingly enough I shared an apartment in for a short time with a grafter who later became one of the leading run out workers in Blackpool. He was a soft spoken and gentle guy before he worked the run out but became very hardened once he started on that path. This is because the people who do this kind of work become very cynical and look on the "punters" (as they are known) as greedy vermin who deserve all they get. They also become very hardened to all the complaints from the public that emanate from their work.

I would never have dreamt of working it myself because it was just too plain vicious. It was operated in an empty storefront and way at the back was situated a sort of high podium although it looked more like a raised counter from which the grafter did his, for want of a better word, "performance". The big empty space in front of the counter accommodated up to a hundred people or so. The operator usually worked with a microphone and was surrounded by all sorts of merchandise such as watches, TV sets, radios, kitchenware, and briefcases. The aim of the promotion was to sell this stuff at inflated prices.

The run out workers worked what was known in grafter's jargon as "mob handed". In other words, there was a full team of around six or so people. There were quite a few mouths to feed. First there were usually two demonstrators taking it in turn to do the sale which usually lasted around forty-five minutes to an hour in duration.

Then there were the floormen. These people worked the floor and their duties were to act as assistants to the grafters who were up on the podium. Most of these floormen looked like they had just come out of jail and in fact they probably had. They acted as bouncers, crowd control officers, and shop assistants (known as retail clerks in North America) all rolled up into one.

One thing that used to amuse me was that all the floormen were called "Walter". Not just in one location but everywhere! No matter what part of the country you saw the run out, the floormen were all named "Walter". You could go to Scotland one day and Wales the next. If you saw the run out in both areas, the floorman would still be called "Walter". This was simply to make identification of staff difficult in case of trouble with the police and consumer protection authorities.

The grafter would draw people in from the street by talking into the microphone and promising astonishing bargains. Once he got a few people gathered he would start to throw out free merchandise such as combs, pens and decks of playing cards to show how generous he was. This material was known in the trade by the name of "plunder". It was generally cheap merchandise that cost pennies and could afford to be given away.

Before long a crowd gathered and the grafter got to work. The showmanship involved is incredible. The crowd was whipped up into what can only be described as mass hysteria. After thirty minutes or so the grafter started to begin the process where he eventually went in for the kill. By a certain process, almost like a stage hypnotist selecting the best subjects, the people who were likely to buy were moved to the front of the crowd. I haven't the space to explain why, but they were all holding up a pound note. The people who were not holding up the banknote were moved to the back. These were not deemed to be good prospects for scamming.

Now came the hilarious bit. Well, hilarious to me, anyway. Out of nowhere all the floormen, usually about four of them, appeared armed with brooms. They literally swept the non-prospects out of the shop calling out, "Closed! You have to leave! Closed!" The brooms actually touched the feet of the punters and they had to leave in order to avoid getting hit by the brooms! It was as if the floormen were sweeping unwanted dust out of the shop! Of course to the run out boys, non-punters *are* unwanted dust!

Once everyone was out then down came the shutters of the shop! The punters could not get out and unwanted people could not get in. Talk about a captive audience! The ram workers now went to work on the selected people in a very ruthless manner. No mercy whatever was shown. Afterwards, when people realised they had been "had" they often complained.

However, the complaints department consisted of the four floormen who looked like gorillas and had tattoos down their arms. They simply told people to go forth and multiply. However they did it in a rather shortened version. They used two words only, the second of which was "off".

Loud arguments and often fights abounded after every demonstration. One lady came in crying to the boss and said that she had spent all her holiday money and couldn't pay the hotel. The "guvnor" was very kind. He offered her a box of tissues. These were "plunder" items. He called out to one of the floormen, "Walter! Get a box of tissues out of the back and give it to the lady for her tears!" She never got her money back though.

I have no idea if the run out is still operating in the UK. I expect it is. However, in the old days there were many attempts to make it illegal. They kept bringing in laws to try and close it down. Newspapers in Britain from time to time would publish articles exposing the operation and warn people not to partake in it. Unfortunately, the warnings did no good whatsoever as warnings tend not to do.

The police were always visiting undercover as were trading standards officers. However, the spiel and tactics used had been approved by top lawyers hired by the run out workers and although they were skating on thin ice, they never really broke it. They came right up to the edge but did not go over the line far enough to be prosecuted for misrepresentation.

One day, however, the ram workers went too far. It seemed that an undercover policeman visited them but they somehow discovered that they had a spy in their midst. I am not sure of the exact details or how exactly it came about but somehow they managed to get him alone in the shop when all the other punters had gone. The shutters were down and they beat the hell out of him. That didn't go over very well with Her Majesty's constabulary and the whole bunch of them ended up in jail including the fellow I told you about that I shared an apartment with.

I noticed that the run out workers usually lived on their nerves. Constant stress, which is not surprising when you consider that every customer was a potential complainant. Added to that, of course, was all the negative attention from the police, the press and the consumer protection authorities.

I preferred a more peaceful way of working so stuck to the trick decks of cards. I didn't approve of the nastiness of the run out in any case. Even though I was developing a very elastic conscience in Blackpool it still wouldn't allow me to get involved in the evil shenanigans even though they did fascinate me.

Perhaps I should have been nominated for sainthood.

CHAPTER SEVEN

More Evil at The University

ONE THING THAT I did do in Blackpool was to change my name to Mark Lewis. Not for any nefarious reason but just because I thought it sounded better than Ronnie McLeod. Later on I wanted to change it back again but by then it was too late since everyone knew me by the new name. Actually, I now think Ronnie McLeod sounds better but there is not a lot I can do about it at this moment in time.

Another thing I did in the town was to take up children's magic shows. Up to that time all my performing was done for adults. I had no idea how to do kid shows so I went along to a local magic shop on North Pier owned by a fellow named Paul Clive of whom more anon. I purchased a whole bunch of magic tricks that looked colourful even though I had absolutely no idea what they did. I also bought a glove puppet and a book on children's magic called *Open Sesame* by Eric Lewis and Wilfrid Tyler.

There was a wonderful opening chapter in that book which explained the best way to present magic for children. I read it completely when I dined alone that evening at a Chinese restaurant. I have always said that when I left that restaurant I had become a children's entertainer and I hadn't even done one trick for them yet!

For years afterwards I performed children's shows as well as adult work. At one point I performed all season on St Annes pier, just outside Blackpool, doing nothing but kid shows.

The shop on North Pier that I had purchased the kid show material was owned, as previously mentioned, by Paul Clive. Paul had written a classic book on card magic entitled *Card Tricks Without Skill* and yet Paul had never done a card trick in his life! Or very few at any rate. Joe Smith who had a trick and joke shop on Central Pier, told me "I've known Paul for over thirty years. I have never seen him do a card trick and in fact he doesn't know any!" It seems that Paul had run around with a notebook asking magicians if they knew any card tricks and he wrote them all up and made a classic book out of it.

Paul was a very upstanding British gentleman of the old school. He was honest to a fault and a very principled person. One of his customers told me that Paul once accidentally overcharged him by a few pence and, lo and behold, that tiny amount came in the mail a few weeks later with a detailed note explaining the discrepancy.

Paul seemed very out of place in such an evil place like Blackpool. In actual fact he once left the town for ten years or so to emigrate to America. It seems that he built up a fantastic business selling jokes and magic tricks and had a few shops in Blackpool. However, he felt that Britain was going communist and he decided to skedaddle to the United States instead. Unfortunately, his stay in the USA did not work out well at all and he made very little money there. I asked him what the problem was and he told me that he couldn't believe how in America nobody trusted him. He was always asked to pay up front for merchandise and advertising and it wrecked havoc with his cash flow. In the UK there is far more leniency with credit and it is granted more on a relationship and intuitive basis than it is in North America where they make a fuss about "credit ratings" and suchlike nonsense. There is no such thing in Britain as "credit checks" or "collection agents" or other such tripe. I often think America should come under British rule once again and this is one example why.

As a good old-fashioned British gentleman, Paul never quite got used to the American cut-throat way of doing business. He said to me, "I have always considered that an Englishman's word is his bond and I found it quite insulting that American business people would distrust me so". I asked him if it was a mistake to go to America and he replied, "Oh yes, a big mistake".

I found it a trifle odd that he thought this way since Blackpool was as crooked and double dealing as you could get. It was just as cut-throat as the United States. I often wondered how he hadn't noticed this living in the town for so many years.

Anyway, poor Paul decided to return to the devil he knew and came back to Blackpool. He reasoned that his name still meant something in the UK because of his famous book. He built his operation back up quite well with a retail shop and a warehouse where he would deal in wholesale supplies. I don't think, however, that his business ever got back to its former glories before he emigrated.

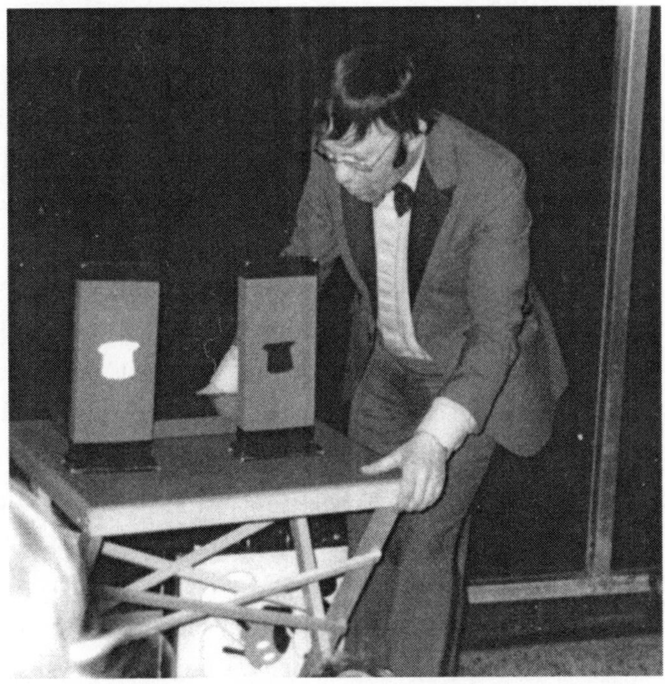

Kid show entertainment

Incidentally, whenever a customer in his shop asked about his book he would never tell them that he wrote it. He was quite modest that way or, perhaps more likely, he couldn't be bothered autographing it.

However, when his wife was in the shop she always insisted that he autographed the book whenever one was purchased.

I used to purchase Svengali decks wholesale from Paul's warehouse and one day I wandered over there for this purpose. I was astonished to find the place crawling with police and CID (Criminal Investigation Department) officers. The warehouse manager whispered to me "we've got trouble. Come back tomorrow".

I wondered all day what prim and proper Paul had been up to. I couldn't imagine him as a hardened criminal somehow. I wondered whether a body or a hoard from a bank robbery had been found on the premises. I found out later that the police had raided the warehouse and confiscated hundreds of trick coins. Magicians would often perform magic with coins that were falsified in some way. They could fold up or had two sides, or were otherwise tricked up in a myriad of different ways. Of course this necessitated the manufacturers of these coins having to deface and alter the money. This was and no doubt still is against the law. You are not allowed to deface coins of the realm. Normally the law is not enforced rigorously, especially in the case of copper coins. Trick silver coins are viewed more seriously since of course they are worth more. Even in this case the law is not applied strictly. Despite this, it seems that for some reason the Blackpool police decided to raid Paul and confiscate all his stock. I don't know if they prosecuted him but I assume not since I never heard a word about it.

Another magic shop owner in the town was the famous escapologist Murray. He was quite a headliner in his day and would escape from jail cells, strait jackets, handcuffs and other assorted restraints. On one memorable occasion he escaped from a strait jacket inside a lions cage at Bertram Mills Circus. He confided in me that when the lions came over sniffing at him while he was trying to escape he thought to himself, "Murray—you've gone too far this time!" However, he did survive and lived to tell the tale.

He claimed to have invented the word "escapology" although this has been disputed by some as showman's talk. However, there is no doubt that he popularised the term even if he didn't actually invent it.

He was a great showman. Some said he was better than Harry Houdini who is renowned as the greatest escape artist of all time. As well as being an escape artist he was also a magician and toured his big illusion show all over the world. One of the places he performed was Nazi Germany. He told me, "Hitler and Goering came back stage to see me. They were standing as near to me as you are standing now".

He was still performing in Germany when the war broke out and he had to escape over the border on a bicycle. He had an illusion show with lots of large props that he had to abandon. It pained him to leave it all behind but he had no choice. As an enemy alien he had to leave or be imprisoned by the Germans. He recovered only a small portion of his show back after the war. I asked him why he didn't leave Germany sooner rather than wait for war to break out. He replied, "I thought sanity would prevail—but it didn't".

I believe it was in the fifties that his career came to an end. Murray loved to drink and I am afraid the devil's buttermilk did him in. He ended up in hospital with alcoholic poisoning and nearly died from it. After he recovered it was obvious that his showbusiness career was finished. He therefore opened a magic shop in Blackpool which he ran until the day he died.

The shop was named "Murrays Magic Mart" and was a fixture of Cookson St, Blackpool for many years. Murray must have been in his late seventies and early eighties when I used to frequent the shop. I always likened him to a wise old man in a cave. Murray was very wise indeed and the place was dark and dingy as a cave.

He really was a great man with much wisdom. He shared many of his philosophies with me, many of which I follow to this day. Here are two that I remember:

"Talk about me good, talk about me bad; it doesn't matter as long as you talk about me".

"If you go through life and never do business with a crook, you will never get anything done".

I would imagine the first of these quotations to be very good advice (if not taken to extremes) for anyone in show business and the second to be very good advice for anyone in the real world of regular business. With regard to the latter it doesn't mean that you have to be dishonest yourself. It simply means that you have to be as sharp as the person you are dealing with.

And old Murray was as sharp as they would get. Legends abound as to the kind of old rogue he was in his shop. He would sell second hand props at twice the price as they were when new. If you protested he would say, "It's a collector's item". Some magicians are avid collectors of rare or antique props and in fact there is almost a separate industry within the magic community for this. And of course collector's items can often fetch a hefty price. Murray knew this and often misrepresented his merchandise as "collector's items". The old coot had been around the block a few times and didn't have the old school ethical and commendable stuffiness that his competitor Paul Clive had.

I well remember being highly irritated when I bought a book from him with five completely blank pages. There had obviously been a fault at the printing presses. When I protested to Murray he simply said, "It's a collector's item and a very rare book". I knew perfectly well that there was nothing rare about the book whatsoever and the only "collection" aspect of it was that it collected money for the old robber who had just sold it to me. I protested to no avail. I never did get a refund. Murray could feign deafness with great effectiveness.

He was famous for not giving the correct change and sometimes, not giving any change at all. He was old and doddery but this belied the shrewd and calculating brain behind the seeming feebleness. He would short change by such a small amount that if the customer did notice they would often not bother trying to explain it to this apparently mumbling, shuffling old man. It was just too much hassle so they let it go. He would even forget to give change and if it was a small amount the customer would often follow the same philosophy that it wasn't worth trying to explain it to the old man.

When Murray was dying in hospital the local magicians naturally wanted to know his progress. The reports usually said there was no change in his condition. One magician reported to a gathering of his fellow conjurers, "There is still no change from Murray" and a wit replied in mock exasperation, "What do you expect? There has never been any change from Murray!"

I well remember being in his shop and an ordinary looking fellow walked in and enquired about the price of a prop. Murray told him some price or other and the fellow walked out. Twenty minutes later another man walked in and made the same enquiry about the same prop. However, this fellow was much more smartly dressed and appeared to be quite prosperous. Murray told him a price which was three times the number I had heard quoted twenty minutes earlier.

After the chap had left with the prop under his arm I asked Murray about the big discrepancy in cost and he replied with a twinkle in his eyes, "Your prices have to be elastic sometimes".

He really was an old rogue but a lovable one. It cannot be denied that he scammed customers in a minor way but his best product was free and in fact quite priceless. His great wisdom and advice was worth thousands of dollars to those who were ready to receive it. I always knew a bargain when I saw one.

One piece of advice applied to magic was "The two most essential things for a conjurer to possess are audacity and bluff". He certainly followed this philosophy to the hilt when serving customers in his shop as I have already explained. Still, in the field of conjuring rather than retailing it was indeed also valuable advice.

Note that he used the word "conjurer". He never used the word "magician" unless the performer had a large show with massive props and large illusions. He considered anyone else a "conjurer". If you used the term "magician" in the usual way he would snort and correct you. If you did smaller magic like most magicians do, you were a *conjurer*.

One magician of the past that he detested was the famous Harry Houdini who died in 1926. Murray's career really took off when Houdini died. Inevitably he would be compared to this past master because he was similarly active in the area of escapes from chains, strait jackets, handcuffs and other methods of restraint. People would often describe him as "a second Houdini" and this would enrage him. He always retorted, "I am not Houdini the second. I am Murray the first!"

Even in his twilight years if you so much as mentioned Houdini you could expect a thundering denunciation of poor old Harry. However, one day I was surprised to see for sale under his glass counter a card trick with a label describing it as "The Houdini Card Trick". Since Murray was so vehement in his dislike of the great escapologist I was surprised to see the item on sale.

I said to him mischievously, "I am surprised to see you selling something with Houdini's name on it". He immediately snorted, "Well, I haven't sold any and I don't suppose I ever will". I couldn't answer that unassailable logic.

Earlier I mentioned Michael Vine as the chap I came to see in Blackpool who was working on Central Pier selling Svengali decks. Murray had arranged this by approaching Joe Smith who owned the demonstration counter in front of his joke and trick shop on the pier. He told Joe that there was a lad new in Blackpool who would be willing to give Joe 25% of his sales if he could sell the trick cards on the counter. Joe readily agreed and assumed that Michael owned the merchandise and that Murray was just acting as a middleman and doing Michael a favour. Little did Joe know that Murray was supplying Michael with the Svengali decks and that he, Murray owned the stock. Murray was paying Michael 25% commission on his sales and Michael at the end of the night would count his money in front of Joe who would take 25% of it. However, Joe had absolutely no idea that Murray had supplied the stock and was paying Michael a percentage.

Michael Vine as he was then

In fact Joe never found this out until years later when I mentioned it to him. Joe couldn't believe it and explained, "I was wondering why Murray was up here all the time talking to Michael. I had no idea that he owned the Svengali decks and was paying Michael a percentage. If I had known that I would have cut Murray out of the picture and dealt with Michael exclusively. I would have given him the name of a wholesaler that he could have purchased the cards from directly".

So Michael. If you are reading this then belatedly eat your heart out. If you had told Joe that you were working for Murray he would have been eliminated and you would have earned twice the money!

Of course Michael probably assumed that Joe knew all about the arrangement that Michael had with the old rogue and no doubt further assumed that Joe was well aware that the percentage he was receiving came from Murray. Well sorry, Michael. I hate to tell you this nearly forty years later but the old goat scammed you!

Michael Vine as he is now

As the reader can imagine from the above description Murray rather liked his money. I well remember two young punks once entered his shop with knives and attempted to rob this seemingly harmless eighty year old man. Trying to force Murray to part with money was an undertaking that no man on this earth could possibly succeed with, let alone two worthless local hooligans. Murray set about them with a broomstick and they ran out of the shop screaming! He got great play with this the next day in the local newspaper.

In his dying days I went to see him in hospital and mentioned to the nurse that Murray was once a famous escapologist. She replied, "Everybody knows that. We all know about you, don't we, Mr Murray?" Murray shrugged his shoulders and resignedly agreed by saying, "Yes. And you know too much". The retort from the nurse was "You can't escape from us, can you Mr Murray?" The old showman let out an audible sigh and amused me greatly by replying, "No. I wish I could!" I don't think Murray was a great fan of hospitals.

When I came to visit him in hospital in the company of another magician he pointed to me and said, "It's good to see this thief here!" Coming from Murray that was a fantastic compliment and I treasure it to this day. It was as if he saw me as a kindred spirit and had a great respect for someone who could "duck and dive" as well as he did. Incidentally, "duck and dive" is a British grafter's expression that I think is self explanatory. In case it isn't I suppose the word "survive" should be enough to explain the meaning.

For those of you who would like to know more about Murray there is a biography out there by the late Val Andrews that describes his adventures and career in more detail. It is entitled simply "Murray" and is published by Goodliffe Publications.

My years in Blackpool were very formative for me and shaped my cynicism and mentality. I must have sold God knows how many Svengali decks there. From time to time I would hire people to help me with this endeavour and here are some details concerning a few of the more memorable ones.

First, there was Peter Snow who helped me in my magic studio as well as assisted me in the sale of Svengali decks. I first met Peter when he was fourteen years old in Bristol or at least so he tells me. I don't remember the incident but it seems that I told him to clear off as he was being a brat teenager and heckling me when I was trying to sell Svengali decks.

Later I got to know him well and he worked for me not only in Blackpool but in other parts of the country. He was a most talented young man and excellent magician with a great personality.

After leaving my employ he travelled the world as a street magician performing in over thirty countries. I bumped into him in Montreal a few years ago at a psychic fair. I hadn't seen him for decades and I didn't recognize him. He lived in Montreal and I thought that it was a strange coincidence that we both ended up in Canada.

He had developed a French accent which was quite a magic trick in itself since he was born and bred in Bristol, England and when I knew him in his younger days his accent was very definitely British west country. I suppose he picked up the French accent after working so many years in France and other French speaking countries. And of course Montreal is in the French part of Canada.

Peter was very talented in his younger days and I am sure that he still is especially as a result of his vast performing experience in the most difficult of conditions. Street entertainment is very challenging indeed since you are not being paid a set fee to perform. You have to earn revenue by hoping your audience will put money in the hat. There can be no such thing as a bad street magician on a long-term basis since if you are no good you don't eat.

Another employee who also hailed from Bristol was Antony Moore. Everyone now knows him as Tony but to me he has always been Antony. I find it difficult to call him Tony but for this description I shall try my best.

Tony is now a highly respected and brilliant musician. At the time of writing he is presenting a music show on Maltese television on a regular basis and I wish him luck with it.

Tony Moore as a young magician

He worked for me in Blackpool quite a bit but at one point I took him to Canada to sell Svengali decks when he was nineteen years old. The reason I know his age is that I well remember he amused me greatly by having an argument with a Canadian bartender who refused to serve him because he looked too young. The legal drinking age in Ontario is nineteen years old. Antony (sorry—I just can't call him Tony) was furious and went to his hotel room to find his passport which had his age on it. He went back to the bartender and thrust his passport in front of the guy's face and said, "Get a look at that, sunshine!" I should explain to North American readers that "sunshine" is a British expression that has nothing to do with weather. For some unaccountable reason it is a form of address to a fellow human being but it does have rather a negative tinge to it. Antony proved that he was nineteen years old and finally got his drink. He certainly had to fight for it.

He earned enough money from selling Svengali decks in Canada to purchase an electric piano and on his return to England he decided to pursue his musical career in earnest. He joined a pop group that were later to become terribly famous. Iron Maiden is the name. I suppose I had better call him Tony from now on since that was the name he became known as in the music business.

Tony Moore, Barry Purkisss, Terry Wapram
Steve Harris and Dennis Wilcock

Tony Moore and the Iron Maiden

He eventually left Iron Maiden and I remember asking him why he departed. He told me, "I don't think they have good prospects". It appears that he was wrong since they went on to become very famous indeed. When I saw Tony recently I remarked that I was surprised that his style would fit into the heavy metal racket that Iron Maiden make. He replied, "Yes, they were rather a noisy lot!"

However, he went on to join another group called Cutting Crew, who actually had a hit record entitled, "Died In Your Arms Tonight". When you listen to that record it is Tony that is playing the keyboard.

The hell with it. I am going to go back to calling him Antony now. Antony is one of my favourite people on the planet and I wish him continued success in his career.

Another fellow that worked for me was Derek Ward. He is still selling Svengali decks to this day and he was always brilliant at doing so.

I wish him well and want him to know that I am still using the instruction leaflets that he wrote for various magic tricks I sell. He must have written them around thirty-five years ago and I am still using them to this day. I hope he doesn't want royalties.

As I was writing this book I was horrified to hear that his daughter Melissa, a probationer police constable was recently stabbed to death by her boyfriend who also died. He murdered her and then killed himself. I was sick to the stomach when I read it on the internet.

I haven't seen Derek for at least twenty years and if I met him today I would have no idea what to say to him concerning this horrific tragedy. The pain for him and his wife Gillian must be utterly indescribable.

If he should ever read this all I can do is to remind him of the wisdom of the serenity prayer.

"God grant me the serenity to accept the things I cannot change,

The courage to change the things I can,

And the wisdom to know the difference".

I wish him well and pray he finds that one day he and his wife can recover somewhat from the trauma of this horrific event.

But now I have to describe one particular Blackpool employee who became a lifelong friend and he means a lot to me for some unfathomable reason. You could even say that he is my best friend. His name is Terry Walker and he is still a grafter to this day over thirty years later at the time of writing. I am afraid that is all my doing as will shortly be described.

I first met Terry in 1977 when I was selling Svengali decks on Central Pier. He was standing in my crowd watching me. He was in Blackpool for his upcoming birthday. I think he was fifteen years old when I met him but he was about to turn sixteen. He was a young magician at the time and he wanted to let me know that he was interested in magic in much the same way I had wanted Joe Stuthard to know that I was a magician too as described in an earlier chapter.

Terry didn't ask about "fanning powder" in the way that I did. Instead he asked, "Are these cut Svengalis?" I had no idea what he was talking about because all Svengali decks are "cut" Svengalis. I won't go into a detailed explanation of the technical intricacies of a trick deck of cards so I hope that you take my word for it. He stood there with a Cheshire cat grin and he was beginning to irritate me in the same way that Peter Snow had irritated me when I first met him. Of course Terry was not heckling me as Peter did but was simply asking stupid questions which was nearly as bad. He then irritated me further by asking, "Have you ever heard of Mark Lewis? I heard that he sells these cards too". He had no idea he was speaking to Mark Lewis especially since people who worked on the pier came up to me for brief moments addressing me as "Ronnie". I decided out of cussedness not to tell him who I was and replied, "I know Mark Lewis. What about him?" Terry replied, "To be honest I don't like him". I decided to have some fun and enquired, "Have you ever met him?" The response was, "No. But I have heard all about him from other magicians. I really don't like him".

The devil in me took over and I informed Terry that Mark Lewis was one of the greatest card magicians in the world and that he was a sterling fellow. Terry was not impressed and went on a diatribe about how Mark

Lewis was a dreadful person and that he was no good at magic at all. I told him that he was talking nonsense and he wasn't able to judge the fellow until he actually saw him perform and that he shouldn't go by uninformed gossip. Terry, however, still argued the point with me.

I was now getting fed up with Terry and his denunciations of the said Mark Lewis and was about to snarl at him and make him go away but then I remembered something which made me change my mind. Two days before I had made a three hour ferry ride to the Isle of Man to do a magic show. I did the show and stayed in a local hotel. The next day, I returned on another three hour boat ride to Blackpool. When I set foot on dry land I realised with horror that I had left all my props behind in the hotel room on the Isle of Man. I have always been absent minded and this was a prime example of it. I console myself that absent-mindedness may perhaps be a sign of genius.

I phoned the hotel to ascertain that my property was still there and indeed to my great relief it was. I knew that I would have to endure another six hours travelling back and forth to the Isle of Man to pick it up.

I intended to do this at some point during the week.

When Terry appeared before me I realised that it might be a good idea to hire him to sell decks on the pier for the one day that I was away. I figured that if I gave him 25% of sales I couldn't possibly lose money since even if he sold only one deck it would have been money I wouldn't have earned anyway. Since I had nothing to lose I decided to offer him a job, selling the cards for one day only while I went back to the Isle of Man to pick up my props. I planned to make the journey the next day, travelling in the morning and returning in the evening.

I asked Terry if he knew how to perform the Svengali deck and he said he did. I asked him to show me and he did some sort of routine with it which I considered adequate since I was only going to be away for one day. Accordingly, I told him to liaise with Joe Smith who owned the location and would hand over the stock to him after counting it. In the evening he was to give Joe 25% of sales and when I returned from the Isle of

Man he was to give me the rest of the takings and I would hand over his commission to him.

Accordingly, the next day I travelled to the Isle of Man and back. On my return I went straight to Central Pier to see how well Terry had done. I was quite pleased to see that he had done quite well so after I paid him we went to eat at a nearby restaurant where I congratulated him and informed him that if he ever wanted a full time job with me in Blackpool he should phone me and I gave him my number.

Terry at work

At this point in the story I am going to pause and reflect on the mysteries of fate. If I hadn't been such a twit as to leave my stuff on the Isle of Man Terry's life would have taken an entirely different turn, as I shall shortly describe. Who knows which path he would have followed? That meeting with me changed his entire life and just thinking about it gives me the creeps. I used to joke to Terry, "If it hadn't been for me you would now be a milkman asking 'one pint or two, love?' I hope you are grateful to me for evermore". Terry usually replied, "Yes, it's all your fault" implying that I had ruined his life.

Terry returned to Winsford, Cheshire where he lived. Two weeks later I got a phone call and heard the caller say, "This is Terry". By this time I had completely forgotten all about him and I had no idea what the caller was talking about. I replied, "Who?" and Terry answered "Terry". I had no idea who the hell "Terry" was so replied "Am I supposed to know you?" The response was, "Don't you remember? You offered me a job". I didn't remember and said, "I have no idea what you are talking about. What job?"

He answered, "I worked on the pier for you for one day when you went to the Isle of Man. Afterwards you said that if I needed a job you would give me one". I then remembered and said "When do you want a job?" and was surprised to hear him say. "Now! I want to come to Blackpool straight away". Since he was only sixteen I asked if it was all right with his parents. He said, "I don't care what they think. I want to get away from them!"

I found out later that Terry's parents were always arguing. He always had an independent spirit and it is not in the least surprising that he decided that he wasn't going to put with it so just upped and left to come and work for me in Blackpool. He had an amazing amount of grit and independence even at sixteen years old.

He came to Blackpool and we got on like a house on fire. He was, and still is, a fantastic mimic and would make me laugh my head off by impersonating various people around Blackpool that we both knew. He had, and still has, a fantastic sense of humour and we hit it off immediately. He was to become my closest friend and we had a lot of adventures together in Britain, Ireland, Holland and Canada. From the moment he came to Blackpool at the age of sixteen he became a professional grafter for his entire life and still is active in this work to this day. I will have more to tell about Terry in chapters to come but suffice it to say for the moment that he took to the grafting business like a duck takes to water. He would watch other grafters work who were selling non-magic products and take it all in. He was learning all the time and soaking in the knowledge that the university of evil known as Blackpool was giving him.

He was working for me for quite a few weeks and still had no idea that I was Mark Lewis. Everyone who was not a magician or entertainer in Blackpool knew me as "Ronnie" so naturally, when they addressed me in front of Terry, he assumed that was my name and I couldn't be anyone else. I still, however, used to talk about Mark Lewis to him and insist he was a nice fellow. Terry would continue to expound on the fact that he had heard from magicians in Winsford, and other places, what a terrible man this awful person was.

Terry and his wife Tracy in a merry mood

This went on for about three weeks or so but my fun came to an end when he wandered into Murray's shop where he had been an old customer whenever he visited Blackpool. Murray asked him what he was up to now and Terry explained, "I am working for that Ronnie fellow on the pier selling Svengali decks". Murray shocked him by saying, "Ronnie? Oh, you mean Mark Lewis!" It then dawned on Terry that I had been winding him up for quite a long time. When he met me after Murray had given the game away he called me a name or two. To this day I remind him of the time he said that he didn't like Mark Lewis not realising that he was working for, and spending hours on end every day, with this dreaded person. He always replies, "I *still* don't like Mark Lewis!" He eventually graduated from being a student at the university of evil to actually becoming a professor there. I have always said that Terry was my star pupil and I am very proud of him.

One year before I met Terry I had visited Toronto on holiday and on a whim booked into three Toronto department stores for the Christmas season with utterly no idea how I was going to get supplies and staff the promotions. However, although it was quite a difficult thing to operate in a foreign country somehow or other I managed to do it. I imported trick decks from the United States although later I found a source in Toronto itself. I took the aforementioned Antony Moore over to Toronto and hired local magicians to cover the three stores. I ran around the three stores to supervise the operation and do a bit of demonstrating myself. I ended up making rather a lot of money.

I had decided to return the next year at the end of the Blackpool season but I had decided to only work one store instead of three but work it myself without hiring anyone. I was quite sad at the end of the Blackpool season to say goodbye to Terry and I wondered how he would make a living since he didn't really want to go back to Winsford. Consequently, I approached my friend Dennis Adams whom I have referred to earlier and asked if he could give Terry a job.

Dennis readily consented and that was that.

Still, I enjoyed Terry's company and I half wondered if I could somehow bring him to Canada and use his help working the one store I was in. I reasoned that the store was open for long hours and he may possibly be of some use in helping me fill those hours. I told him that I would bring him out to Canada with me if it turned out that I could afford to do so. I proposed that I would go over to Toronto and test the waters first and, if I were able to, I would bring him over.

However, when I arrived in Toronto, it soon became apparent that, although I was doing well enough sales wise, the store slowness in paying what was owed to me was playing havoc with my cash flow and I was rapidly running out of money. I realised that I was never going to be able to bring Terry over. I could hardly keep myself let alone support another person in a foreign country.

I had promised Terry that I would do my best to bring him over but I realised that it wasn't going to happen and I felt very bad that I would have to phone him and tell him the bad news.

I phoned Dennis in England and told him to tell Terry that I couldn't bring him over after all. Dennis replied, "You can't do that, Ronnie. Terry is very loyal to you. You can't let him down". I said, "I don't want to let him down but I have to. I can barely pay my own way let alone his".

A few days later I got a phone call from Dennis saying "Terry is coming to Canada! I just paid his fare! One of you bastards had better pay me back!" I protested to Dennis, "You shouldn't have done that. I can't afford him!" Dennis replied, "It's too late. I've paid the money and he has his ticket. He's coming whether you can afford him or not. He is very loyal to you and you can't let him down". I spluttered, "When is he coming?" I was utterly floored when Dennis replied, "Tomorrow!"

And so he arrived in Canada the very next day. The very first thing I asked him as soon as he got off the plane was how much money he had on him because I was about to run out. Thus Terry received a lesson in "ducking and diving" in a foreign country.

For weeks we were living on our wits trying to exist without money until the store finally paid out. Without going in to the ins and outs of it we managed to survive by various nefarious means that had better be imagined rather than explained. In addition, I was able to get a few entertainment bookings from local variety agents which helped us get through the cash flow crisis. We finally made a profit and came back to Britain with satisfactory revenue.

For years to come I would often return to Canada for the Christmas season. Another country, however, was soon to beckon. I used to call this country "my big green piggy bank" because of all the money I made there.

Why green you may ask? The answer will be in the next chapter.

CHAPTER EIGHT

The Emerald Isle

WHEN I WAS SELLING Svengali decks in Blackpool, the best spenders were Irish and Glasgow holidaymakers and the worst were people from Yorkshire. There was something known in Blackpool as the "Glasgow fortnight". These were the two weeks in July that Glaswegians came down in their droves to invade the town. Sales doubled during that period all over Blackpool and the local shopkeepers and traders looked forward to this period.

On the other hand there was something known as the "Yorkshire Wakes" that were dreaded by the locals who wanted to make money. There were periods known as "wake weeks" in Yorkshire when factories and other businesses would close and all the workers would come to Blackpool for their holidays. However, Yorkshire people were terrible spenders owing to their famous frugal nature and sales would inevitably take a dive during this period. In fact the famous saying in the town was "Yorkshire wakes while Blackpool sleeps".

Fortunately, the Irish and the Glaswegians more than made up for the tight fisted Yorkshire visitors. I had always known that the Irish were "good punters" (grafter's vernacular for good customers) since I had sold Svengali decks in Northern Ireland on many occasions and had always taken in far more money than I ever had in England, Scotland or Wales. I had never worked, however, in the Republic of Ireland but I noticed that whenever holidaymakers from this southern part of that country showed up in my Blackpool crowd they were just as fantastic as the Northern Irish punters.

I had a hunch that it might be a profitable move to check out Dublin in the Republic of Ireland to see if was a good venue to set up a Christmas promotion with the Svengali decks. Accordingly, I took a trip over with Dennis to have a look at the place. We took a plane over and at the time I was terrified of flying. Dennis said, "Don't worry, Ronnie. If the plane crashes I will knock you unconscious and you won't know anything about it". I regret to say that I did not find this "assurance" terribly comforting.

When I arrived I checked out the various department stores and they seemed very busy indeed with lots of foot traffic. I decided that one day I would operate a Christmas promotion one day in this city but in reality it didn't happen for a couple of years.

However, when it did happen it happened with a bang. I went over to Dublin at the end of the Blackpool 1978 season to see what I could arrange. I approached a leading department store called Switzers and made an arrangement to sell the cards in the store. I was to give the store 25% of sales in the way that I had done with many department stores but I was astonished at the casual way the Irish did business. In England and Canada there was always quite a lot of red tape involved with dealing with department stores. One of the main problems was that the money would be taken in the store's cash registers and processed through their accounts department. After what was sometimes an interminable interval I would eventually receive a cheque from the store minus their percentage.

That wasn't the way the Irish worked. Not only did they not give me a cash register they didn't take the money to their accounting department. To my astonishment they were quite happy to have a share out at the end of every evening when the store closed. I would count out the money in front of them and give them 25% and just put the rest of the money into my pocket. When I would attempt to count out the reasonably large amount of coinage as opposed to paper money the department manager would say, "Ah no, don't bother counting out all that change. It'll take far too long. Let's ignore it. Just put it in your pocket and we'll simply count the notes".

I found this casual approach to be quite a peculiar way for a large department store to operate but I didn't object and found it terribly convenient.

One day the general manager of the store took objection to the way I was collecting the money and I thought he was going to insist that I use a cash register. Up to this point I had just been using a cardboard box to put the money in since no register had been offered to me. He said to me "You can't use a cardboard box". Naturally I assumed that he was going to make a big fuss and organize a cash register. To my utter astonishment he went on, "Ah no, you can't be putting money in a box like that. You might have the money stolen. Put the cash in your pocket—that's the best way!"

This way of operating in a department store in any other country apart from Ireland would be quite unheard of, not least because the store would have no way of monitoring that their percentage was accurate. I used to give them the correct percentage every night but I found out later they expected me to shave a percentage and skim off the top. It was the strange Irish mentality at work. As long as they made enough out of it and had the entertainment of the magic demonstration they were quite happy. I never did cheat them but sometimes I almost wish I had. No doubt I should be given some sort of honour for resisting temptation.

Sales were utterly fantastic. I sold an average of 400 decks a day and my top day was 478 decks. I was making an absolute fortune and my hardest task was to find supplies of Svengali decks. Ron MacMillan by this time had stopped importing the cards from Czechoslovakia where they had originally come from, so in Blackpool I had purchased a guillotine that would cut through playing cards and made my own from regular cards that I had purchased wholesale. I decided to follow the same procedure in Dublin and found a wholesaler to supply me with decks of regular playing cards. My main problem, however, was to find time to make the cards.

I was selling so many that it would have been impossible for me to keep up. I therefore purchased a guillotine in Dublin and hired two students to do nothing but make the cards in their own homes. They worked long hours to churn out the amazing amount of decks that I required.

To go off on a little tangent here, one of the store detectives whose duty it was to catch shoplifters used to come over and watch my demonstration quite frequently because he found it so entertaining. Two years later I was doing a Christmas promotion in Simpsons department store in Toronto and to my amazement I saw the same guy wandering around the Canadian store. I couldn't believe my eyes so to check it was really him I asked him the time to see if he replied in an Irish accent. When I did that he recognized me and looked quite surprised. I found out that he had emigrated to Canada and had got a job as a store detective in Toronto in Simpson's. He used to watch me demonstrating the cards in Canada just as much as he watched me do them in Ireland! It just goes to prove that it really is a small world!

Anyway, I made so much money in Dublin that I resolved that I wanted more where that came from. Accordingly, I worked more venues in Ireland such as the *Cork Ideal Homes Exhibition*, the *Limerick Ideal Homes Exhibition*, the *Dublin Horse Show*, the *Dublin Spring Show* and many other places. I also worked in Northern Ireland at the *Royal Ulster Show* and the *Belfast Ideal Homes Exhibition*.

Sales at all these places were wonderful but the main problem was that there were not as many venues to work as there were in Britain. However, I worked in as many places as I could because I knew that I could treble the sales that I made at comparable venues in the UK.

Of course as I already mentioned I had worked before in Northern Ireland. I am going to backtrack a few years on my story to tell you a little about this. I had worked in Belfast many times for Ron MacMillan but when I went out on my own I decided on one memorable occasion to book space at the *Londonderry Ideal Homes Exhibition*. That is the title of this consumer show for my Protestant readers. For my Catholic readers it is the *Derry Ideal Homes Exhibition*. To those innocent of the politics of the Holy Province of Ulster (Northern Ireland) it is rather a peculiarity that if you call the city of Londonderry/Derry the wrong name to the wrong people you can get into mighty trouble. I am, however, going to be brave and call the place Derry since whenever I have been there the majority of the population in the city call it by that name.

This was at the very start of what became known as "the troubles" in Northern Ireland. Anybody that reads newspapers or watches television news will know about the bombs that went off and the bullets that were flying about during this long period with the dreadful loss of lives that resulted from this long and nasty political conflict. In actual fact the problems go back hundreds of years but there was relative calm in the streets until the late sixties. However, all hell broke loose in the streets of Derry in October 1968 when there was three days of rioting. The situation remained tense until August of 1969 when the British Government sent the army in to supposedly keep the peace.

All this was a trifle unfortunate for the Derry Exhibition since it was scheduled for early September and the British Army had only been in the city for a couple of weeks or so. I had scheduled and paid in advance for this show months before when things had been relatively quiet. As I read the newspapers, however, I began to have second thoughts about exhibiting. At the time I was safely ensconced in London and reading about riots in the streets and shops being burned to the ground does have a somewhat discouraging effect. I called the promoter who informed me that I had nothing to worry about and that everything was calm although there had been a bit of trouble a couple of weeks before. He said that now that the army had arrived everything was hunky dory. I wasn't convinced by this and came to the conclusion that perhaps the Svengali deck and myself had better seek safer pastures.

Accordingly, I decided to sell the show to a local London magician that didn't seem the sort who kept up with the news. Of course he knew that there had been riots but I convinced him that it was all in the past and everything had now calmed down. He agreed to take on the show and promised to mail me a cheque. Unfortunately, just before he did so there were riots and mayhem galore reported in the press which did put a damper on his mood concerning the matter. He rather rapidly called up to inform me that he wished to live and that travelling to meet the good citizens of Ulster he considered not to be conducive to his good health.

I was stuck and therefore had no choice but to do the show myself since I had already booked and paid for it in advance. In September 1969 I got on a plane to Northern Ireland with great fear and trepidation. I wondered if I would come back alive. I decided that if I did so that would be a feat in itself and any financial profit would be a mere bonus.

When I arrived I promptly booked into a bed and breakfast, which I later found out was the only Roman Catholic house in a Protestant street. Of course this was way before I became psychic and perhaps was not the best judgement call to make. However, it worked out well despite subsequent events and I did eventually check out alive and well as evidenced by the fact that you are actually reading this story.

I then went down to the Guildhall where the exhibition was being held. As I was setting up the day before the show two Irish workmen came over to me. I assume they were standfitters or were involved in setting up the exhibition in some way. They started to make conversation and one of them said, "You people in England must read the papers and think we are all mad over here. We are all ashamed by it. I want to thank you for coming to Northern Ireland. You can go back and tell people what we are really like. Not all of us are at each other's throats. I am a Protestant and my friend Jimmy here is a Catholic. We love each other and we need each other. We are the greatest of friends. Now you go back to England and tell them that!" It was quite a moving statement and I was very impressed by it. I was to discover that the people of Northern Ireland were the salt of the earth and very upfront. Their friendliness was unbelievable.

To my surprise the exhibition turned out to be a very good one and I was making money hand over fist. I was at the top of some stairs near the entrance and I was able to attract every person who came in off the stairs. And of course when they left I got them on the way out. The main reason for my success, however, was that I was situated right beside the toilets or to use the polite North American term washrooms. It was a very narrow corridor and people had to pass me on the way in to the toilets and again on the way out. I had crowds gathered around me all day.

The streets were quite calm and I used to walk home unmolested in the dark every night after the show closed at 10.00 p.m. There was lots of street lighting and little shops that were open along the way even though it was quite late. I was actually surprised to see these little shops open and they were mainly newsagents and tobacconists.

Since the exhibition opened at two p.m I had plenty of time to look around the town and it did look a mess with burned out buses and badly damaged shops and buildings. The army was everywhere and I was shocked to see soldiers standing guard with sub machine guns outside Boots the Chemist, which was and for all I know still is a leading pharmacy chain in the United Kingdom. To see such a thing in another part of Britain was quite a shock to me.

It took quite a while to get used to all the guns that were displayed by soldiers and police. With regard to the latter the police wore green uniforms rather than the dark blue uniforms that were the norm in the UK. This was the Royal Ulster Constabulary and I had first come across them when I worked in Belfast in previous years for Ron MacMillan. I remember being surprised that, unlike the rest of the police in Britain they were armed. Of course not everyone agreed that Ulster was part of Britain and that was the root cause of the unrest when it all boiled down to it.

In North America where I now live people know very little about the Irish situation and imagine everyone in Ireland is fighting to free themselves of British rule. Some of them are quite surprised to hear that there are a very large proportion of Northern Ireland people, in fact the majority of them, who want to remain part of the United Kingdom. This is mainly the Protestant faction.

I am not going to comment on Northern Ireland politics in case I get myself into trouble. I will only say that on both sides of the conflict are the most friendly and wonderful people on the face of the earth. The obvious exceptions to this are the thugs and killers on both sides of the divide.

Although the streets were calm and the people friendly there was an atmosphere of tension in the air as if something was going to erupt at any moment. Although trouble was brewing everywhere in Northern Ireland particularly in Belfast, Derry was a flashpoint and being a small city it was particularly vulnerable to an uncomfortable feeling of being on the edge of an explosion.

During this time I was constantly told by the population who were mainly Catholic that they were very pleased and grateful that the army had been sent in to keep the peace. They felt that they would get a far better and fairer deal from the British Army than they would get from the Unionist Protestant Government of Northern Ireland and the Royal Ulster Constabulary. The police at that time were mainly Protestant and it was felt, rightly or wrongly, that they were prejudiced against the Catholic population.

At this early period at the very beginning of "the troubles" there were no bombs going off and no bullets flying as were to later occur with such horrific effect. At that time the violence was limited to throwing bricks and burning down houses with of course, frequent kicking of heads in. I was, therefore, horrified to hear one exhibitor at the show state that he could bring in as many firearms as were required to defend us all in case of trouble. I later found out that this fellow was a member of the Irish Republican Army (the IRA for short). At the time the IRA were very low profile and virtually a joke in Northern Ireland. Of course later on they were no joke at all.

The chap was actually a very nice man and all I remember about him is that his name was Pat and he played the guitar. I have no idea what happened to him.

This kind of talk concerning firearms had been provoked by rumours of the exhibition itself being attacked because it was so prominent in the city centre and of course there were quite a few English exhibitors that extremists might take exception to.

I didn't think this was going to happen but there was no denying that you could cut the tension in the air with a knife. The atmosphere wasn't helped by the constant police and army presence. One day before the opening of the show I nearly had a heart attack when walking down an aisle to see the muzzle of a machine gun pointing at me. A soldier was there bended on his knees looking under a carpet for something or other. His gun was somehow pointing straight at me while he was looking elsewhere. I hoped to God the safety catch was on and I moved very quickly out of the way. I found all this tension fascinating as well as fearful. I was instinctively aware that I was present as a witness to history and I wondered what was going to happen next. I didn't have long to wait.

One night as I was leaving to go home as usual I noticed a lot of activity going on in the street outside the exhibition. I normally walked home by strolling up a hill outside the Guildhall where I eventually arrived at "The Diamond" which was a big square. I then would turn left and walk for about fifteen minutes or so to the street where the bed and breakfast was located.

This night there was a hell of a lot more people than usual walking up the hill and it was obvious that something was going on. This was confirmed to me by the promoter of the Derry exhibition whom I noticed in the street. He greeted me with, "Hello, magic man. Make sure you don't get killed walking up there. I want to see you at the show tomorrow!"

Of course curiosity and the need to get home compelled me to walk up the hill regardless. I asked various people what was going on and they informed me that there was a raging riot going on at the top of the hill where the Diamond was located. I was told that petrol bombs and bricks were being thrown and I had better be careful.

Suddenly I noticed beside me a young boy who could not have been more than twelve years old. I recognised him as one of the kids who hung around the exhibition doing odd jobs for the various exhibitors. He was carrying a bottle that he had filled up with petrol. I asked him what he was going to do with it which was rather a daft question now that I think about it. He replied, "I am going to throw it and kill some proddies (Protestants)".

I decided to reprimand the urchin and did so by informing him that I considered such actions to be socially unacceptable and a mite dangerous. He didn't seem convinced by my argument and seemed irritated that I wanted to spoil his fun. I argued back saying, "How would you like it if someone threw something like that and it set your mother on fire?" He answered, "It depends on who started it. And the proddies started it".

He then looked at me aggressively with some suspicion. "Are you a Catholic or a Protestant?" he enquired. I answered, "Neither. I am Jewish" whereupon he responded, "Yes, but are you a Protestant Jew or a Catholic Jew?" I was a trifle bemused by this but nevertheless I replied, "Neither. I am a Jewish Jew. Not everyone is a Catholic or a Protestant, you know".

The little mini terrorist stared at me and came back with a devastating reply that still sticks in my mind to this day. "Well, you go and fight for Jerusalem. I am going to fight for free Derry!"

No doubt the little monster went on to join the I.R.A. or did time in prison. Either that or he became a cabinet minister in the present government of Northern Ireland.

When I got to the top of the hill I was confronted by massive crowds of people in the Diamond throwing stones and petrol bombs at each other so I decided that discretion was the better part of valour so I headed back down the hill again.

Beside the Guildhall was a very expensive hotel known as the City Hotel. British journalists who had been sent to report on all the riots and mayhem used the hotel as a base of operations and the place was teeming with reporters and photographers. A few of the richer exhibitors at the Guildhall exhibition stayed there but not too many. I certainly couldn't afford the prices myself. I decided, however, that it might be a good idea to enter the hotel and have a drink and something to eat until the riot died down and I could then go home. It was perfectly obvious that there was no way that I could get back to the bed and breakfast place until there were signs of calm outside.

When I arrived I met up with various exhibitors and grafters from the show who happened to be there. We all sat in a lounge area drinking, eating and making merry by gossiping and singing songs. There was also a fair bit of discussion concerning the riot going on outside. Most of the local exhibitors present were Irish republican sympathisers and I remember one fiery woman saying, "I hate violence but I also hate injustice".

The English exhibitors were mainly grafters who had no idea about Irish politics and had very little understanding of why people were rioting in the streets so they tended to talk more about other things. However, the Irish exhibitors chattered away about how the solution would have to be an eventual united Ireland but of course, they had no idea how it was going to be achieved.

After a few hours the alcohol began to take effect and everyone started to sing louder and play musical instruments such as a guitar and harmonica which someone happened to have. It got very loud indeed and the hotel manager came in a few times and gave us all frosty looks. Word was that the riot was still going on outside and, in fact, it was getting worse with buses being set on fire and property ablaze with a number of injuries being reported.

Suddenly a jolly reporter from the Daily Express newspaper opened the door and looked in on us. I remember he talked with a posh accent and had a handlebar moustache. He surveyed the scene and remarked, "I say, old chaps. I came in to see what all the noise is about. I can see you are all fiddling while Rome is burning outside". I asked him if the riot was still going on since I was beginning to wonder when I was going to be able to get home. He replied that all hell was still breaking loose and we had better not leave the hotel.

He left the room and the party got even louder and the Irish exhibitors began to sing Irish rebel songs. This was the last straw for the hotel manager who came in and demanded quiet saying, "Look, no party political songs please. Especially rebel songs. A man has been killed out there tonight".

And indeed he had. I am hazy on the details after so many years but I seem to remember the story was that he tried to save his teenage son and ended up getting stoned to death himself.

After the reprimand from the hotel manager the atmosphere became a lot quieter and after an hour or so the party broke up. Word had come down that the riot was over. I figured it was time to leave so I nervously left the hotel and tentatively walked up the hill to go home. The streets were now very quiet and indeed it was actually an eerie silence. It was about three in the morning and I needed to get to bed.

Suddenly an army jeep drove up beside me and a couple of soldiers got out. One of them asked, "Where do you think you are going?" I answered, "Home". They continued, "Where do you live?" When I told them they said "You can't go home. We have cordoned off that street and nobody is allowed down there right now. We want everyone off the streets until morning". I replied in an irritated fashion, "Where am I supposed to sleep tonight?" The rather aggressive answer with a tone to match was, "We don't care where you are going to sleep tonight. That is not our problem. I just told you that the streets are out of bounds tonight. Now we just saw you come out of the City Hotel. I suggest you go back in there and see if they will give you a room".

I replied, "I can't afford that place" to which the response was, "Not our problem. Now get off the street, please".

So I began my trek down the hill again and the soldiers drove off. I realised that I had no choice but to book a room at the hotel for just one night.

The next morning I went back to the bed and breakfast and the landlady gave me breakfast and told me that she had no idea there was a riot going on and she slept straight through it. She only found out about it when she listened to the radio early the next morning. She checked my room and realised that I didn't make it home. She thought that I had been caught up in the riot and was about to call around the hospitals to find me and report my disappearance to the authorities. She seemed greatly relieved that I was still alive and told me that she had the only Catholic house in a Protestant street. She was worried that she would be targeted one day because of it.

Interestingly enough despite all the mayhem I had a very good week financially and went back to England with pots of money and a new interest in Irish politics which has never left me to this day. I must say that this was one of the most memorable weeks of my life.

However, there was rather an odd sequel to this story. While I was in Northern Ireland I purchased a deck of cards which I thought looked rather pretty. It had a great big and bloody red hand pictured on the back. I had been booked to perform some card tricks on a TV show in England and decided to use this deck. Just before I went on a cameraman saw the pack and remarked, "I wouldn't use those cards if I were you". I asked why and he said, "You have the red hand of Ulster there". I had no idea what he was talking about so I just went ahead using the deck as planned.

When the programme went out all hell broke loose at the BBC switchboard with people phoning up to complain about my dreadful pack of cards. To balance that letters came in to the producer over the next couple of weeks saying how wonderful my card tricks were. Of course all the letters praising me to the skies were from Northern Ireland Protestants and all the phoned complaints were uttered in Ulster accents and presumably were from the Catholic side. I had no idea that the Red Hand of Ulster was a divisive Protestant symbol full of partisan meaning. I never used the deck on television again.

Of course, as I said, I had to backtrack to tell the tale of my experiences in Derry but now I will fast forward to the point where I departed from my story. If you recall, I described how I went over to Ireland to work the various stores, fairs and exhibitions. There was not enough work there to keep me going so I would also work in England, Scotland and Wales. In addition to this I would sometimes travel to Canada and work there too.

Eventually I was working so much in Ireland that I decided to move there permanently. So one day I packed up and left Blackpool for the place that I called my "Big Green Piggy Bank". Green because it is known as the Emerald Isle and the piggy bank reference was because I made so much money over there. I rented an apartment in Dublin and started my Irish adventure in earnest.

One Christmas season I decided to expand my operations somewhat and instead of booking into one Dublin department store I took on two and just to complicate matters further I decided to go kind of international and book a store in Belfast too. So I had two stores in Dublin in the Republic of Ireland and one store booked over the border in Belfast which was the part of Ireland under British jurisdiction.

I brought Terry over from England to work in Switzers and hired a local magician named Daniel O'Donoghue to work in Arnotts department store. Dan was a brilliant close up magician that I had worked with in Blackpool at a concession in the Pleasure Beach. We had a concession where we would present close up magic shows in a sideshow type of operation. We called it the "Theatre of Mystery". However, it was terribly unprofitable and we ended up calling it the "Theatre of Misery" instead.

Dan is still following his career as a magician in Ireland and he is a truly wonderful performer and the odd thing is that he is not very well known in the world of magic although he could be if he wanted to be. In fact he keeps well away from other magicians and he is probably wise in doing so. He works for the public rather than for the profession and he does very well at it.

It will be remembered that in earlier chapters I mentioned what an influence Ron MacMillan was on my career. By an odd coincidence the MacMillan family also had an influence on Dan's life too. He married Ron's daughter Georgina! They live happily in Dublin today.

I decided that I would not work at any of the stores and devote my time to running around between them doing the odd demonstration here and there, supplying stock and keeping things as organised as best I could. That meant that I would have to find a demonstrator for the Belfast store. This was the Anderson and Macauley department store a rather upscale emporium in the centre of Belfast.

I couldn't find a local magician so I resolved to put an advertisement in the Belfast Telegraph newspaper. I knew that I was unlikely to hire a magician for the position but I reasoned that I wouldn't necessarily need one because I could train the person how to do this one trick known as the Svengali deck and the advantage of a non magician is that the person would be sales minded instead of magic minded. In other words if they were paid commission they would have money on the brain instead of magic.

Lo and behold, I ended up hiring the most amazing character that I worked with for many years. Her name was Ann Fuller, a dark haired girl in her twenties, and she was such a character that I have devoted the next chapter of this book to her. You can read it later and hopefully marvel at her with great amusement as I did on many occasions. In fact she was so much of a character that Anderson and Macauley couldn't handle her and consequently they kicked the demonstration out of the store. I will relate the story in the Auntie Annie chapter that is devoted to her.

I hurriedly arranged a new place for Ann to work and this was the Co-operative department store which was the biggest store in Belfast. She adapted quite well there and took in loads of money even though, as a non-magician, she couldn't do the tricks properly. However, that made no difference whatsoever because she had the ability to sell.

Meanwhile Dan was having trouble with the management of Arnotts in Dublin. They had exactly the same arrangement as Switzers in that it was cash every night—the store took their cut, Dan took his cut and I took mine. It was wonderful for the cash flow I must say. In Belfast I had to do things in a more official manner and all the money went to the store and they paid me after getting invoices and I had to suffer the usual delays in payment. Of course Belfast was under the British influence while Dublin was subject to the more casual Republic of Ireland approach.

However, Arnotts did not like Dan putting the money in his pocket even though Switzers seemed to be all for it. They wanted things to be slightly more official and insisted that Dan used a cash register which they would supply. Dan, however, found it interfered with his sales and he plain couldn't be bothered with the register. The department manager was always arguing with Dan over it and insisted that the sales were rung up properly. Dan was very stubborn in refusing and despite my efforts to keep the store happy, resisted even my attempts at persuasion. Finally, the department manager pleaded with Dan, "Just ring up a sale or two for show. You don't have to do it every time. Just put the money in the till and don't bother ringing up a sale unless you see my boss come by. We just don't want you putting the money in your pocket since it looks bad". Dan finally gave in but this should give you an idea of the eccentric way the Irish do business. That Christmas I did very well despite the difficulty in working in two jurisdictions. In fact I did so well that I decided to repeat the promotions again next year for the Christmas season.

The following year I cut down on the Dublin end of things and only had one store running. That was Switzers where I had Terry working and two in Belfast one of which was the Co-op and the other was known as Leisureworld which was essentially a toy store. I had Ann in the Co-op and hired a little fifteen year old Belfast hooligan called Jimmy to man Leisureworld.

Jimmy never bothered to attend school and he used to sniff glue. I threatened to tell his parents if he didn't cease. My threats were empty and they certainly didn't stop him. He was an ardent Fenian (Irish republican) who hated Protestants because he lived in a very poor section of Belfast, which was very republican in nature and the IRA had a lot of influence in his district.

I was walking down a Belfast street with Jimmy one day and he started spitting on the sidewalk. I told him, "You can spread germs and diseases doing that" whereupon he replied "It doesn't matter as long as it kills a few Brits". I explained to him that it was a "Brit", namely me, who was paying his wages.

When I worked certain venues I would say to him, "Would you mind asking your IRA friends not to plant bombs in here? It will affect business and you won't earn quite so much". He seemed to find this amusing. The ironic thing is that he got on quite well with Ann despite the fact that she was a staunch Protestant.

Jimmy wasn't a very good demonstrator and there was also a subtle discrimination against Catholics in certain spheres of employment. I tried to put Jimmy in the Co-op but they didn't like him at all and I detected anti-Catholic bias. They seemed to know that Jimmy came from a poor part of Belfast and in Northern Ireland they also have a way of knowing if someone is Catholic or Protestant by the person's surname which gives the game away to those in the know. Catholics have Irish sounding names and Protestants have more British (particularly Scottish) sounding names. I therefore placed Jimmy in Leisureworld and Ann worked in the Co-op.

Again it was a good Christmas.

I worked the rest of the year sometimes in the North of Ireland, and sometimes in the South. Whenever I worked in the North the political situation was always a factor lurking in the background. One little incident sticks in my mind. I was working at an indoor market in the centre of Belfast. There were a ton of marauding kids present who were aged ten to twelve years old. They were a bunch of little hooligans whose main object seemed to be heckling and trying to steal my merchandise when I wasn't looking. I tried everything to get rid of them including threats of mayhem upon their persons but none of it worked. I asked a neighbouring vendor who was at the market regularly if these kids were in there all the time and he replied that they were. I told him that I couldn't get rid of them and all threats to them fell on deaf ears.

He replied, "It is no good threatening these kids. They are scared of nobody. They are the same kids that go out at night and throw stones at the British army".

How utterly charming I thought.

One day I was exhibiting at the Royal Ulster Show at the Kings Hall in Balmoral, Belfast. I was talking to a Scottish grafter named Frank who was working the Zyliss Vice. Suddenly there was a massive bang and Frank looked at me and said, "We all know what that was, don't we?"

And of course he was right. Everyone knew that a bomb had gone off somewhere. I looked round and saw a frightened girl who was selling ice cream start to cry and the walking crowds came to a standstill frozen to the ground.

Actually the bomb had not gone off in the building we were in but rather on the grounds outside. Of all places it has been planted on the RUC (Royal Ulster Constabulary) police booth. They were ironically exhibiting there to promote community policing. Fortunately nobody was killed although a few people were taken to hospital with injuries caused by the explosion. The next day the exhibition was sparsely attended because people did not want to bring their kids to the show after they read about the bomb in the newspapers.

Normally the IRA phoned in a bomb warning but I don't think they did on this occasion. There used to be a code sent to the exhibitors if a bomb threat had been received. It was put over the tannoy and it said, "Would Mr Green please come to the exhibition office". This was a secret notice to the exhibitors to check their booth area for suspicious objects that could contain a bomb such as unattended luggage or bags.

False alarms came in from time to time and I would occasionally hear an announcement saying, "Ladies and gentlemen. A bomb warning has been received. A search of the building has been made and nothing has been found. If you wish to leave then slowly and without panic please depart the building by the nearest exit".

The amazing thing is that nobody took any notice of this announcement whether exhibitor or member of the public. Hardly anyone left the building. They all seemed to be quite used to it and seemed to know that it was a false alarm. It used to make me nervous though.

On the occasion of the specific incident described above the "Mr Green" announcement wasn't made so I assume no telephone warning was given. Or perhaps because the bomb was outside rather than inside it was deemed unnecessary to make the announcement. Of course if the bomb hadn't been planted in the first place then I think that would have been far more polite than a telephone warning anyway.

It reminds me of the time that I experienced another bomb going off. I had booked into a branch of the Co-op in Bangor, Co Down which was a small seaside town not far from Belfast. Ann was working with me at the time and she lived in the town. I was staying at a bed and breakfast place, a five minute walk from the department store.

I had just had breakfast and was leaving the guest house to go to work when I heard a great explosion. The noise was very loud and it was again obvious that a bomb had gone off. People were hurt by flying glass including someone in my guest house and were taken to hospital by ambulance. Again nobody was killed but quite a bit of damage was done to property including the Co-op Store where we were working. This was because the bomb had been planted in an unoccupied car that was parked just outside the store. The massive glass front and windows of the Co-op were shattered to bits but luckily the store was closed at the time of the blast and nobody was inside. The bomb had gone off in the morning just before the store was due to open for business.

Ann later told me what had happened. She was strolling down the street when she noticed a parked car outside the Co-op. In Northern Ireland at the time cars were not allowed to be parked in what were called control zones in case there were bombs primed to go off in the car. Quite a few errant motorists would come back to find that their parked car had been blown up by the army in a case of "better safe than sorry". Of course the populace was then safe but the motorist was then sorry.

This was a control zone and Ann knew that the car shouldn't have been there. She stared into the car but could see nothing suspicious and went on her way thinking it was just one more idiot motorist who had parked his car illegally in forbidden territory. However, a bomb warning had been phoned in and the police knew it wasn't a hoax since the IRA had special code words that were private between them and the Royal Ulster Constabulary. A sort of gentleman's agreement that wasn't all that gentlemanly when you come to think of it. The IRA would anaesthetise their consciences by usually giving bomb warnings thus enabling the police to clear the area.

The cops soon figured out that the bomb was in the car but had to clear the area as fast as possible so that army bomb squads could get to work and defuse the offending device.

However, they didn't have a lot of time to clear the crowded street. They drove up and down with loud hailers telling people there was a bomb in the street and that everyone should leave the area immediately. Of course, nobody took the blindest bit of notice either because they assumed it was another hoax call of which there were many or in typical Northern Ireland fashion in a perverse way they decided that if they ran like hell, they would be giving in to terrorism.

Since nobody seemed to be leaving the streets the cops decided to take more aggressive action and Ann told me that she saw the police leave their cars in frustration and start pushing and swearing at people to get off the street. Once the cops started to scream at people to leave and physically push them to do so, it eventually had an effect and got everyone to leave the street which was cordoned off. However, just after the street was cleared and before the army had a chance to get to the car and defuse the bomb it went off with a bloody great bang with the result described.

When the street was eventually given the all clear Ann and I went to look at the mess. The car had naturally been blown to smithereens and the glass windows of all the shops on one side of the street had been blown out and in particular the Co-op store.

To my readers who are not used to bombs and bullets on a daily basis it may seem odd that the Ulster population would not leave the streets quickly or as I described earlier would not leave an exhibition hurriedly when a bomb warning was in effect. I can only say that you get used to anything and after a while it almost becomes no big deal.

I remember this casual attitude when one day I was walking down a Belfast street and came across a big crowd watching the army defuse a bomb. The street has been cordoned off but you could watch from a distance. Two teenagers were watching the "entertainment" and one seemed fascinated by it. The other wasn't interested at all and kept trying to get his friend to come away so they could both wander off down the street to other amusement. He kept saying, "Come on Sean, let's go!" and his friend kept delaying. Finally in exasperation he said, "I'm going without you" whereupon his friend responded, "Just a minute. I want to see them defuse the bomb. It's really exciting". His impatient friend responded, "Ah Jaysus! When you've seen one bomb, you've seen them all! Let's go!"

I imagine some people like bombs and some people don't. No accounting for taste I suppose.

CHAPTER NINE

Auntie Annie

I SUPPOSE I HAD BETTER explain the title of this chapter before going on to the subject of it. In Blackpool I had picked up the nickname "Uncle Ronnie" which persists to this day. It all came about because of my activity doing children's magic shows. In Britain there are lots of children's "uncles" who perform magic shows for kids. Thus a magician will often call himself "Uncle Harry" or "Uncle Fred" as a stage name. I had never used this "Uncle" moniker myself but friends of mine found it fun to call me "Uncle Ronnie" and occasionally "Wicked Uncle Ronnie" because of the wickedness inherent in the grafting profession coupled with my streetwise education. However, I think the origin of the nickname came when one day in the company of others, with a touch of irony I remarked, "Here I am. Uncle Ronnie—the kiddies friend!" I was actually being extremely cynical since it was well known how I would growl at kids and chase them away when I was selling Svengali decks.

Actually, when entertaining children I am sweetness and light itself but when selling to them I am the Devil incarnate.

The nickname stuck, however, and Ann, the subject of this chapter, used it a lot. In return I nicknamed her Auntie Annie and that is what I always called her.

As explained in the previous chapter, I hired her during the Christmas period by placing a classified advertisement in the newspaper looking for demonstration staff. Quite a number of people phoned me and I whittled it down to Ann. She had mentioned that she had connections with Canada and I figured that this might prove useful in the future. And indeed it did because she was to eventually work with me in Canada as well as Ireland.

Ann was a glorious eccentric who used to drink quite a bit. When she would imbibe a little too much she would start singing in the street, which could be somewhat embarrassing if you were in her company. I well remember walking through a mall in Toronto with her one evening when all the shops were closed and she erupted in full force.

There was some sort of big sports game going on called the Grey Cup. I have no idea if it was hockey or baseball or whatever the hell it was. I have no interest in sport whatsoever either British or Canadian. It would be very easy for me for the purpose of this book to research it and find out what kind of game it was but I plain can't be bothered so I am not going to. The reader will probably know or if he doesn't, can go and look it up if he cares that much.

All I can tell you is that two teams were playing and one was called the "Argos" and the other the "Eskimos". The reason I know the names of the teams despite my complete disinterest in the game was that there were hundreds of marauding fans, many of whom were more than a little tipsy, wandering the streets of Toronto yelling "Argos" or "Eskimos".

Ann picked up on this and started to mimic it like a parrot. She became very prone to shouting "Argos-Eskimos" which I suppose showed neutrality and that she wasn't supporting either team or perhaps that she was supporting both.

Her shouting in the street wasn't too much of a problem since everyone else was yelling in the same manner. However, when we went into a quiet mall her shrieking became a trifle embarrassing especially when a security guard came by. I thought he was going to ask us to leave and waited for the verbal eviction notice. He saw me cringing with great embarrassment and trying to look as if she was not part of my company and in fact I actually walked away from her when he came by.

Instead of kicking us out or telling Ann to pipe down he smiled at me and said, "I know—you're not with her! Right?" and went merrily on his way. Perhaps he was a sports fan himself.

Ann didn't always need booze inside her to show eccentric behaviour. She would make me cringe on the Toronto subway transportation system by taking a deck of cards and perform ostentatious flourishes with them such as springing the cards from hand to hand with a loud noise or making giant fans of cards. I had taught her all these maneuvers with a deck of cards and my tuition came back to haunt me. Other passengers would give her very odd looks.

Another thing she used to do on the subway concerned a little item we used to sell and as a matter of fact I still do. It is called the "Squirmle" and it consists of a little furry snake that crawls around the hand, fingers and even up the sleeve. Ann used to rack up fantastic sales with this item and took quite a liking to it. In fact she took such a liking to it that she carried it wherever she went including, unfortunately, the Toronto subway system. On the train she would let it run through her fingers and onto her hand and sleeve while I would cringe in embarrassment. In fact I would cringe so much that I would leave my seat and pretend I wasn't with her. She attracted great attention and she never seemed to notice that everyone was looking at her and I expect that if she did she wouldn't particularly care anyway.

But of course I am running ahead of myself as I find I often do when describing my adventures. Let me backtrack to where I was a few paragraphs ago. I had hired Ann to work at Christmas from the newspaper advertisement and in fact when I used to get exasperated with her (which was pretty often!) I used to say "I got you as a Christmas present from the Belfast Telegraph. I have a good mind to send you back to Santa Claus as defective merchandise!" Of course Ann wasn't defective merchandise in the slightest when it came to her selling skills. She was simply phenomenal at selling magic yet she knew nothing about the subject whatsoever. She had never done even the simplest party trick in her life until she met me. In fact she couldn't even do the Svengali deck properly. She did all the tricks wrong and yet she still sold the decks in amazing quantities.

I think this was because she was such an amusing personality. When she fouled up a trick she would hit her hand and say, "Ann, you really are a silly girl!" and the punters loved it. Terry and I would watch her and cringe inwardly when she got all the tricks wrong and in fact I was so conscious of the fact that the tricks weren't working that I hardly noticed her sales and just assumed that she was plain lucky when she sold the decks.

However, Terry said, "I know. I can hardly bear to watch her either. But have you noticed how much money she is taking in? I should leave her be and let her do things her own way. Why should you care how badly she does the tricks as long as she is taking in good money?"

And of course he was right. Ann did not know how to do magic but she did know how to sell which was infinitely more important. In fact over the years I have had superb magicians work for me but they didn't have the sales knack which was much more important in the grafting business.

Actually, after a long period Ann eventually mastered the Svengali deck and the other small tricks we sold. Of course her sales were as good as ever. There was no particular difference, however, in her sales when she mastered the deck compared to the days when she got all the tricks wrong.

I started her off in Anderson and Macauleys department store in the centre of Belfast but before long I got a call to come in to see the store manager. He showed me a letter from an irate customer complaining that Ann had been very rude to him. They wanted Ann out of the store forthwith. Ann denied to me that anything had happened and had no memory of the incident—or so she said. At any rate I had to find another place for her to work so I abandoned Anderson and Macauley and instead quickly organised a spot for her at the giant Co-operative department store. It was a blessing in disguise because in that store Ann really came into her own and was soon taking money hand over fist.

And so started my long association with her. She was intelligent, funny, charismatic and a wonderful character. In addition to this she also had a fiery temper of which more anon. However, this was more than balanced out by her marvellous sense of humour and, best of all, she knew how to sell.

She sold Svengali decks for me in England, Ireland and Canada. Naturally there was quite a bit of activity in Northern Ireland where she hailed from. One of the places we worked was known as "the field" and in order to describe it I shall have to wade into the volatile world of Ulster politics once again.

The Twelfth of July is a special day in Northern Ireland. It rejoices over the Battle of the Boyne in 1690 and is strictly a Protestant celebration. It is a day that Protestants love and Catholics love not so much. In fact hate might not be too strong a word.

The reasons that Catholics aren't quite so enthusiastic over the celebration is that their Protestant fellow countrymen have rather a bad habit on that day of marching through Catholic areas banging drums and riling up the locals who respond in a very traditional and time honoured manner by throwing stones and petrol bombs. As can be imagined it is rather a troublesome day for the police and army and is usually a flashpoint for mayhem and rioting.

There are parades taking place all over the province and they are quite fun if you happen to be on the correct side of the political divide. The bands and the parade eventually congregate in a nearby field where speeches are made denouncing the Pope who isn't the slightest bit offended because he has never been invited to attend so of course doesn't get to hear the speeches.

This gathering place is known traditionally as "the field" and of course there are many, many "fields" dotted all over Ulster on this special, if volatile day. In the field are several vendors selling various wares to the public who follow the parade and congregate in the field to listen to the political speeches and sit on the grass eating, drinking and generally enjoying themselves.

I decided in my great wisdom that it would be rather a splendid idea to cash in on all this activity and rent vendor booth space in the field. Although, as I previously mentioned, there were parades and "fields" all over Ulster we decided to work the event in Bangor, Co Down where Ann lived at the time.

In order to secure selling space at "the field" it was necessary to obtain a vendor's permit from the Orange Order. This is a Unionist Protestant organisation who arranges the marches and festivities connected with the Twelfth of July. The fellow who was in charge of the permits for the field had a house in Bangor. I decided it would be best for Ann to speak with him since she was a staunch Protestant and her Ulster accent was better suited to dealing with him that my heathen British accent.

A very odd paradox of Ulster politics is that although Unionists demand to be part of the United Kingdom and insist that they are British through and through they don't actually like the English that much. The Scots they tolerate better since they themselves are to a large degree originally descended from Scottish farmers but even so it is a very odd fact that they can take the British or leave them and the latter seems to be a more prevalent attitude than the former.

Anyway Ann phoned him and found out that the permit was a mere seven pounds. She arranged to trot down to the man's house and pay him the money in exchange for the permit. She later relayed to me an amusing conversation she had with the man that gives an idea of how ridiculous the sectarianism of Ulster politics can be.

Apparently the man said to Ann, "Yes I can give you a permit but I must ask if you are a Protestant". Ann responded "Yes, I am a staunch Protestant". He seemed satisfied and said, "Will there be anyone working with you?" She answered in the affirmative, saying, "Yes, my boss will be with me". The inevitable question followed, "Is he a Protestant too?"

Ann replied, "No. He is Jewish". The Orangeman responded, "Oh that's all right. As long as he isn't Catholic".

I laughed my head off when Ann told me this. Of course I was once told that there is absolutely no anti-semitism in Northern Ireland since Catholics and Protestants are so busy fighting each other that they leave the Jews alone.

The fellow went on, "You know I heard that there were Catholics working in the field last year. I don't believe it. I think it was just a rumour—I can't see it myself".

The funny thing is that once I got the permit I thought it would be an amusing concept for little Fenian Jimmy to work in the field and take money from all the Protestants that he hated so much. However, Jimmy told me that his life would be at risk if he went there and he considered it to be too dangerous.

The danger was confirmed when I and Ann went to work in "the field". I decided that it would be a good idea for me to work at one end of the field and Ann to work the other. Since the place was so busy and the vendor's permit covered both of us I figured that this way we could make twice as much money.

After half an hour I was surrounded by a bunch of rough looking men who snarled that they wanted me to leave. I asked what in hell's name was the problem and they accused me of being a Southern Irish Catholic. I told them that I had never heard anything so ridiculous and they only had to listen to my British accent to realise that this was nonsense. They started to get very threatening and nasty but luckily a neighbouring vendor who knew me came to vouch for me. They trusted this fellow since they knew he was a loyal Protestant who had worked the field for years. They apologised to me and walked away. However, I couldn't figure out what had set them off but later on I got word back through the vendor's grapevine what the problem was.

I had often taken a booth at the *Royal Ulster Agricultural Show* and had innocently put a sign up on my stand which had the name of my company. I called it Irish Magic Service and a few of the standholders at the show knew that I was based in Dublin.

It may seem odd to North American readers that to use the word "Irish" in Ireland can cause certain people to become very aggressive indeed. You are quite safe to say the word "Irish" in Southern Ireland but if you say it in Northern Ireland the Protestant Unionists do become a trifle aggressive. If push comes to the shove they will admit with great reluctance that they actually are Irish themselves but they tend to be in a bit of denial over the matter.

I had innocently put the sign up at the *Royal Ulster Show* not realising that it would be an unwise thing to do. Since Ulster is very small you get known very quickly especially if you are in the public eye and just selling magic put me in that public eye. Because of my presence at the *Royal Ulster Show* the rumour had gotten around to the rather nasty Orangemen that I must be an Irish Catholic because they heard that I was based in Dublin and that my company was called "Irish Magic Service". I realised that I had a close call and it was just as well Jimmy wasn't there to complicate matters.

I went to work and was taking in loads of money. However, I kept getting irritating comments from the punters as to how there was a girl at the other end of the field who was much better than me. Time after time they kept coming up to me saying that Ann was absolutely fantastic and that I could take lessons from her. I swallowed my ego and reasoned that it really didn't matter who was better since I was getting all the money anyway.

And then Ann appeared looking furious. I asked her what the matter was and she refused to tell me at first. I told her to go back to work and she refused. I asked her if anyone was harassing her and she denied it. Finally the truth came out. She was upset because all the punters kept telling her that there was a man at one end of the field demonstrating the card tricks and he was much better than her. Ann had quite an ego but it was a fragile one. The slightest attack on that ego would get her very upset and she would either attack her critic with great ferocity or she would plain give up as she did that day on the field.

I assured her that people were coming up to me all day long saying that I wasn't as good as the girl at the other end of the field but she didn't quite believe me. I convinced her that it was just the sort of thing that punters said and she shouldn't take it so seriously. Eventually she believed me and went back to work. We both took in a lot of money that day.

With regard to Ann's sensitivity to criticism I well remember we had a young man working for us who rather foolishly remarked that her demonstration was a little long. She said nothing for a full three minutes or so thinking about what had been said and then she erupted and tore the poor fellow to pieces for saying such a silly thing. After that day his career with us was toast and she tried everything she could for me to get rid of him and eventually she succeeded.

Another memorable place we worked was the *Ballinasloe Horse Fair*. This is a world renowned horse fair held in the Republic of Ireland so at least I didn't have to worry about agitated Orangemen. People come from all over Ireland to buy and sell horses and it is a major event of the year.

We set up in a big green field where all the activity was. There were various vendors but we were the only ones demonstrating and getting a crowd. And get a crowd we did. Massive crowds in fact. It was somewhat disconcerting, however, to look up and see that half the audience consisted of horses! As you can imagine the horses didn't buy anything but that wasn't the main problem. Nobody else did either! Now normally when people don't buy anything it isn't a real problem. You let the crowd disperse and start all over again with a fresh crowd. We were confronted, however, with a horrific problem. The crowd wouldn't leave! They wouldn't buy but they wouldn't leave. And they did this all day! I have never experienced this in my lifetime and I expect I never will again.

We just couldn't get new people to watch the demonstration and it was hampering our sales tremendously. Since the crowd wouldn't leave I would decide to repeat the show hoping that some of them would get bored seeing it all over again or perhaps they would buy on a second demonstration. But my ploy didn't work and they *still* wouldn't leave. And neither did they buy.

After three or four repeated demonstrations, which resulted in nobody purchasing and nobody walking away, I told Ann to take over and see if she could get better results. However, she got nowhere either and eventually made a little speech saying, "Look. Let me explain the procedure here. First we do the demonstration and then you have to make a decision as to whether you wish to buy or not. If you wish to purchase you give us your money. If you don't wish to purchase then the normal procedure is that you are supposed to walk away".

Auntie Annie

It didn't work. All the farmers and their horses just stood there with their eyes twinkling (the farmers—not the horses!) and it was beginning to dawn on me that they were winding us up with typical Irish humour. In the end I whispered to Ann, "We're getting nowhere here. Let's take a break and come back later and they should all be gone by then".

So we covered up all the merchandise and went away for around thirty minutes assuming that when we returned the assembled crowd would have disappeared. However, to our astonishment when we came back they were still there! We couldn't believe that the crowd hadn't shifted one iota and that they had waited a whole half hour for us to come back.

We had no choice but to start up again. We worked and sweated sometimes trying to get rid of them and sometimes doing another demonstration hoping for a sale. We tried going away for breaks time after time and we still couldn't get rid of them even when we started to insult them. I have never seen anything like it before or since.

After two hours of no sales I couldn't stand it any more and decided to call it quits. I said to Ann, "This is a complete waste of time. Let's go home". Ann agreed and we started to pack everything up. Once we started to do so someone in the crowd said, "You're not going home are you?" I replied, "We certainly are. We have more chance of selling something to the horses than trying to get money out of the rest of you. Goodbye!"

And then it happened! I couldn't believe it but suddenly money appeared from everywhere. Virtually everyone in the crowd purchased a Svengali deck and the other small magic tricks we were selling. Best of all, they dispersed and went away! From then on we took money hand over fist and had one of the best days we had ever had in our history of selling the decks together.

Weird.

Ann had a knack of working successfully in the most difficult of venues. One of these was Honest Ed's famous discount store in Toronto. Ed Mirvish was a well known and respected Toronto entrepreneur. In addition to owning this store he was the proprietor of several theatres and restaurants in Toronto. He also owned the Old Vic theatre in London.

I approached him to see if he would have the Svengali deck in Honest Ed's. I joined him in his boardroom where he was in the company of other store executives. I showed them the Svengali deck and it caused quite a lot of laughter to erupt. Ed seemed to quite like the demonstration but insisted on heckling like a school kid. He did this in a jovial manner but it was distracting nevertheless. I was able to turn the tables on him, however, and this made his executives laugh even more.

He agreed to have the promotion in his store and the venue turned out to have many challenges. The store had a crazy atmosphere about it. There was (and still is) garish neon lighting outside and lots of eccentric signs all over the store such as "Honest Ed's a nut but think of the 'cashew' will save!" or "Honest Ed ain't upper crust but his bargain prices will save you dough". That was just a couple of examples but there was many more.

The main obstacle to our sales was the ethnic make up of the customers. The store catered to a multi-racial demographic who would be attracted to the low prices offered on most of the merchandise on sale. Many of them couldn't speak English and it was a nightmare to get them to stand still and watch the demonstration. They would often walk away halfway through the show and disrupt the crowd.

I found it too difficult to work so I put in other demonstrators to see what they could do. None of them had any success in Honest Ed's. Then I put Ann in there and she had no problem whatsoever! She was the only one who was able to sell the Svengali deck in this particular store and it was quite a remarkable achievement.

Honest Ed's is quite a landmark in Toronto and the store exists to this day. Unfortunately, Ed himself passed away at the age of ninety-two while this book was being written. He was quite a remarkable businessman and a Canadian icon.

He was awarded the Order of Canada which is a very prestigious honour that is only awarded to terribly important people. I remember once jokingly saying to a magic shop owner "I wonder if I will ever get the

Order of Canada". The reply was, "You will probably get the order *out* of Canada!"

Incidentally, the owner of this particular shop and the person who uttered the awful remark above is Jeff Pinsky and the store is a wonderful place for people to learn and buy magic in Toronto. It is called the Browser's Den of Magic and is situated at Bathurst and Eglinton. The phone number at the time of writing is (416) 783-7022. The website is www.browsersden.com There. I shall expect commission from him for this blatant commercial.

One of the most difficult places I worked on a regular basis was the Dandelion Market in Dublin. The main problem was all the thieving kids that used to frequent the place. These horrible urchins who ranged in age from eight to twelve years old stole everything in sight. It was so bad that I had to work with a suitcase holding the stock between our legs in case they would run off with it. The stock itself I hardly dared to display on the table since the little horrors would steal the stuff and run away.

One day I saw a more respectable kid watching the demonstration and I offered him a free deck of cards if he would go and buy me a hamburger and bring it back. I couldn't leave the table unoccupied otherwise all the merchandise would be gone. I gave the kid some money to purchase the hamburger and I felt confident he would be back since he seemed to be a decent kid unlike the other dirty ragamuffins that were hanging about bent on larceny.

Ten minutes later the kid came back looking quite woebegone and without either the hamburger or the money. Some of the nasty kids had seen me give him the money and had actually mugged him on his way to where they sold the hamburgers. They forcibly took the money from him and ran away.

That was the Dandelion Market. I even remember a policeman being sworn at by a kid in the market and there wasn't much he could do about it since the kid was too young to be charged with anything.

Terry worked there and shrewdly beckoned one little brat over saying, "Can you steal me a shirt?" Of course he didn't really want a stolen shirt but it was his way of gaining rapport with the kids and stopping them bothering us. It did work to some degree with this particular urchin anyway.

Ann, however, was the master at stopping the kids thieving. Somehow she had a knack of spotting them shoplifting and would say, "You are supposed to pay for that, you know" and make the kid put the stolen item back. I heard one kid say admiringly, "Jaysus, the woman must have eyes in the back of her head. She always catches us".

Actually Ann had a knack for handling difficult kids. I remember once demonstrating in Dublin and Ann had gone for a break. A bunch of obnoxious and nasty marauding children surrounded me and I plain couldn't get rid of them no matter how much I threatened them with mayhem upon their persons.

Suddenly, Ann appeared from a short distance away. She beckoned over to the kids and said, "Come over here, I want to tell you something". The kids complied and Ann whispered something to them. They went as white as a sheet and as quiet as a mouse. Within seconds of her calling them over they walked quietly away like well behaved choir boys.

I asked Ann what she had said to them to obtain this magical effect. She merely smirked and refused to tell me. To this day I have no idea what she said to make them change from little terrorists to innocent little angels.

But back to the Dandelion market. Ann could sell in that particular venue and not everybody else could. However, she would never draw people over. She would infuriate me by just standing there until people came over to her. I would tell her that she should ask people if they wanted to see some magic as they walked by or use some other method of drawing people over but she always refused saying, "That is a very low class way of working. It is typical of you to work that way but I wouldn't dream of it".

One day, at the Dandelion Market, I and Terry secretly watched her from a distance. She had a display box consisting of twenty-four decks of cards. She made no effort whatsoever to draw people over and just stood there whistling and flipping a coin in the air. I was seething with annoyance to see all the people walking by. She would make no attempt to stop them and show them something. I was about to go over and make rude remarks to her about it but Terry advised me not to. He said we should just go away and come back a little later.

So indeed we did. We came back an hour later and resumed watching her from the secret position. To my utter fury not only was she still whistling and flipping a coin in the air and making no attempt whatever to draw people over, the display box which had twenty-four decks in it still had the same number and I could see that she hadn't sold a single deck of cards.

I went over to her seething with anger and said, "You haven't sold a bloody thing! How can you expect to sell anything just whistling and flipping a coin without asking people to come and watch you?" She glanced at me contemptuously and picked something up from under the table. It was a display box but it was completely empty! The full box she had on the table was a new box and the empty one was the one I had seen originally an hour before. She had sold twenty-four decks in one hour and that was a remarkable number considering the venue in question. She held the box by one corner and just let it drop dramatically on the table and gave me a triumphant and dismissive look as if to say, "See? I know what I'm doing. Now go away".

I took the hint and left. I couldn't argue with that.

For a while Ann took an interest in magic but I don't think she pursued it to any great extent. One day, however, I took her to a big magic convention where magicians from all over the world attended. They had various performances and one in particular was called the Gala Show. Every year one of the organisers of this convention insisted on performing himself on this particular show. Let us say that he was a little stage-struck. He was an amateur magician and not very good. However, he was in a position to book himself every year and of course he did so. He is somewhat dead now but to spare his posthumous blushes I shall alter his name and simply call him Percy.

He was so bad that magicians in the audience would dread the moment he came on. I remember one well known professional leaving the theatre and I asked him where he was going. The reply was. "I am getting out before Percy comes on. I'll be back when he finishes".

One year Terry came to the convention and suffered through Percy's act. I remarked, "He performs as if he is the school headmaster and it is the annual prize day at the school". Indeed, Percy was terribly pompous on stage and in a way it was quite funny to watch although perhaps not in the way that Percy intended. My remark was enough to set Terry off who was, and still is, a gifted mimic. He suddenly started to impersonate Percy, even mimicking his voice saying, "Now pay attention that boy at the back while I put this silk handkerchief in my hand. Now class 3C I want you to watch how I make this pack of cards disappear". Terry went on in this vein and we both ended up loudly laughing our heads off and got some very frosty looks from members of the audience.

However, this incident was nothing in comparison to what happened the following year when I brought Ann to the same convention. I warned Ann that Percy was not the best performer but she insisted on judging the matter for herself and wanted to be objective about it. After a few minutes of watching him, however, she started to loudly shriek with laughter saying so everyone around her could hear, "He's so bad!"

The frosty looks she got were far more than Terry received the year before. History repeated itself with me collapsing into laughter as Ann loudly and hysterically kept saying how bad Percy was. The audience started to shush Ann who now had become uncontrollable. I never did get her to calm down and it was a wonder that no official came over and asked us to leave.

Ann was a fierce critic of incompetent magicians of whom there are a great many. After the gala show she was heard to loudly complain about how bad the acts were, especially poor old pompous Percy. I was embarrassed and amused by her at the same time. We wandered outside the theatre and down the street. Suddenly she spied a parked car that obviously belonged to a magician because of all the advertising of his services plastered over the car. The back window was covered in dust and Ann took advantage of this and on a whim with her finger she wrote in the dust the words, "Magicians are boring" in great big letters.

She certainly wasn't a dull person and as I write I am nostalgically remembering what a character she was.

I had taught her a magician's maneuver known as the "coin roll". This wasn't really a trick but more of a flourishy showing-off type of thing that sometimes you see actors do in movies. The magician takes a large coin and rolls it back and forth across the fingers of his hand. It looks terribly skilful and indeed it takes an awful lot of practice to master it properly. After my tuition Ann could do it very well.

One day we were at an exhibition selling Svengali decks. Terry by now had gone out on his own and was selling merchandise such as kitchen gadgets, rolling rulers, glass cutters and other demonstration products. At this particular show he also had a stand of his own. I don't remember exactly what he was selling since he tried different items at different times over the years. A real professional grafter in fact.

Terry could also do the coin roll and during a quiet period when there was little foot traffic about he idly started to play with a coin and before long was merrily rolling it back and forth across his fingers. A customer noticed him and was duly impressed. He asked if Terry could teach him it. Just as Terry was doing so Ann happened to walk by and said "That looks amazing. Can I try it? How do you do it?" She pretended that she did not know Terry and he went along with it and pretended to teach her. She intentionally fumbled at first and then started to do it properly. Gradually she picked up speed as the coin went merrily across her fingers.

The punter was utterly amazed and said to Ann, "I can't believe how quickly you learned that. Why can't I do it as well as you?" I then happened along and saw what was going on and I decided to join in the fun. I pretended that I did not know Ann or Terry and asked, "That looks amazing. Can I try it?" Again Terry went through the motions of pretending to teach me and just like Ann did a moment before, I pretended to fumble. Suddenly I mastered it and ran the coin across my fingers with great skill. I even added to it by turning my hand palm up and continuing the maneuver. This made it seem more difficult and spectacular.

I am afraid that we gave the poor man a great inferiority complex over it. He just couldn't figure out why he couldn't master this stunt while two casual passers by like me and Ann could do it without any trouble. I think we probably traumatised the poor fellow for life.

If Ann had a fault it was her Northern Irish temper. She admitted to me once that it didn't take much to set her off and she accused me of always riling her up for my own amusement. Alas, she was correct and I was very wicked in this pursuit of mine. On reflection after so many years I think I was far too hard on her and I wish I had treated her better.

Her temper sometimes came out when she was grafting. One thing she could not bear was when someone would come up to her and demand, "Show me a trick!" She would stare at them and simply say "No!" and that would be the end of that.

Of course you could say that wasn't really temper—just irritation. Temper came out if she was being heckled. I well remember two young men giving her a hard time. She lost patience with one of them as he bent forward to scatter the cards on the table. As he did so his tie was hanging down and this proved to be too much of a temptation for Ann who promptly pulled it so hard that the fellow came down with a jerk and banged his head on the table. After that he and his friend took fright and he scampered away in a painful daze with his friend following after him.

Once we were working on a Sunday market known as Notts Corner on the outskirts of Belfast. Grafters paid twice the price there that other market traders did no matter how little space they used. I suppose this was because grafters tend to disrupt the aisle flow and crowd out other vendors. According to one exhibition organiser, "The definition of a grafter is someone who buys ten feet, uses fifteen feet and kills fifty feet".

Neighbouring vendors often get very aggressive and unfriendly when they are located next to a grafter who tends to draw interest and customers away from them. I myself have had a knife thrown at me from a disgruntled market trader at the Waterloo Market in London. It came over and missed my hand by an inch and embedded itself into the table beside me.

Grafting is a tough business and not for babies.

At Notts Corner Ann and I would get the same problems from the neighbours and we just ignored them as much as we could. However, one day the "Toby" (grafters slang for the person in charge of the market) came and told us we had to move because the neighbours were complaining.

We put up some resistance to this but eventually gave in and went somewhere else which as it happened was quite a good location so it seemed to be a blessing in disguise. However, after an hour the Toby came by and again asked us to move. We asked why and he gave us the same story about the complaining neighbours. I could see Ann building up steam but we did indeed move again. After half an hour the guy came back and—you guessed it—he apologetically asked us to move once more.

Ann erupted and screamed at him, "We are NOT moving! You have already moved us twice and we are NOT moving again! You charge us twice as much as anyone else so we have just as much rights as anyone else!" When the poor fellow tried to explain his point of view she yelled and screamed at him and to top it all threw our table over with all the merchandise on it. The Toby decided that discretion was the better part of valour and made a hurried exit saying, "It is all right. Just stay there". As he left he whispered to me, "Where did you get that girl? She has one hell of a temper. I had better get out of here before she kills me!"

I helped Ann get the table straight and retrieve all the merchandise laying on the ground. We then went back to work. Of course the complaining neighbour saw Ann's fury and was in mortal fear and terror. We never got a peep out of him the rest of the day.

Of course, that wasn't the last time I was to see Ann throwing merchandise all over the place. I well remember one time at Eaton's department store in Toronto a similar occasion of great eruption. It was during the Christmas period and sales were tremendous. I remember we were selling around two hundred decks a day. In fact business was so good that I decided that it might be an advantage to have two demonstration tables running instead of one. I therefore arranged with the store management that Ann would be demonstrating at one end of the toy department and I would be at the other, both of us selling Svengali decks simultaneously. However, a friend of Ann's came in to chat to her and wouldn't leave. I was getting increasingly frustrated to see this woman yapping to Ann when there was so much business around.

After an hour of this I could stand no more. I have never been the most tactful of people and I went over to the two conversationalists saying to Ann without looking at her friend, "Get rid of the visitor". The poor girl scampered off leaving Ann to do the work she was being paid for and I thought that the objective had been achieved. However, a few moments later Ann came over to my table and erupted in great fury saying, "You are a horrible, obnoxious little man and I never want to see or work for you again". So saying, she swept all my Svengali decks off the table throwing them all over the floor. The table was too solid and heavy otherwise that would have gone over too. She then stormed off down the escalator. Standing at my table witnessing the furore was a magician named Martin Sommers who is now a Toronto lawyer. Marvin always had a good sense of humour and remarked, “Wow. She didn’t even wish you Merry Chrismas!”

Of course I did see Ann again and although we used to fight like hell we had great affection and respect for each other.

Eventually, I lost touch with her around sixteen years ago and I have no idea what happened to her. I don’t know which country she lives in now or anything about her life at present. However, who knows? This book might bring her out of the woodwork. I wish her well wherever she is and whatever she is doing.

She was one hell of a grafter and one of the funniest, albeit quick tempered, characters I ever met.

CHAPTER TEN

How I Became Psychic

EVENTUALLY ANN EMIGRATED TO Canada and I lost touch with her. I still operated in Dublin combining the sale of Svengali decks with my showbusiness activities. With regard to the latter fully 90% of the shows I did were children's magic shows since there didn't seem to be much going on in the area of adult work.

I started to sell Svengali decks less and less but still worked at some of the major Irish venues. Occasionally I would go over to England to work and I would visit Terry there. One day I had the idea that he might do well in Ireland with the glass cutters he was selling at the time so I arranged a Christmas promotion for him in one of the Irish department stores that I worked. He also started to visit Ireland a fair bit to work at some of the exhibitions there. He did very well and he told me later that his Irish work helped him to buy a house in England.

One day he phoned me from England and asked me to check out an exhibition in Holland that he had heard of. I did so and he told me that he was going over there to work his glass cutter. I decided that it might be an amusing idea for me also to go over and sell the Svengali decks there. I knew that English was spoken widely in the Netherlands and language would not be a problem for either me or Terry but at the same time I thought it would be an amusing idea to learn the Svengali demonstration in the Dutch language.

I had remembered that when I was in Germany, magician Jerry Bergmann, of whom I have already spoken, had told me that he worked in Japan doing a talking act rather than a silent one accompanied by music as some magicians did. I knew he spoke several languages so I asked him if he also spoke Japanese. He said he didn't so I asked him how on earth he was able to do his show in a foreign language and a difficult one at that. He told me that he simply learned his act by rote in Japanese and I decided that if I ever had a chance to perform in a foreign land where English was not spoken that is exactly what I would do too.

However, nobody has ever asked me to perform in foreign climes that do not speak the Queen's English so I have never had the opportunity to try out the idea. I therefore jumped at the chance to try it out in Holland which on reflection was rather a daft idea since everyone spoke English fluently there anyway.

I searched Dublin high and low for a Dutch translator but they seemed to be in short supply. Finally I found one chap who for all I know was the only one in Dublin who could do the work. His name was Robert Kortenhorst and he did a fantastic job of it. I knew he was good when he asked for a sheet of the Svengali deck instructions in addition to the script of the demonstration which I thought would be all that he would need. After a few days he translated the entire demonstration into Dutch and put it on tape as well as on paper. That way I could get the pronunciation right. I practiced it hard and went back to him so he could listen to it. He said that it wasn't perfect but it was pretty good.

I then went over to Holland to try it out. The exhibition was held in Amsterdam and was known as the Huishoudbers. It was a giant show with many exhibitors including some Dutch grafters. I do remember Terry being a bit worried that people might not buy from him since he was British but a Dutch exhibitor assured him that it wasn't an issue. He was told, "Of course you will have no problem. We love the British. You were our liberators in the war. Mind you, that German bastard over there selling vegetable slicers is going to have trouble". So saying, he pointed to a German grafter working the aforementioned slicer.

The prediction turned out to be correct since this poor unfortunate Teutonic demonstrator did indeed have trouble selling his product because of anti-German prejudice which, to my astonishment, still resonated with the Dutch people so many years after the war. This no doubt was because of the German occupation and the miseries inflicted on the Dutch population during this period. I was amused to hear that the German grafter had to apologise for the war at the beginning of every demonstration and in fact had it scripted into his sales pitch. He hardly sold a thing during the entire length of the fair.

Mind you I wasn't selling a great deal either but I was deriving great amusement from working in Dutch. It was the creepiest feeling imaginable to ask people to select a card or cut the deck and to see them actually doing it. I had no idea what I was saying but the spectators did and I could hardly believe it. I would ask someone in Dutch to blow on a card or hold on to one and wondered whether they would actually do it. When they did it felt quite surreal.

However, the greatest amusement I got was when I called people over to watch and asked if they would like to see a card trick. I did this in English and then suddenly started to demonstrate in Dutch. The expressions of astonishment on the faces of everyone made my day! They were more amazed by the fact that someone with an obviously British accent started to chatter to them in English and then switch to what seemed fluent Dutch. Hardly anyone outside Holland and Belgium bothers to learn Dutch so this was a matter of great astonishment to them. They all assumed that I was a fluent Dutch speaker and they would sometimes ask me questions in Dutch that I didn't understand. I would then reply in English, "Sorry, I don't speak Dutch so I have no idea what you are talking about". I would then retrieve the Dutch script from my pocket that Robert in Dublin typed out for me and showed it to the spectators saying, "I just learned what to say off by heart". It used to get a massive laugh.

I found the Dutch to be fantastic audiences for magic and in fact some of the world's greatest magicians come from Holland, which is quite remarkable considering the small size of the country.

I would often show them tricks that were not the ones I sold and I did so for the sheer fun of it. The reactions were quite fantastic and I think that the best responses I have ever received for my close up magic since my Brady Boys Club days were the ones I received from the Dutch public.

The thing that makes me marvel at the Dutch is their impressive command of languages. Virtually everyone in Amsterdam, for example, speaks not only English but French and German fluently. I was mouth agape to find that ten year old kids were heckling me at the exhibition in fluent English. Heckling from kids was pretty normal when selling Svengali decks but for it to be done in a language that was not a native one I found to be remarkable. One passing Dutchman who noticed my incredulity at the kids' fluency remarked, "It is amazing isn't it? Of course they get an English lesson every day when they watch television since all the programmes that come from America and Britain are not dubbed into Dutch but come in the original language and have Dutch subtitles underneath".

Mind you, even the Dutch command of English isn't perfect. I well remember meeting a Dutch girl who was an exhibitor saying to me in English, "I had better get going—I don't want to get caught in the traffic marmalade". Of course she meant to say, "jam" instead of "marmalade" and it did give me great amusement.

I did find that quite often when I spouted their language when selling Svengali decks that the Dutch would say to me, "Why are you talking Dutch? Speak English". They said this so that they could show off how well they spoke English and it was a source of justifiable pride for them.

The only problem with working to the Dutch was that neither Terry nor I made much money out of them. I went back to do the Huishoudbers the following year and also booked an exhibition in Borne near the German border but again with indifferent results. The poor sales resulted in the novelty of working in Holland wearing off but I enjoyed the experience nevertheless.

However, there were other novelty venues that I decided to try and one was psychic fairs where palmists, tarot card readers, astrologers and other metaphysical people were plying their own unusual trade. These were all located in England and I travelled over to do them. They were quite profitable and a cynical person would say that anyone that believes in psychic stuff would be daft enough to believe that a trick deck of cards would be value for money. I shall ignore those distrustful types but would certainly admit that the people that came into psychic fairs were also good customers for the Svengali deck. In fact they would often get their money out before I had even finished the demonstration.

One memorable fair I did was in London at the Mind, Body and Spirit Exhibition. I was working with an old friend from my Ron MacMillan days. This was Roger Blakiston who had also worked for Ron in the old days. He is better known nowadays as Jolly Roger. Roger eventually emigrated to Arizona where he is now a full time children's entertainer.

I remember there were all sorts of odd exhibitors at the fair including a chap called Merlin who insisted to us that he was actually from the planet Mars despite the fact that he had a Cockney accent. I am not sure if he really was from Mars but I think I can say with complete certainty that he was definitely from another planet.

Then there were the Scientologists who had a stand at the exhibition. Many readers will know that this is a very controversial group who call themselves a "religion" and their critics call them something else that is a trifle less saintly.

They had massive signs on their stand proclaiming that Scientology promoted clear thinking. This statement proved to be at the core of the incident I am about to relate.

Roger was an excellent Svengali demonstrator and he had gathered a large crowd around him. In the crowd was a visitor from the Scientology booth who was having a break from his duties. Unfortunately, he had committed an unpardonable sin for which he was about to be reprimanded. The chap was smoking and to Roger this was the end of civilisation as we know it.

He stopped his demonstration cold and stared at the offender, saying, "Excuse me, sir. I see that you are a Scientologist. Is this correct?" The chap could hardly deny it since he was wearing a Scientology t-shirt. He answered in the affirmative. Roger then continued, "May I ask you a question about Scientology?" The smoking Scientologist warily replied, "Yes, of course. Go ahead". Roger then enquired, "Is it true that Scientology promotes clear thinking?" I awaited the response with bated breath but wondered what on earth this had to do with the sale of Svengali decks. The fellow answered, "Yes. It does indeed".

There was rather a large crowd witnessing this exchange and I was wondering where it was going to go. I didn't have to wait long to find out because Roger then enquired, "If Scientology promotes clear thinking why are you smoking? Smoking is not a way to promote clear thinking. How can you think clearly if you smoke?" The poor chap was quite dumbfounded and dreadfully embarrassed to be singled out among the crowd and mumbled something or other. Roger then went on a rampage against the poor chap and nearly reduced him to a bumbling, quivering wreck. Roger railed against the evils of smoking and gave the cowed Scientologist a dreadful tongue lashing.

The poor chap who was just minding his own business watching a card trick, had not expected to be verbally assaulted by a raging anti-smoking fanatic who did card tricks and talked in a posh upper class British accent. Roger again demanded the fellow explain to the now greatly amused crowd how he could smoke and at the same time espouse Scientology which promoted clear thinking. The fellow certainly didn't show much of the aforementioned clear thinking when being bombarded by Roger's aggressive questioning and weakly said, "If you are that interested come back to my stand later and I will explain it to you". Roger wasn't satisfied with this and demanded, "No. Why don't you explain it now?" I was now beginning to wonder where all this was taking us and I could see all the potential

Svengali deck sales going down the tube. The unhappy Scientologist declined to explain himself to Roger and in fact very wisely decided to scamper hurriedly back to his stand never to come near us again.

Roger then continued with his demonstration and needless to say, nobody purchased a single thing. Nevertheless, he certainly presented a devastating case against smoking and Scientology being compatible with each other.

Another psychic fair I worked was in Birmingham. Sales were good but there seemed to be a problem. My method of working was upsetting the neighbouring psychics. They wanted to work quietly away and the slightest noise disturbed them. And of course, the noise they got from me wasn't the slightest. In addition I also drew large crowds that they found distracting. I suppose it affected their psychic vibrations.

Suddenly the promoter of the show confronted me and said, "You can't work like this. It affects the other exhibitors". I told her that there was no other possible way for me to work. I had to draw a crowd and I had to demonstrate. I promised to lower my voice if that would help but she would have none of it. She said, "Our other exhibitors don't draw people over in such an aggressive manner" and I responded saying, "They are psychics. I am a demonstrator. Demonstrators use different sales techniques than psychics do". She then retorted, "It won't do. You will have to move your table right back to the wall of your booth so that your crowd doesn't come into the aisle". I told her that if I moved my table back to the wall my sales would go down to zero but she insisted and I acquiesced. She moved my table right back to the wall and then disappeared.

Naturally I moved it forward again once she had disappeared out of sight but I forgot one thing. She was a psychic herself and must have got a vibe that I had pushed the table out again so within a few moments she reappeared and angrily said, "I told you to push your table back to the wall and you have pushed it back out again. We expect our exhibitors to cooperate with us and if you are not going to do so then we don't want you to come back next year".

She then stormed off in a great huff. I realised that the situation would have to be saved somehow so I ran after her and said, "I'll tell you what. To save any trouble next year I will come back and do what everyone else is doing. In other words I will be a psychic. That way there will be no crowds and no loud demonstrations. I will work quietly away just like everybody else".

She suspiciously responded, "Do you have any experience doing psychic readings?" I lied saying that I had been doing it for twenty years whereupon she enquired what kind of readings I did. I told her that I used tarot cards and palmistry, which of course was a downright lie since I had never done a psychic reading in my entire life. She then said, "All right. You can come back next year and do psychic readings but we don't want those trick cards back in here".

I figured that I would have a whole year and that was plenty of time to figure out how to do readings. I had a vague notion that I would study the subject and fill in any gaps in my knowledge by simply making it all up but in actual practice I didn't do anything about it because of other commitments. However, as the exhibition approached I started to wonder if I should go over to England and do it.

I was on the verge of chickening out when I got a phone call from the promoter wanting to know if I was going to exhibit this year. Since I was caught on the hop I impulsively said yes. However, I didn't actually send any money for the booth rental as they requested. I still wasn't sure that I should exhibit since I really had made no preparation or study to do psychic readings. I deliberately didn't send any money or sign the contract because of this. However, nearer the date I got another phone call demanding money and the signed contract back. I stalled saying that the show was starting very soon and by the time I mailed a cheque from Ireland and by the time she cashed it I would be in Birmingham anyway. I told her that I would pay her in cash on the opening day of the fair. She reluctantly went along with this. I then felt obliged to attend notwithstanding the fact that the fair was only a few days away and I had made no preparation or had any experience in the art of psychic readings.

I decided that the best way to handle things was to learn a script that would fit anyone and everyone. I noticed from my acquaintance with Blackpool seaside fortune tellers that this is precisely what they did. Of course the gypsy fortune tellers in Blackpool were a far cry from the more serious readers in Birmingham but I reasoned that it would probably work. I therefore wrote out a script that I would say to everyone regardless of who they were. The only trouble was that I found that learning the script off by heart in the limited time span I had was damn near impossible so I soon gave up that idea. Instead I had a half-baked idea in my mind that I would secrete the written script in my lap as I did the reading. My idea was that I would read the script in my lap and the client wouldn't know the difference.

I then made up a few signs proclaiming that I was a psychic and purchased a plane flight to Birmingham. However, on the flight I had quite severe misgivings about the whole concept and I changed my mind in mid flight. I figured that I would never get away with it and talked myself out of the whole idea. I decided instead that once I got to Birmingham I would have a few days off and make a holiday of it. My brother lived in Birmingham and I would take the opportunity to visit him instead of attending the psychic fair. After all I hadn't signed a contract or paid any money so I could get out of the agreement to exhibit very easily. When I made my decision I relaxed completely and the weight of becoming a psychic when I actually wasn't one was taken off my shoulders.

I checked into my Birmingham hotel and I discovered that it was quite near the hall where the psychic fair was being held. I resolved that I would visit the fair but not exhibit. I just wanted to have a look but now had no intention of setting up there. I figured that I would make myself scarce if I happened to see the promoter there. My plan was to disappear before she saw me.

However, as Robert Burns, the great Scottish poet once said, "The best laid plans of mice and men gang aft agley". For those of my readers that do not speak the Scottish language it simply means that plans sometimes go wrong. As they did in this case since on wandering round the hall and congratulating myself on deciding not to exhibit I felt a tap on my shoulder and when I looked round I saw the psychic fair promoter glaring at me. She said, "I need some money from you before you set up". Alas and alack I was now caught red-handed and I didn't have the nerve to tell her that I had changed my mind about exhibiting since she would have been furious and, being a psychic herself would probably have put a hex on me. I duly paid up and resigned myself to two days of being a rookie psychic.

I put up my display signs that I had brought with me, and sat at the table which had been provided. I remember charging five pounds (around ten dollars) for the reading which would have been about fifteen minutes or so in duration. Nowadays at a psychic fair I would charge sixty dollars (around thirty pounds) for about twenty minutes to half an hour which shows that times and prices have moved on.

Of course I had to then decide how to do a reading when I had no psychic power whatsoever. I still had the little script with me and I decided that this, combined with a bit of astute guesswork, would be enough to do a successful psychic reading.

I sat there in abject fear hoping and praying that nobody would sit down and have a reading and started to curse my stupidity for attempting this nonsense. I felt that all the psychics were looking at me and thinking, "That was the fellow who was doing card tricks last year. How come he has suddenly become psychic?"

And then I got my first paid customer for a psychic reading and I remember her to this day. She was in her mid-twenties and even more stressed out than I was. She was literally shaking with nerves. I could see that she was trembling and on the edge of tears. I used a deck of regular playing cards for the reading but had no idea of the divinatory meaning of the individual cards. I asked her to select ten and I laid them out in a spread.

I didn't actually have to look at the script on my lap and since I could see that she was very stressed out the reading was very easy for me. Her body language and my street wise cunning showed me what was on her mind and I was able to waffle successfully for about fifteen minutes and she seemed pleased with the reading and more importantly the message I imparted which was designed to give her courage and hope.

After she departed I left my stand to go outside in the fresh air to relieve my tension and meditate upon what I had just done. It was my first paid reading ever and I remember being a bit upset over it even though it had been quite successful. I had no idea that people would be in such distress in their lives and it bothered me. To this day I get upset over other people's stresses and strains. I am sure it is rooted in my horrific childhood and other traumas that have been present in my own life at various times.

I remember once a psychic telling me that "the best psychics are the ones who have had hard lives". There might be something in the statement since someone who has had it hard has empathy with fellow sufferers and, as I was soon to learn, clients don't go to a psychic when things in their lives are hunky dory. They visit when things in their lives are not quite right. Of course there are the short entertainment readings that sometimes people will do at a party on a non-professional basis but once a reading lasts more than ten minutes and money changes hands then the odds are that the client is in trouble of some sort.

This first reading distressed me because of the troubles that this young lady had. I resolved that as soon as this fair was over I would never get involved in this work again. Alas something went wrong with my resolution because since that day I have done thousands upon thousands of readings over a period of twenty years or so. And many of these readings have been far more distressing than this first one I did in Birmingham so many years ago.

After walking around the block for half an hour to relieve my stress I felt strong enough to go back into the fair and continue my charade. Eventually another client sat down and I did another reading which was not quite as successful as the first. There was no trembling this time and no body language to give me an idea of what was going on in this person's life. I tried to read the script in my lap but I couldn't bloody see it properly so that idea was a washout. However I came out with some waffle for around fifteen minutes and the client did not look too pleased when she paid me.

Again I went outside to relieve my tension after this reading. I remember thinking "How the hell did I get into this?" Come to think of it, I am still considering that question to the present day.

Over the course of the day I did about seven readings, most of which weren't bad but one or two were distinctly iffy and the clients did not look very pleased. I was also having great trouble with the written script. Since I discovered that I couldn't read it in my lap I decided to stick it to the inside of the table with some wax. I felt very vulnerable doing this because the paper became much more visible. I also kept imagining that the neighbouring psychics would see it and would be very disapproving of my wicked ways.

The question soon became moot since the damn paper kept coming off and falling to the floor. I therefore had to do without the script and make the whole reading up as I went along. My experience as a grafter helped me quite a bit with this, as did my knowledge of people coupled with my street smarts having lived among rogues and vagabonds for such a long time in Blackpool.

I went back to the hotel that evening with the little piece of paper that kept falling to the floor and tried to put some work into memorising it properly in preparation for the next day which would be the final one since it was a two day fair. I also said a little prayer for the first girl that I had read. I just couldn't get her out of my mind and I felt that I had to pray for her. I am a very odd person because I don't believe in God but I pray anyway. God knows why. And you can read that last sentence in any way you want.

I ventured forth the next day relieved that it would all soon be over. I used to dread customers so I wouldn't encourage them. I used to look away and avoid eye contact and hoped that they wouldn't sit down with me and for the most part they didn't. If I had truly wanted customers I would have done very well financially and would have had many more readings. However, I was in such abject terror of the whole procedure that business was slow for me. I would waste a lot of time going outside after every reading to calm down and, of course, this affected business too.

Still, despite my best efforts to deter customers I actually got a few whether I wanted them or not. Most of the readings weren't bad at all since I had memorised the script a bit better. An odd one or two were awful but I was encouraged because a few people complained to me about the other psychics too. The fact that the other psychics were getting moans and groans about their bad readings made me feel that I wasn't alone.

After a few hours I decided to go on my usual trip outdoors but just when I reached the exit door an exuberant girl in her twenties covered in jewellery asked me, "Are you Mark Lewis?" I was quite astonished by this since my name was displayed nowhere on my stand and I had no literature there with my name on either. I answered her in the affirmative and she enquired, "Are you going out? I wanted a reading". I felt instinctively that this would be an easy reading so I replied, "I don't have to go out. I can do a reading now if you want me to".

She was delighted to hear this so we headed back to my stand and on the way I asked her how she knew my name. She responded gushing, "Oh, my friend had a reading with you yesterday and she said that you were absolutely marvellous and you were a great help to her. She has been going through a really bad time lately and she said that you made her feel much better. She asked you your name yesterday and she gave it to me to come and see you. She thoroughly recommended you".

I then put two and two together and realised that her friend was the first person who came to me the day before. The one that was a nervous wreck and that I had felt the urge to pray for the night before.

Armed with that knowledge and the fact that this girl in front of me was so accepting and easy to read made this one of my most successful readings of the fair. She paid me and at the same time praised me to the skies and kept chattering about how wonderful I was.

She departed and I again started to make my usual escape to the fresh air outside. However, when I got to the exit she was there again but this time with an older woman. She said to me, "You're not going out again, are you? I want you to do a reading for my mother". The older woman was indeed her mother but I am afraid that she didn't look the slightest bit enthusiastic about having a reading and in fact she looked so miserable that I hoped she wouldn't.

In fact, she did refuse and said haughtily, "I don't need a reading". However, her daughter pleaded and begged with her saying, "Mother, he is absolutely marvellous. I have never come across anyone as good as him!" Unfortunately, this made the mother look quite resentful and it was plain that she had no interest whatever in having a reading. I didn't want to read her and she didn't want to be read by me so you would think this would result in a happy mutual arrangement not to bother each other.

However, the daughter insisted and cajoled so much that the woman reluctantly consented. I went back to my table accompanied by her with a feeling of great foreboding. As I sat down I had a bad feeling altogether and she confirmed it by exuding negativity galore which quite unsettled me. Her whole body language indicated that she did not want to be there and considered me to be an inferior psychic. On this occasion she was right because my reading was way off base and I got it all wrong.

In the end I made such a mess of things that I said to her, "I am sorry. I can't get any vibes through. I just can't read you. Let me return your money". She softened and said, "That is all right, dear. That sort of thing happens when you do a reading. It happens to me from time to time too". I got a little confused by this and responded, "It happens to you? Do you do readings yourself?" She smirked and told me her name in such a manner that she expected me to know it. She then went on, "I am a professional clairvoyant, dear".

I then asked her if she had a booth at the fair and she looked quite insulted saying, "I don't do readings at fairs, dear. My clients are exclusive and I do readings internationally". I responded, "Oh, no wonder I couldn't read you. I can't seem to do it with other psychics".

She responded, "Don't worry, dear. I can. I know all about you for example". She then started to show off her great superiority by rattling off a whole bunch of facts about me which shocked me with their accuracy. Then she said, "You are going down to the seaside in a few days, aren't you?" To this day I have no idea how she knew that because in fact I intended to visit Great Yarmouth in Norfolk to visit Terry who lived and worked there. It is indeed a seaside resort on the east coast of England.

She went on, "One day you will live in Canada and have a son there". She got that half right since I am at the time of writing indeed living in Canada. I don't have a son though and I don't think it is likely to happen. However, she did pretty well and I was greatly impressed. I tried to figure out how she knew those things. At first I wondered for a moment if I had said something to her daughter about my life but I knew perfectly well that I didn't. I then went over the memory of her daughter's friend who came in the day before and I was quite certain that I had said nothing there either that would give away information. I later realised that I had met a genuine psychic who had no need of hidden scraps of paper or reliance on body language and a gift of the gab.

I finished up the fair later that day still in a great state of awe and wonder. However, the amazing sequel came a couple of years later when I was in a bookshop browsing through a volume in the New Age section. This book consisted of mini biographies of famous psychics. Lo and behold, there was a photograph of her staring right at me! And there was also a few pages written about her. Unfortunately this happened so many years ago that I have quite forgotten the woman's name or the name of the book she was in. It was quite a surprise though.

When I returned to Dublin I resolved that I would never indulge in psychic readings again. I had made no profit from the fair but I hadn't lost money either. The whole exercise was just a break-even proposition although it certainly had been a fascinating experience. In any event I didn't feel comfortable with this weird way of making a living.

I did know from my days in Blackpool that it was a profitable business. I knew a few of the gypsy seaside fortune tellers and was familiar with the way they operated and the money they made. There was also an incident that I remember when I was walking along a Blackpool beach with a grafter called Bruce. He kept picking up pebbles and I asked him what he was doing. He said that he was picking up the pebbles for his "clients". I had no idea what he was talking about and asked him to explain. It seemed that he did mail order readings on a cassette tape recorder and sent the tapes to the client along with a lucky charm. The charm in question was one of these pebbles on the beach! He called it a lucky stone and told the clients it would be a blessing for them and would bring them good fortune. They certainly brought Bruce good fortune at any rate.

I forgot all about the psychic business for a couple of years but one day I decided to try the mail order idea of Bruce's without the lucky pebble aspect. I reasoned that the advantage of only doing it by mail was that I would not have to go through the terror of actually being in the client's presence and could turn off the tape recorder if I got stuck without something to say. I could then resume when I gathered my thoughts and thought of some further waffle.

This time, however, I resolved to study the matter properly and started to learn palmistry from books. To my amazement when I tried it out on friends it turned out to be remarkably accurate and I realised that it was quite a genuine method of divination that went back thousands of years. In fact, palmistry is actually mentioned in the Bible. In any event I decided that if I were going to do readings I would be on a surer footing if

I were to do things the genuine way and rely less on guesswork in the way I did at Birmingham.

When I decided that I was competent enough to do the readings for money I advertised in various magazines that I could do palmistry by mail order. Now my reader is wondering how it is possible to do palmistry by mail. No—the clients didn't have to cut their hands off and send them to me by post! Instead I would get them to send me a photocopy of their palms and I would send them back a taped reading based on what I saw on the photocopy. I would tell the client not to press too hard on the glass when making the photocopy and when they did that quite a good copy of their hand emerged.

To go off on a little tangent here it is quite interesting that if you take a copy of your palm print as indicated above and then take a similar copy a year later you will see that there have been some subtle changes in the lines. Some will have disappeared and some new ones will have appeared. Sometimes the lines will develop breaks in them or they may become either stronger or weaker. The lines on the palm are always moving and growing as the person's life changes.

I made a little money from these mail order readings but certainly not a fortune. I did get feedback that the readings were terribly accurate. It was beginning to dawn upon me that palmistry was a very real method of divination.

During this period I decided to bring over to Ireland a young Canadian magician named Adam Harmes. Nowadays Adam is a distinguished professor who is going to be somewhat less distinguished now that I have decided to include him in this book. Adam used to work in Canada for me and I would tell him stories about Ireland. Finally I thought it would be a good idea to bring him over there to work in the same way I had brought Terry and Antony over to Canada years before.

Terry happened to be in Ireland at the time and he agreed to pick Adam up at the airport since he had a car and I didn't. We waited for him and lo and behold he appeared. Adam in those days was, and no doubt still is, a cynical and outspoken type with a good sense of humour and as a result got on with Terry like a house on fire. It wasn't long before they started to trade friendly insults with each other. In fact I don't think it was fifteen minutes after they met that they started to make jibes at each other. Terry who knew Canadians very well because of his visit to the country years before said to me in Adam's presence, "Where did you find this twit? (actually he used a stronger word than twit!). He certainly isn't a typical Canadian".

And Adam wasn't in the sense that Canadians are very polite and not too outspoken, especially when meeting strangers. Adam was the opposite and has always had a cynical bluntness about him that was quite a refreshing change from the usual Canadian "niceness".

Terry got on so well with him that in the evening on the very day he arrived he ended up in a Dublin bar having a ridiculous competition as to who could hold the most drink. Adam bragged that he could out drink Terry any time which, of course was absolute nonsense and I advised him not to compete. Regrettably he took no notice and they both embarked on a childish competition to see who could imbibe the most alcohol. I am afraid that Adam lost the competition and to this day there is a stain on the carpet of the bar in the Sheiling Hotel in Dublin where Adam spewed up.

This was over twenty years ago and Adam hasn't seen Terry for a long time but to this day Terry can't resist making little jibes about Dr. Harmes as he is now known. Adam has written two books as well as many articles in obscure academic journals that would be outside my realm of reading material. One is entitled "Unseen Power" and the other "The Return of the State". The first tome is about mutual funds and the second political globalisation, whatever on earth that means. Terry has always referred to the subjects sarcastically as "edge of the seat material" and when I sent him a copy of one of Adam's books he thanked me and told me to tell Adam that it would make a great doorstop.

Eventually Terry went back to England and Adam worked the summer of 1987 with me in Ireland. Alas we didn't do that well with the Svengali deck mainly because of the lack of suitable venues in Ireland so we were both running low on money. I tried to figure out how to make some quickly and I hit on the idea of becoming psychic again.

I had an untidy office in Dublin that Adam always used to refer to sarcastically as "corporation headquarters". The office was costing me rent so I thought I might as well make use of it. I thought that it might be a good idea to do readings in the office. I told Adam that my plan was to place a classified advertisement in the newspaper saying "Famous Scottish psychic arriving in Dublin. Half hour taped readings. Phone for appointment at...". And then I filled in the phone number.

Adam in his usual cynical manner scoffed that I wouldn't get a single call. I told him that it would be worth a try. And it certainly was. We were both taken by surprise at the response. To my utter astonishment about a hundred people called for appointments within the first week of running the advertisement. Many of them didn't show up for the session but a hell of a lot did. Before I knew where I was I was rushed off my feet with readings.

The only snag was that some of my sessions weren't very good and I got very mixed receptions to my psychic ability. Some people thought that I was great but a great many thought that I wasn't. I made sure to get paid in advance because of this. Despite the negative reactions of many to the readings I was very busy indeed and was becoming financially solvent once again.

The main problem with the readings was that I was quite inexperienced and was trying to bluff my way through it. After a year and a half the readings had improved to a great extent, especially when I studied how to read tarot cards but in the beginning some of the results were abysmal. I knew I had potential talent in this area since many of the clients were very happy but I would say that fully one third weren't. However, as a trained grafter from the University of Evil I managed to get by without blinking too much of an eyelid at the dissatisfied customers. Of course, a thick skin developed from years of selling Svengali decks helped.

On one memorable day, however, things came to a head with the bad readings. I had three appointments booked in one after the other.

The first was a lady who was alone and the other two were a mother and daughter who had come together.

The first reading went badly and I could see that the woman wasn't satisfied. I resolved to get rid of her as quickly as possible and away she went with her money safely in my pocket. Then the two other women appeared, mother and daughter, and I took the daughter first. She was underwhelmed by the reading and it showed in her body language and general attitude. However, as always, I had her money and wasn't too concerned. I then dismissed her and brought her mother in while she waited outside.

Unfortunately, unbeknown to me trouble was brewing. The first lady had left the premises no doubt fretting about how bad a reading she had, and how the awful psychic had scammed her. She decided to return and ask for her money back. She met Adam in the waiting area who told her that she would have to see me about that. However, in the waiting area was sitting the daughter of the woman who was in having a reading. She had just had a reading herself from me and was also dissatisfied. When she heard the other lady complain they compared notes and decided that I was a complete fraud and they both conspired together to make an almighty fuss and get their money back when I came out. They both harassed Adam to give them a refund but he refused to take the responsibility for it. Of course, nowadays he pontificates about economics as a university professor. I am glad to see that he got his first education in these matters from working with me. He realised that it would not be an advantage to him personally if he gave these women a refund. Very astute of him if I may say so and good training for his future career as a professor who later wrote books about money related matters.

However, Adam also realised that it might not be a good thing for me to come out and face two irate women without some warning. He therefore went outside to a pay phone to call and warn me of impending trouble. Unfortunately, when the phone rang in my office I ignored it as a courtesy to the lady I was reading at the time.

Adam was nothing if not persistent and resourceful so he climbed up on to a neighbouring roof and repeatedly threw stones and pebbles at my window to get my attention. I excused myself to the client and went to the window to see what on earth was going on. I looked out and saw Adam on the roof next door frantically trying to signal to me by sign language that something was amiss. I had no idea what he was trying to convey since I wasn't really psychic so I merely ignored him by shrugging my shoulders and went back to work.

The lady I was reading was mightily impressed and was far more receptive than her daughter and I thought that all was well. When I opened the door, however, I was to find two irate women snapping at me and demanding their money back. They were threatening all sorts of dreadful scenarios if I didn't refund the money such as the consumer protection authorities and the press. I decided that the least troublesome option was to just give the money back and get rid of them. However, the mother who had the good reading looked terribly uncomfortable and told her daughter not to make such a fuss and that she was quite happy with her reading. The poor woman then scampered outside in great embarrassment leaving me with the two battle axes.

I handed them their money back and just waited for them to go but the daughter said, "Now what about the money for my mother's reading? I want that back as well". I refused saying, "Your mother was quite happy with her reading. If she comes back to me herself and wants a refund she can have it. However, I can't let you speak for her". Of course I knew that the mother wouldn't be back to me.

Eventually I got rid of them and I resolved that from now on there would be no more complaints and from that day forth I studied divination methods properly. In fact I spent hours and hours studying astrology, palmistry, tarot, auras, numerology, rune stones and every divination system you can think of. At one point my psychic book collection became bigger than my conjuring library.

In addition to this I studied books on counseling and tried to develop my own true psychic ability. I believe everyone has this ability but when you do it all the time as a professional clairvoyant your intuition and innate psychic ability sharpen. As the old saying goes, "practice makes perfect". As time went by I seemed to know all about people just by looking at them. I just knew what was going on in their lives. I would get flashes of names and situations that I couldn't possibly know about and they turned out to be correct. All my shenanigans and trickery went out the window and it was no longer necessary to use them. In fact, I was far better off without them and the moment I abandoned that nonsense was the moment my intuition started to sharpen.

It is a very odd thing in the psychic business that skeptics become believers when they start to do readings themselves. And the longer they do readings the more they believe in it. Many people come into the business just wanting to make money out of but not really believing in it. Before very long, however, they find that there *is* something in it and they end up with a lot of faith in metaphysical matters. That is precisely what happened to me.

One surprising offshoot of all this spirituality is that it made me a more understanding and compassionate person and transformed the hardened, unscrupulous grafter in me to a softer, kinder human being.

In the early days, however, some of my readings were a bit hit or miss. Among the more memorable and thankfully successful ones I can remember a few examples.

There was one lady whose dog had been killed by a person unknown and my client wished me to contact the said canine in the spirit world and ask it the identity of the perpetrator of this dreaded deed. I did indeed contact the dog who had somehow acquired the ability to speak English in the spirit world and who gave a good description of the person who was guilty of the atrocity. Unfortunately, the dog wasn't able to provide the name, address and phone number of the assailant. The psychic world of the animal kingdom does have its limitations, I suppose.

Then there was the lady who believed that she was herself psychic. There had recently been the murder of a child reported prominently in the Irish newspapers of the time and this lady was convinced that the mother was the perpetrator. In fact, she had gone down to the police station and insisted to the detective in charge of the case that she had psychic abilities and insisted that he arrest the mother of the child. The officer in question had some doubts as to the lady's psychic ability or indeed her sanity and declined to cooperate.

The woman then came to me and wanted my opinion of the matter. I told her that she might be right but then she might also be wrong which of course covered both eventualities and was 100% accurate. She seemed happy with that and made me promise that once I got a more certain vision of the guilty person that I contact the detective in charge of the case. She dutifully wrote down the phone number of the police officer, handed it to me and departed my office leaving her money behind in my pocket, which of course was of more concern to me than solving a crime that was more properly left to the authorities to figure out.

Another memorable reading was of a young man who seemed happy with the session but yet I felt that there was something troubling him that hadn't yet come out in the reading. I asked him if I had covered everything he wanted to know and he said "yes". However, I still got the feeling that he wasn't telling me everything. Anyway at the end of the reading I accompanied him downstairs because I knew the door to the premises was locked on this one occasion and I would have to let him out. We made small talk and just as we got to the door he said, "Oh, can I ask you just one more question?" I knew that now what was really bothering him would be revealed so I replied, "Yes, of course". He then floored me by saying, "Can people read my mind?" I said, "What makes you say that?" and he responded by saying, "There are a few people I know and I think they can read my mind and I don't like it". I then assured him that nobody could read his mind, including even me or any other psychic for that matter. He asked if I was sure of this and I assured him that I was 100%

certain. He looked greatly relieved at this and I knew immediately he had gotten value for money from the reading. Incidentally I believe that I was correct in my assessment of the situation. I really do believe that people could not read his mind....

Psychic publicity

Adam went back to Canada and I continued to improve my readings and genuine psychic ability. I studied and studied and studied. I eventually expanded my readings from a half hour session to an hour and charged more money for it. I became very good at what I did and achieved massive publicity in Ireland as a psychic, with many newspaper articles, and I appeared on many television and radio programmes as a psychic consultant.

I read for noted entertainers, politicians and people of celebrity status. I was swamped with requests for readings and I became very well known indeed from massive newspaper articles that were written about my work. Some of the articles were a full page long and there were even a few two-page spreads.

One day the late but famous pop star Michael Jackson came to Ireland to tour and the newspapers asked me to do an astrology reading for him from his date of birth. I did not meet him personally. I put this on a cassette audio tape and gave one copy to the paper. It got me a full page write up in the newspaper and from that point on I was booming with business. I tried to get the audiotape to Michael Jackson through various intermediaries. I am not sure if he ever received it.

CATCHING UP ON PAST LIVES

KATHRYN ROGERS meets a man who helps people come to terms with past existences.

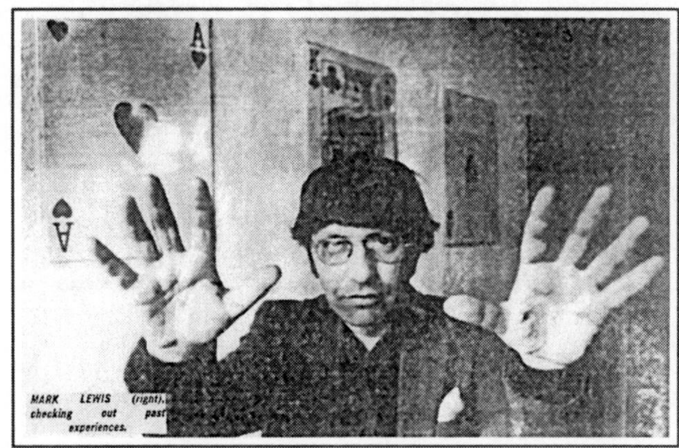
MARK LEWIS (right),
checking out past
experiences.

Article on past life regressions

I interspersed my readings with children's magic shows and the advantage of this was twofold. One, the ordeal of dealing with the sadness of people's lives contrasted well with the fun of entertaining children and two, it was a very easy matter to schedule the readings in between the

Evening Herald, Thursday, July 28, 1988 17

EXCLUSIVE: We peer into Jacko's astro future

Born under a BAD sign

CORK could change Michael Jackson's life!
That's the startling prediction I make today following my investigation of his astrological chart.

Michael is a private person. There are few people who can claim to really know him. He keeps himself to himself. His public image is carefully controlled and he rarely allows the media pry into his innermost thoughts.

In an attempt to learn more about the enigmatic superstar I decided to consult the occult. Since time began people have scanned the heavenly bodies in the hope of finding some pattern for the craziness of life on earth.

COUNTDOWN TO CORK

Eamon Carr gazes at a red hot supernova

STAR QUALITY: Michael has staying power, energy and drive

I reckoned there was one person who could help me discover the REAL Michael Jackson, and that was Mark Lewis, astrologer, numberologist and renowned clairvoyant.

He didn't know what he was letting himself in for. But here's what he reckons.

"The subject is a sensitive person who's either a technical wizard or a precise craftsman," he says having consulted Michael's astrological charts. His view is based on a configuration of planets at the time of Michael's birth on the 29th August, 1958. The location of Gary, Indiana is also important.

Energy

Mark tells me that the subject "is nearly on the cusp of Leo and Virgo". Oh, yeah. What does that mean? Well it seems that Michael "is a careful person who likes to help people". Sounds like our man!

"The willpower of Leo combined with the industrious application of Virgo would make him capable of hard work and concentration. A real perfectionist. He'd also have a strong urge to help others. A definite humanitarian."

Already on his British tour Michael has donated over £300,000 to children's charities. He also made a morale-boosting visit to Great Ormond Street Hospital, to visit the children's wards.

The fact that he has Mercury in Leo would indicate that he has an open exploring mind. He sees the world through the eyes of a child. No wonder he relates to the smaller folk. However this can sometimes lead to insecurity and a need to impress others.

It's interesting to note that prominent Irish personalities with Virgo sun signs are Charlie Haughey and Dick Spring. Soul brothers, perhaps? Yo!

However, Michael shares something with both Stalin and former FBI chief J. Edgar Hoover. They all have the planet Mars in Taurus. This suggests they have staying power, drive and energy. However it sometimes means they can be a little inflexible.

Mark Lewis feels his subject is likely to be "an expressive, creative individual. A generous, warm, natural out-going leader." The hordes of loyal fans who'll flock into Cork this weekend will undoubtedly agree.

While not wishing to tempt fate I asked Mark to look into the future and tell me what he saw.

August, it seems, will mark a new phase in Michael's life. He's likely to make a new start which might well mean considering new projects. The way the planets are lined up suggests the end of a definite phase in his life. By my unspecialised reckoning this ties in with his blockbusting appearances at Pairc Ui Chaoimh.

Whatever the outcome of his Irish sojourn, Mark feels he may diversify. "He's got a wonderful ability to take what's at hand and turn it to his advantage."

SOUL BROTHERS: CJ and J. Edgar share Jacko's sunsign

Although Mark Lewis probably doesn't know it, Michael has already proved his ability to diversify by buying the rights to all the old Beatles' songs. It's been claimed that he turned his friendship with Paul McCartney to his advantage. I guess there's something in this astrology business after all.

Looking ahead for Michael, it seems likely that he'll have to use all his powers of diplomacy in September.

Creative

"He's a sensitive person. His feelings can easily be hurt. And his feelings will be hurt in September. He'll have to use a lot of diplomacy to smooth over troubled waters. Perhaps he'll get some hassle from the media," says Mark, knowingly.

However October and November seem more attractive. He's expected to use his creative powers to their fullest extent then and there'll be lots of hard work.

December and January are months of major change. Business and personal matters undergo a dramatic transformation around then. It's likely to involve family and friends and Michael will either experience emotional turmoil in his love life or his spiritual beliefs. Either way it's all for the good. We can only speculate. There are those who'd like to see the Jackson 5 re-form. Others would hope that Michael will settle down and get married. Me? I just hope he keeps on making excellent music in the full of his health.

I'm sure that's the heartfelt wish of all his loyal Irish fans who are intent on extending a traditional Irish welcome to the world's most dazzling supernova this weekend. The real star gazing takes place in Cork on Saturday and Sunday.

Astrology reading for Michael Jackson

shows. The shows were fixed dates but the readings could be arranged to my convenience.

I ended up writing horoscopes for newspapers which I found very tedious indeed. I did this in conjunction with various psychic phone lines that I had arranged. These were voice activated by the client and very general readings but they did raise my psychic profile and brought in decent revenue that at least I didn't have to work for.

One day I bumped into legendary stage hypnotist Paul Goldin who lived in Dublin. He remarked to me, "I don't know why you don't do stage hypnotism. You have the chudspah for it". Chudspah is a Yiddish word meaning brazen audacity. I can liken it to a man who murders his parents and pleads for the mercy of the court on the grounds that he is an orphan.

I did eventually take up stage hypnotism and did very well with it. All this happened when I officially immigrated to Canada. Up to this point I had worked in Canada for years on a temporary basis. I had tried for some time to be allowed in as a landed immigrant with permanent resident status. I failed to achieve this time after time until an odd incident involving card tricks at the Canadian Embassy in Dublin turned events in my favour. Turn the page and you will find out how it all transpired.

CHAPTER ELEVEN

Canada and the Psychic Fairs

I HAD TRIED FOR YEARS to immigrate to Canada but got nowhere. The Canadian Government was very strict in deciding who they would let in to the country and whom they wouldn't. In fact I heard later that they would reject nine out of ten applicants and the red tape and bureaucracy involved was quite discouraging.

To give you an idea of how difficult it was, you had to apply for the application form. In other words there was a pre-application form that you had to fill out. If you passed muster with this you would then be given the real application form. It was a pre-screening tool and it eliminated most applicants.

In many cases the immigration officers stationed at the various embassies and consulates in Britain and Ireland weren't Canadians at all and in fact had never even been to Canada! I found it quite astonishing that persons who could decide if you should be allowed into Canada had never actually been there themselves! It was the policy, however, of the Canadian Government to hire local staff to work at the immigration and visa sections of the various consulates and embassies. These people were nationals of the country that the consulate was located in but had not necessarily ever been to Canada themselves.

One day I got the notion that I could possibly gain admission if I opened a magic shop in Canada so I phoned up the immigration section of the Canadian Embassy in Dublin. I asked if opening a retail shop would be considered good criteria for potential immigrant status. They replied that I would have to invest $100,000 before they would even consider the application. Since I had absolutely no idea what that kind of money even looked like I thanked them and decided to end the call. However, they asked my address over the phone so that they could send me literature about immigrating to Canada. I told them not to bother but in typical Canadian fashion they told me that they were obliged to send me material whether I wanted it or not since it was "policy" to send stuff out to anyone that made an enquiry.

I shrugged my shoulders and told them that they could send the material if they really wanted to and I mentally made a note to throw it in the garbage when it arrived since I had seen loads of similar literature over the years.

True to their word a big glossy publication arrived and I looked at it cursorily and was about to throw it out when my eyes came upon a tiny little paragraph with no more than three or four lines in it. It simply said words to the effect that if a person had a business proposition that they would like to discuss with a representative of the Canadian Government then that person should simply phone up and make an appointment.

I realised that I had found a loophole since it was virtually impossible to meet a human being to discuss immigration with when going through the normal channels. As I have explained you had to fill out a form to get another form. If you passed muster on the second form you might get to see a real human being to be interviewed. All this red tape was very uncertain and even if it worked it could take months and even years.

However, anyone that wanted to set up a business wasn't necessarily going to emigrate but could just want to set up a branch in Canada of their existing business. I assume that is why they made it fairly easy to see a representative of the Canadian Government to assess whether the business had potential in Canada. I expect they were looking for people to invest money in Canada rather than necessarily emigrating there.

I called up the embassy and enquired about the matter. The girl that answered asked, "Are you considering emigrating or did you just want to come in for a chat?" I immediately took the cue that was offered to me and said, "Just for a chat". They then fixed an appointment time for me a few days later.

On the appointed day I was ushered in and I was pleased to see that my contact actually had a Canadian accent. In past years of dealing with the Canadian Embassy I had not found the Irish employees to be terribly efficient. At this stage so many years later I forget the fellow's name so for the purpose of this narrative shall simply call him Mr. S.

I told him that I had a business proposition to offer Canada and when he asked what it was I told him that I was a psychic whereupon he raised an eyebrow or two. Actually, now that I think of it he actually raised three eyebrows which was quite a feat since he only had two. At any rate he was a mite astonished since it didn't fit into the category of the usual business propositions he sat down discussing with potential entrepreneurs. I showed him copies of my extensive newspaper coverage in this activity. He was quite impressed by it and asked, "Is this a religion or something?" I told him that it wasn't.

I could sense the conversation was going into rather eccentric territory so I changed the subject and explained that I had been to Canada many times before and transacted business there selling trick decks of cards. I think this rather confused him further so I brought out a Svengali deck and proceeded to demonstrate it for him.

His eyes nearly popped out of his head when he saw the deck change from a regular pack to all nine of hearts. He lost all interest in my odd business proposition and demanded to be shown the secret of the deck. To gain rapport with him I did indeed show him how it worked. I then told him that I was a professional magician as well as a psychic. He asked if I knew any more tricks. Naturally I did and to prove the matter I proceed to show him some with a regular deck of cards. I explained that these were not the ones that changed to the nine of hearts and in fact they were just normal playing cards that he could examine to his heart's desire.

He was suitably impressed and amazed. I don't suppose he had ever experienced an appointment like this in the past and I don't suppose he has ever experienced one like it since. Suddenly, he stood up and said, "I want you to follow me please". He left the room and I traipsed after him. I had no idea where we were going and he didn't enlighten me. I wondered for a moment if he was going to take me to security to be escorted from the premises.

Instead he took me into a room where the telephone switchboard operators were. All ladies as I remember and there were about five of them. He said, "Girls, I have something I want you to see". He then turned to me and said, "Show these ladies a few card tricks!" I did so and before long they were laughing and screaming with amazement. In fact they shut the switchboard down for half an hour or so while they watched a funny little man do some card tricks and read their palms. Mr S leaned against a wall smirking with great pride as if to say, "Look what I found!" He then said, "Come back to the office. I want to talk to you".

Dutifully I returned with him and he remarked to me, "I think you will be a cultural and artistic asset to Canada". I nearly choked when he said that since other people would have regarded me in a somewhat different light but I didn't argue the point. He then went on and said, "Have you ever before thought of immigrating to Canada?" I told him that the thought had crossed my mind but I hadn't had much success in the past at getting in. He said "Oh, that is standard. We reject nine out of ten applicants. I think the best way for you to apply would be as a magician rather than as a psychic".

This actually surprised me since I had the impression from past dealings with Canadian embassies and consulates both in Ireland and in Britain that entertainers were not the highest priority for the country. I found out later that the performing arts were actually quite highly regarded in Canada.

He advised me to fill out an application form to emigrate and he helped me to do it. I was mouth agape at this since the form was, in fact, the one that you actually had to fill out another preliminary form in order to receive it. In this case I was able to miss this pre-screening form and get right to the meat of the thing. In addition to this I was actually being advised how to fill out the form in the most advantageous way possible.

I then left the embassy feeling that I had just done an audition consisting of card tricks in order to enter Canada. Or reflection I think I probably brightened Mr S's day not to mention a bunch of bored Irish telephonists.

I was told that I would have to wait in the mail for the next step. Now normally after an application form is received it can take several weeks or even months to receive either a refusal or much better, an appointment for an immigration interview. In fact I have even heard that in some cases where there is a backlog in applications it can even take a couple of years or so. I received my own notification about three days later! Card tricks have a rather positive effect on bureaucracy sometimes!

The letter informed me that I had been granted an interview a few days later to see if I could be accepted as a landed immigrant to Canada. It also requested that I bring eighty pounds with me as a processing fee that would not be refunded in case of refusal. However, a girl at the embassy told me unofficially to ignore that. She said that "Once we take your money, you are as good as in".

I then showed up for the interview with great trepidation. I had no idea how the interviewer would take to me or whether I could pass muster with him or her. However, when I went in, I was quite surprised to see a familiar face. It was Mr S again! I didn't realise somehow that he would be the interviewer and as soon as I saw him I knew it was going to be a mere formality.

He ran through a list of questions that I suppose he was obliged to ask. The one that amused me most was when he enquired if I had ever been convicted of war crimes. I couldn't think of any offhand so I answered in the negative. He wished me luck and told me that I was to be accepted into Canada.

Normally an application takes a minimum of eight months or so to be accepted and in some cases several years. I was accepted within three weeks of applying! It is amazing what a few card tricks can do.

At some point in the process I had to get a medical examination by a local doctor approved of by the embassy. That was no problem. I also had to get a certificate of character from the Irish police who are known as the Gardai. That proved to me more of a challenge not because I had a bad character but because of the laissez-faire attitude of the local constabulary. I could write page after page about the amusing incompetence of the Irish police but I would end up writing another chapter so I had better not. Perhaps they have improved and are better now than they used to be. However, in the days that I lived in Ireland I saw such a casual attitude to enforcement of the law that I couldn't believe it. I got the impression that laziness was at the root of the matter.

I discovered that when I went down to my local police station to get this certificate which they never seemed to have heard of. I told them that they were merely to check out if I had a criminal record—which I didn't—and if everything was hunky dory to give me the certificate which I would present to the Canadian Embassy.

The cops seemed very reluctant to do this and I got the impression that it was more because they plain couldn't be bothered than anything else. One of them said to me "Canada eh? You're English aren't you? Canada has the Queen. We in Ireland don't have the Queen. Ah Jaysus, Canada is part of the British thing, they'll let you in if you're British. You don't need anything from us". I explained that it wasn't quite as simple as that and I asked to see a superior officer who might know what I was talking about. They showed a distinct lack of enthusiasm for going that route and promised me that they would deal with it and send it on to the Canadian Embassy. Suddenly they seemed to know all about the correct procedure and made me fill out a form. I then realised that they had done all this before and knew exactly what it was all about. Their previous seeming ignorance was purely a sham because they couldn't be bothered with the paperwork that had to be done. Of course the Gardai had recently had some bad publicity regarding another certificate of character they had given out and perhaps that incident had some bearing on their reluctance to process my application.

It seemed that a certain Irish disc jockey thought that it would be rather a good idea to murder a fellow citizen for some reason or other. He became a prime suspect in the killing and he was under investigation by the police. He very wisely decided that this might be a good time to emigrate to the United States. The only snag was that the American authorities required the same certificate of character that the Canadian ones did.

He therefore had to apply for this certificate from the same police who were investigating him for murder which one would imagine would present him with some difficulties. However, it didn't and the said certificate was given to him with which he promptly used to obtain American immigration status and promptly left the country.

The national press did not take kindly to this and neither did the family of the victim so there was a big hue and cry in the newspapers concerning the matter with great criticism of the Gardai who self-righteously defended themselves by saying that a man was innocent until proven guilty, and since he hadn't been charged with anything yet, and had no previous criminal record they were compelled to give him the certificate. This reasoning regrettably did not go down well with the Irish public. However, all's well that ends well since the silly chap made a rather daft decision to come back to visit Ireland on holiday and when he did so he was promptly arrested and charged with murder. Obviously Irish eyes weren't exactly smiling for him anyway.

This might be a good place to recount an adventure that I had with the Irish police. I had found out that there was a horse show in Westport, County Mayo and I decided that the Svengali deck might do well there. Consequently, I phoned the fair secretary, a Mr Saunders, and told him what I had in mind. He readily consented to me exhibiting but didn't mention any fee for the space. I think he thought that I was a magician who wanted to entertain people and was a kind of busker rather than someone who wanted to sell things. I did mention, however, that I sold trick decks of cards but I am not sure it sunk in properly.

I showed up in Westport and booked into a hotel then went down to the nearby showgrounds. I went to see Mr Saunders who told me to set up in a particular spot. The fair was on for three days, Friday, Saturday and Sunday. The Friday was more of a setting up day with few people around. However, I seemed to be quite busy and was surrounded by kids all day. The kids had plenty of money and they bought the decks of cards with great enthusiasm and I was doing very well. I couldn't seem to get any adults to come over and watch the demonstration but I didn't really care since I was taking in plenty of money anyway.

However, one old farmer came by and stared at me. He tut-tutted and shook his head disapprovingly at me saying, "Ah Jaysus, those are the cards of the Devil. They won't let you sell them here". I just ignored him and he went away. A little later a couple of weather beaten country people came by and muttered, "The Devil's cards!" and went on their way. On the few occasions an adult walked by they gave me disapproving glances. Then one old woman came by and cursed me to high heaven saying, "Ye should be ashamed of yersel' showing the Devil's cards to the children!" At this point I was beginning to think everyone in the town was nuts except the kids who were sensible enough to be spending money like water.

The next day I returned to the location and the same pattern emerged. Kids spending money like crazy and adults walking by glancing at me with great disapproval. Suddenly the old farmer from the day before appeared out of nowhere. He came sidling up to me and whispered, "Ye can expect trouble. They won't allow you to sell the Devil's cards to the children. I just want to help you by warning you in advance".

I retorted that the cards had nothing to do with the Devil whatsoever and that they just did magic tricks. He then made a statement that quite amused me saying that people were going to call the police about me. He bade me good day and went on his way. I was beginning to think all this was something out of Alice in Wonderland.

I didn't take him seriously and it never occurred to me for one moment that anyone would actually call the police to complain that an evil man was selling the "Devil's cards" to innocent children.

However, I was wrong and at one point I saw two Gardai watching my demonstration in an unsmiling and unfriendly manner.

When the crowd dispersed I was approached by the full majesty of the law embodied in two country yokel policemen from Westport. One of them astonished me by saying, "We have had complaints that you are selling the Devil's cards to children". I defended myself by stating, "These are trick cards. They are nothing to do with gambling or the Devil. They do magic tricks. You just saw me do them. I sell these cards in Switzer's and Arnotts" naming the department stores in Dublin that I worked at during the Christmas period. I thought that the mention of Switzers in particular would mean something because it was quite an up market store that would be far too posh to be associated with selling works of the devil.

However, instead of mollifying the cops it seemed to irritate them further and one of them snorted, "Ah, you wouldn't be selling these in Switzer's!" I assured him that I was and he could phone the toy department there if he wished to check. He showed no inclination to do so and instead snarled, "Have ye got a hawker's licence?" I knew perfectly well that a hawker's licence was something that vendors needed if they were selling door to door or casually setting up in the street. I didn't operate that way and only worked in legitimate venues. I was therefore perfectly well aware that I did not require such a licence and told them so saying, "This is private property. I don't need a hawker's licence".

However, anyone that has ever been to Ireland knows perfectly well that logic has no bearing on conversations and the Garda (singular of Gardai) retorted, "Ah yes you do!" although I could tell by the look in his eye that he was just bluffing and had no idea if I needed a licence or not. I wasn't fazed by this and insisted that I was trading on private property of the Horse Show and that he had no jurisdiction in the matter and hawker's licences were not even an issue legally.

I knew that I was in the right and he was in the wrong but he insisted on arguing the point. "Ah, ye keep repeating this private property thing as if you have a trump card. Well I'll tell ye—we have a local magistrate here who is very good at deciding what is private property or not. We can let him decide the matter". I knew this was an empty threat but again tried to argue logic by responding, "Look. I was invited here by Mr Saunders who runs the Horse Show. He was the one who placed me in this location. He and I know perfectly well that a hawker's licence is not required".

Then the other garda chimed in, "Ah no, no. We know Mr Saunders very well. He didn't invite you. We understand you invited yourself". I realised then they had been talking to Saunders and he must have told them that I phoned him. The best way to deal with the Irish lack of logic is to become illogical yourself so I responded, "Yes. I phoned Mr Saunders and invited him to invite me and he consented. So in effect he invited me to invite myself and since he agreed to this invitation that of course means that I did not invite myself but he did. So here I am".

This nonplussed the country bumpkin officers of the law somewhat and a fresh crowd had begun to gather to take in the entertainment afforded by the spectacle of the ridiculous discussion under way. While the conversation was going on kids were coming up with money to buy the cards from previous demonstrations and I was serving the kids at the same time as arguing with the two gardai. This seemed to irritate them even more.

They seemed to become uncomfortable with the uninvited audience especially since they weren't making a terribly good argument and were beginning to make an incompetent spectacle of themselves with grins from the crowd and sniggering from the kids.

I then asked in front of the assembled crowd, "Well, are you ordering me to leave? Or what do you want me to do?" They then shrugged their shoulders and slowly walked away looking terribly embarrassed. They didn't tell me to stay but they didn't tell me to leave either. I therefore decided to take the most profitable option and that of course was to stay put.

I knew that they realised that they didn't have a legal leg to stand on and they just wanted to harass me.

I continued selling the rest of the day and did very well especially after the confrontation with the gardai which had been witnessed by a crowd of very amused people who also purchased the cards despite their status as being the works of Satan.

However, at the end of the day Mr Saunders came by and said, "I am sorry. We have had complaints from the public and the gardai that you have been selling playing cards to children. I decided to let you finish the day off but I cannot allow you to trade tomorrow".

I protested that I was selling a magic trick and was not encouraging gambling or the works of the devil and that I sold the decks in Switzers. He seemed to sympathise saying, "Yes, I know that it is a legitimate product but I thought you were just coming here to entertain people. I didn't realise you were going to sell things". I told him that I explained plainly to him on the telephone that I was going to sell magic tricks but he either didn't remember or pretended that he didn't. I was irritated since I knew that the next day would have been the busiest day of the fair and I would have made the most money. However, I had no choice but to leave town. The only consolation was that I didn't have to pay for vendor space.

Anyway, I have now had my belated revenge by writing about the incident in this book. I wish to inform the world not to go to Westport in Ireland in case they run you out of town for dealing with the Devil. And don't bring playing cards or do magic tricks otherwise you will be harassed by the country bumpkins who make up the local constabulary.

And if Mr Saunders is reading this after the event of two decades ago and he is still with the Westport Horse Show I hope it rains every year at the show for the next fifty years. In fact since I now have psychic powers I wish to inform him that I am putting a hex on the fair from this day forth. Now watch the weather. Serves you right.

Never let it be said that Mark Lewis does not have a vindictive nature.

At any rate I abandoned Ireland and came to Canada and started off my new life by returning to my old life. In other words selling Svengali decks in Eatons department store where I had worked many times before. I needed assistance, however, so that I could be available if an outside show or psychic fair came up. I found psychic fairs in Canada to be quite lucrative so I did them whenever I was able to.

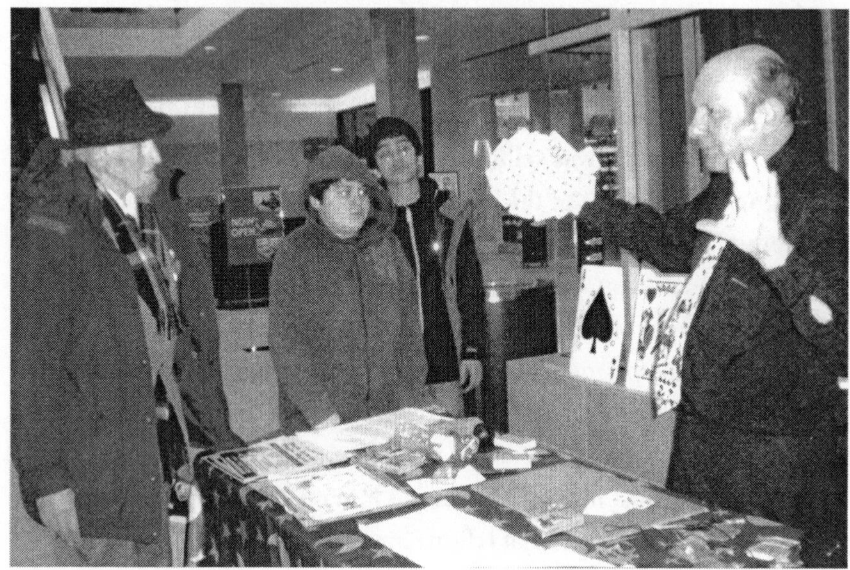

Grafting in Toronto

I searched for suitable staff to help me in Eatons but I got absolutely nowhere. I tried magicians and non-magicians but the quality just wasn't there. The magicians were actually worse than the non-magicians and I found them to be quite unprofessional in their approach to the job. None of them lasted. Finally, somebody recommended a young female magician named Lisa Moore. As I explained in the very first chapter of this book female conjurers are a rarity in magic. I remembered however, how effective Ann was as a salesperson and knew quite well that a woman could take in just as much money as a man when selling magic. Of course Ann wasn't even a magician but then as I have already explained she didn't have to be.

Lisa showed up for an interview and I knew immediately that I had found my new demonstrator. She was much more professional and businesslike than all the other incompetents that I had tried out for the job. She wanted to study the deck carefully before trying it out with the public and was quite meticulous in the way she went about planning how to do the demonstration work before she even started. She took the deck into a corner and studied it with great care before she even attempted to perform it.

And when she did eventually start to demonstrate before the public her sales were quite excellent. Her style was quite different from Ann's but just as effective. Whereas Ann was flamboyant and eccentric, Lisa was much quieter and worked in a manner which I can only describe as "sweetness and light". Typically Canadian in the sense that she was polite and very charming. I would work in a harsh carnival style and Lisa would work in a much more low key and leisurely manner. It was an interesting contrast and we made a good team working together in Eatons. Her "nice" style wasn't the normal way of working since grafters are very cynical and can be quite tough in their attitude to the customers mainly because the punters can drive the demonstrator crazy over a period. She would often exhort me to "be nice" when I showed great irritation with the public and I retorted to her that I had never been "nice" in my entire life and I wasn't going to start now.

I was the obnoxious street hardened grafter and she was the sweet and innocent polite Canadian and it made quite a contrast. I well remember we were both wandering round the toy department of Eatons when a member of the public approached us somehow knowing that we worked there. He asked us, "I am trying to locate 'Beauty and the Beast'. Do you know where it is?" He was referring to a toy product based on the movie of that title. I looked at him and then looked at Lisa remarking, "Beauty and the Beast? Just look at us. You've found them, sir!" I can't remember if he found this amusing but we certainly did!

The contrast was also in evidence when I tried to extract money from Eaton's accounts department who were always atrociously slow in paying out and it interfered badly with my cash flow. I would go up to their office and snarl at them to no avail and then later on I would send Lisa up there to try her sweetness and light approach. It was a bit like the good cop and bad cop scenario. One day Lisa went up there and they were actually co-operative and they remarked to her "Please don't send that horrible man up here any more".

Lisa Moore and Paul Pacific

Lisa went on to work for me for years not only selling Svengali decks but assisting me at various psychic fairs and she even helped me do a children's magic show or two where we would do a sort of double act. She would assist me in my hypnosis show and introduced me to the wonderful world of computers that I knew nothing about. We travelled all over Canada working at various psychic fairs and had quite a few adventures together.

Eventually she moved to Las Vegas and married a well-known magician named Michael Close and consequently, from that moment on became Lisa Close instead of Lisa Moore.

However, I am still in constant touch with her and she still assists me in various projects and handles my website since she is a bit of a computer genius. We remain very close friends to this day. We have fought like cats and dogs over the years and almost murdered each other, but when the chips are down she's always been there for me and vice versa.

The way that Lisa got into magic is an interesting tale in itself and I shall relate it here. Her father was a sheriff's officer in Canada, which is a kind of bailiff who enforces court judgments and collects debts of various kinds. It seems that years and years ago when Lisa was about nine years old a magic shop of the day was encountering financial difficulties and her father went in to tell the owner he had to pay certain debts otherwise he would have to close down the shop. Fortunately the owner and the bailiff worked out a satisfactory payment arrangement and all was well. The shop owner was greatly relieved at this and out of gratitude to the bailiff for his flexibility he asked, "Do you have any kids? Here are a few tricks that you can take home to them". So saying he handed over a few magic tricks that were on sale in the shop.

When the bailiff got home he gave the tricks to his daughter Lisa and her future was set. She became excited by the magic and from that date she was hooked. Ironically over the years she probably spent more in that magic shop than the owner owed when he got into trouble in the first place!

Eventually Eatons went out of business after one hundred and fifty years and I do hope that I and Lisa had nothing to do with it. I therefore devoted all my attention to the psychic fairs that were quite big business in Canada. In fact the Canadian psychic fairs were generally far better organised that their counterparts in America and Britain and far more lucrative. Terribly hard work and somewhat stressful but lucrative nevertheless.

My first Canadian psychic fair was in Richmond Hill on the outskirts of Toronto. When I first set up I had no display material to speak of and my set up looked a little shabby. The other psychics took pity on me and gave me candles and silk handkerchiefs to make the place look a little better. I found out later that they were all muttering among themselves that I wouldn't make any money and I am sure they were all quite pleased about it since new psychics are competition. However, they didn't know that I was a grafter and used grafter's techniques to get business. When they found out they were quite horrified by it and didn't feel sorry for me any more. In fact, I think they wanted their display material back but didn't quite know how to get it since possession is nine-tenths of the law. I was doing magic tricks and making people laugh and before long I was booked up and busy all the time with reading after reading.

The other psychics went nuts with envy and complained to the promoters about what a circus I was creating with all my showmanship. I think the last straw was when I would take a sponge ball and do a magic trick with it. I would introduce the trick by saying, "These other psychics use crystal balls. I am different. I use sponge balls". I would then hold the ball up to the light and ask bystanders, "Can you see any visions in the ball?" This suitably irritated my psychic neighbours. Another thing that used to upset them was the fact that I had a small stone Buddha that I kept pushing through the table by magic. I suppose they thought it was rather a disrespectful and non-spiritual manner of handling the little chap.

My favourite way of irritating the other psychics was to sell the Svengali deck at the fair and say, "Now anyone can do this trick. You don't have to be Houdini to do it. Which is just as well because he's dead. Mind you, there are people in here who can get in touch with him" referring to the spiritualist mediums at the fair who claimed that they could contact the dead.

This used to infuriate the psychics in a most suitable manner. However, over the years they got used to my flamboyant ways and in the end I became quite popular among them. There was still the occasional complaint about me but the fair organisers ignored them. One promoter remarked to one complaining psychic, "Look. We are here to keep the public happy and hope they enjoy the event. They walk away from Mark's booth happy and laughing and that is good for the fair. They don't look like that after walking away from *your* booth".

Some odd things happened at the fairs from time to time. I went to Edmonton, Alberta to do work a fair and was very busy. Doing readings at psychic fairs is hard and stressful work but I was soon to experience a welcome distraction.

Fundamentalist Christians are not fans of psychics, with all their perceived wickedness, and they sometimes picket psychic fairs to warn the public of the work of the Devil going on inside. In Edmonton, however, the local anti-psychic activists tried a much more novel approach. A group of about six of them hid a lot of placards under their overcoats and paid their admission fee to enter the fair. The placards denounced the Satanism that was going on in the fair and told everyone that Jesus loved them, which I thought was terribly nice of him.

At a given signal they all produced their placards and unrolled them after which they all joined hands and started to sing hymns rather loudly, which nevertheless, I thought were terribly melodious. I had been a little stressed out at the fair but this was a welcome distraction and it amused and delighted me very much. However, the promoter of the show was not quite so amused and seemed to experience something akin to apoplexy. She scampered off to find security but by the time she did so all the holy people had brought their protest to an end and left the premises having made their point. The infuriated promoter arrived with security to find they had vamoosed to wherever good Christian citizens vamoose to after causing havoc at psychic fairs.

Deprived of her prey she said, "We'll be ready for them if they come tomorrow". Alas they never did so I was deprived of that amusement the next day.

I have to backtrack a little now and go back to Ireland temporarily because mention of this happening brings to mind another incident that happened in the Emerald Isle where a similar group of good Christian people did not get quite such a successful result.

In Ireland they don't seem to have psychic fairs or at least they didn't when I was there. However, a group of enterprising psychics from England decided that it might be a good idea to stage a few of these events in that country. Consequently about five or so of them came across the water (in other words the Irish Sea) to try their luck. I saw that they had a fair advertised in the Gresham Hotel in Dublin so I went along to see them.

The fair looked deserted and it didn't look like they were doing well. I introduced myself to them and remarked upon how quiet things were. The lady promoter complained about how she had great difficulty organising the fair and found that she had experienced no cooperation from anyone. For example, newspapers were reluctant to accept their advertisements no doubt because in holy Ireland the press were a trifle nervous that the Catholic Church would not approve. Hotels were similarly reluctant to rent function rooms to them for the same reason. Surprisingly they also received no cooperation from a new age bookshop in Dublin where they would have expected some help in putting up a notice in the shop advertising their fair. No dice.

I asked them if they were promoting any other fairs and if they were I was game to try my hand with a table doing readings. They told me that in a week's time they were going to promote a small one day fair at a hired room in a pub in Dundalk which was about one hour away from Dublin and I was welcome to join them. They were very easy going and didn't require any deposit from me and simply said I could pay them on the day.

One week later I got on a train to Dundalk and arrived at the pub around 10.30 a.m. The psychic fair was scheduled to open at 11.00 a.m. There was already a queue of people waiting for readings in the bar. It looked like it was going to be a very busy fair and much more successful than the one in Dublin a week before.

There appeared, however, to be a great snag. The function room where the fair was to operate above the pub was locked and there seemed to be no sign of any psychics or indeed activity of any kind. I went to the pub landlord to ask where all the psychics were and he told me they must be late but not to worry because they were bound to show up as they had paid for the room in advance and not only that they had purchased extensive advertising space all over town.

However, at 11.30 a.m. there was still no sign of anyone and I thought it was a bit odd since surely the psychics would have needed time to set up their display and I would have thought that they would have arrived around 10.00 a.m. in time to do so.

The waiting clients were getting very restive and impatient so again I went to the landlord who told me that he had no idea what was going on but I should just sit and wait. After another fifteen minutes of this he called me over and said, "I just heard something on the radio. It says on the news that all the psychics have gone back to England after having their van broken into! The fair must be cancelled".

I rushed out to buy a newspaper to see if there was anything written up about it and sure enough there was a story mocking the psychics who couldn't see in their crystal ball that they were going to have so much trouble trying to promote psychic fairs in Ireland. It detailed all the troubles they had been having and that the final straw was when the van was broken into with all the display material, posters, tarot cards and crystal balls stolen. At that point the psychics told the press that they had now had enough of Ireland and they weren't coming back. In fact they abandoned the psychic fair in Dundalk even though they had paid for the room and the advertising. They were just so sick of their Irish trials and tribulations that they just packed up and went home never to return.

Meanwhile, there was a pub full of people wanting readings so I had a brainwave and approached the landlord saying, "Did you say they have already paid for the room upstairs?" He said "Yes, they have" whereupon I proposed to him that I take the room over instead and do readings for all the disappointed people that were waiting. He agreed readily because he knew that all the waiting people would be purchasing drink from him.

Consequently I had a bonanza of one reading after another. It was a fantastic and profitable day for me since I was the only psychic there and

I was able to take advantage of all the advertising that the promoter put out. Not only that I didn't have to pay for the room or booth space!

One of the clients told me, however, that outside there were Christian picketers with placards telling people not to go in to the pub because it was full of evil psychic people. The pub landlord was concerned about this and went out and tried to get them to go away but since they were full of a divine mission they took no notice of him and quite rightly informed him that they were within their legal rights. I told him that I would deal with the matter so I went outside and made friends with the picketers but neglected to tell them that I was one of the people they were picketing against. Actually, the only one they were picketing against but they hadn't read the papers and didn't know that.

I told them that I was also a Christian and I also didn't approve of the wicked goings on inside and had intended to join their protest. They were very welcoming to me and quite elated when I gave them some good news. I told them, "I have a happy announcement to make. Have you read the newspaper yet?" I then told them that the psychics had their van broken into and all their tools of evil stolen. I also told them that I had been in to the pub and found out that the fair had been cancelled. I showed them my copy of the newspaper with the story of the psychics whereupon they looked mightily relieved and thanked me wholeheartedly for the good news. They informed me that God would bless me and that Jesus would always love me. I told them that I was quite sure that God would also bless them and that I knew perfectly well that Jesus loved everybody. I bade them good day and was greatly amused to see them pack up and leave. Once they were out of sight I went back to work and cleaned up. I made a ton of money and had to work until midnight. I suppose you could say that this was proof that Jesus did indeed love me. Of course some people might see this a little differently.

I shall continue with my saga where I left off and get back to Canada.

I went to Vancouver to do a psychic fair and witnessed a most astonishing incident that amused me greatly. I heard an awful commotion and looked in the aisle to see what was going on. I was amazed to see two women wrestling on the floor. I was even more aghast to see that one of the protagonists was a middle-aged psychic lady who had rented a booth at the fair. To add to my astonishment when I looked closely at the other party to the wrestling match it became obvious that it was a man dressed as a woman!

I began to think I was seeing things and stood there in great wonderment at what I was witnessing. My fun however came to an end when the rather large and well-built lady promoter came along and separated the two warriors and peace reigned once again.

It seems that the cross-dresser came in to the fair the day before and had a reading from a particular psychic. When he/she got home it was discovered that the audio tape supplied with the session wasn't working properly and the sound quality was incomprehensible. This is a problem that occasionally crops up for psychics who give out tapes with the readings. Most of them usually give out a leaflet explaining their services and the leaflet will tell the client that the tape is given only as a courtesy and the psychic cannot be responsible for a bad recording. I personally take this a little further and inform the client that they can have a free astrology book as compensation.

The cross dresser was unhappy with the situation and came in to confront the psychic the following day. However, that day she was ill and her booth was empty. The frustrated client became even more frustrated when discovering this and asked someone where the psychic was. He was informed of the lady's illness but was also told that another psychic at the fair was a close friend and they travelled together.

He/she then approached the friend and, venting his frustration, demanded his money back. This particular psychic took umbrage at the tone and told her/him in no uncertain terms that the matter was not her responsibility and basically told him to buzz off. Before long the argument escalated and ended up in the wrestling match on the floor that delighted me so greatly.

This was an example of one of the few crazy moments at psychic fairs which helped to lighten my stress level. I found the fairs to be even more stressful than selling Svengali decks which has its own stresses and strains. One great advantage of doing the fairs, however, apart from their lucrative nature was the fact that I could practice my hypnosis show in the lecture area.

All the psychics had the option of doing a thirty minute lecture on their work so as to encourage clients to get to know them and entice them onto their booths for a reading. At first I used to talk about psychometry and other psychic subjects but I quickly came to realise that this might be a good place to practice hypnosis on real live people.

Since Paul Goldin in Dublin originally told me that I would make a good stage hypnotist I had studied the subject assiduously. I had asked Paul how to rehearse such a thing without live people to try it on and he told me to simply practice on the tables and chairs at home! In other words imagine that the furniture was the audience and rehearse my words to them. I was simply to assume that the hypnosis would work if I recited the script properly and that one day I should just simply have the nerve to go out and try it on stage. A very nervy proposition I must say.

I realised that if I were to practise my act at the psychic fairs it would be a very good thing indeed. Accordingly, one day I abandoned my usual lecture and tried out the hypnotism. To my utter astonishment it worked perfectly and before long I had enticed various audience volunteers to do crazy things like get stuck to their chair and lose their belly buttons.

I was on cloud nine and terribly pleased with the outcome. However, the next day I tried another hypnosis lecture and it didn't work at all. After hypnotising the volunteers I couldn't get them to do anything whatsoever and I realised that my technique was faulty somewhere.

Nevertheless, over the course of the next few weeks at psychic fairs I tried the hypnosis act again and again and, regrettably, it still didn't work. I would have given up trying if it hadn't been for the fact that it had already worked when I performed it in public for the very first time as previously explained. At the time I had made contact again with Adam Harmes who was back in Canada and he used to assist me at the fairs. I asked Adam if he would act as a secret confederate on stage to help things along and he promptly refused saying, "I don't want to be part of a sinking ship". No staff loyalty nowadays I am afraid.

However, as time went on I got the hang of it and before long I got all sorts of crazy reactions from my volunteers such as chasing invisible canaries and incessantly singing the national anthem. The other psychics soon got fed up with my hypnosis demonstrations because they made such an awful racket. I suppose they found it a bit disconcerting when hypnotised clients would come up to the booth and ask where their missing belly buttons were located. I would emphasise, however, that I only sent those clients to the psychics I didn't like.

Hypnosis show

Another thing that annoyed the psychics about the demonstration was that they came to the erroneous conclusion that I was giving post-hypnotic suggestions to people to come to my booth for readings. Of course anyone that knows anything about hypnosis will realise that this is an impossible scenario since people will not do what they don't want to do under hypnosis. For example, you cannot force people to rob a bank under hypnosis unless they were the sort of persons that would want to rob a bank anyway. However, if they were indeed that sort of person they would do a far better job of the crime if they were wide awake rather than being in a hypnotic trance.

Still, even if the psychics disapproved the promoters loved the demonstrations since they were so entertaining for the visitors and before long they allowed me to do an hour demonstration instead of the usual half hour normally allotted to lecturers. Then one day a leading promoter offered me a free booth to do the hypnosis show. His assistant panicked a bit because hypnosis was illegal in Ontario at that point. However, her boss said, "Let Mark do his thing. The whole fair is illegal!"

And so it was. I think there was some obscure law against fortune telling and kindred nonsense on the statute books somewhere but it was regarded as quite unenforceable and on a par with such regulations as not being allowed to walk three abreast on the sidewalk. Yes, this is actually a law that they have in a Scottish city but there are also myriad silly laws that are never enforced in Ontario too. The psychic law was one of them.

However, the hypnosis law was also on the books and it made life difficult for stage hypnotists in Ontario for quite a while. The story behind the law was quite interesting. It seems that there was a local amateur magician who was a physician and who held a post in the Ontario Ministry of Health. He lobbied against hypnosis and caused a law to be brought in saying that only a doctor or dentist could hypnotise anyone. This put paid to stage hypnotists of course but it also affected hypnotherapists who were not always medical doctors.

Now here is the amusing part. When this fellow retired from the ministry he also retired from medicine. However, he took up a new career. What was it? A hypnotherapist of course! By bringing in his law he effectively eliminated a great deal of his competition. Some people have all the nerve!

However, when I first came to Canada and started to practice my hypnosis show I realised that this statute would be an obstacle to my ambitions in this regard. There were still a few stage hypnotists around despite the ruling because after the regulation had been in for a few years it wasn't enforced terribly strongly. However, the stage hypnotists felt very uncomfortable concerning the matter. One fellow called himself a "mentalist" rather than a hypnotist. This caused confusion since up to that point the term "mentalists" referred to magicians who perform tricks with a mind reading theme in their acts.

Another stage hypnotist tried to get around the regulations in a clever way by advertising "The hypnotic artistry of..." filling in his name.

This was quite ingenious because it put the idea across that he was a hypnotist but it also could have meant that he was an excellent acrobat or ballet dancer.

I wanted no part of all these verbal shenanigans and I resolved to see if there was another way around the regulation. Consequently I phoned up various government departments to see if anybody knew anything about this law. Nobody did and in fact nobody had even heard of it. Finally I was referred to the Ministry of Health and, of course, they had never heard of the law either. They told me to get in touch with their legal department and gave me their phone number. I called and spoke to someone in a position of authority and guess what? You got it! They had never heard of the law either!

I explained that I was a stage hypnotist who had just emigrated from Ireland into Canada and I was anxious to comply with the law. However, in order to do so I needed to know what that law actually consisted of. They congratulated me on my good citizenship and responsible attitude informing me that they would get back by telephone after researching the matter.

After a week or so they were as good as their word and called me back to inform me that there was indeed a law against stage hypnosis but the reality was that it was never enforced. I told them that if it wasn't enforced then what was the point of having it in the first place? Since the staff in the legal department knew nothing whatever about hypnosis they couldn't

These are photographs of a recent stage hypnotism show at an outdoor event. To my horror when I stepped out on stage there was nobody in the audience. My assistant thought it would be terribly amusing to take secret pictures of the impending catastrophe. I have learned not to panic and slowly a crowd gathered bit by bit and in the end I had a very successful show.

My friend Jeff Pinsky was very impressed by the pictures and became very philosophical, finding in them a deep meaning about the struggle of life in general and my own life in particular. He felt that they sent a message about resilience and not giving in even when the odds are against you.

It is because of Jeff's thoughtful take on the pictures that the sequence has been included. I hope my readers see the same motivational message in them that Jeff did.

Art imitates life: at first, nobody shows up...

... then, slowly, a few brave souls venture...

... encouraged, people start entering...

... word spreads and a crowd builds...

... until, finally, the show can begin!

answer the question. However, they advised me to just carry on doing my shows unless there was a complaint and someone in authority specifically told me to stop.

That was good enough for me for a while although I wasn't entirely satisfied. However, I did notice a very odd thing. I would keep getting phone calls asking for hypnotherapy sessions to stop smoking or lose weight. I did indeed do a bit of this and have had good results but I hadn't advertised it in any way so I was a trifle puzzled as to where all these new enquiries were coming from. I asked the clients where they had heard of me and was greatly amused to hear that they had got my phone number from the Ontario Ministry of Health! It seems that when people phoned them up to recommend a hypnotherapist I was the one that they sent the referral to!

I reasoned that they therefore viewed me with favour and I called to thank them and kept in touch dropping joking hints that they were in fact breaking their own law by sending me clients when I wasn't actually a doctor or dentist. Then one day, to my surprise, they phoned to inform me that the law had now been repealed. This was a cause of rejoicing among stage hypnotists and hypnotherapists. The amateur magician doctor turned hypnotherapist did not object since he was extremely dead at that point in time. I have always suspected, and in fact am reasonably certain, that I had something to do with making that particular law disappear.

I am a magician after all.

CHAPTER TWELVE

The Showman and the Shaman

AND NOW FOR A strange, one-sided love story. Once upon a time I took a booth at a big psychic fair in Vancouver. I had with me my good friend, the aforementioned Lisa Moore who assisted me in these matters. She would act as a sort of secretary whose job was to sweet talk clients into signing up for readings with me and to keep track of the appointments. The technical name for this function is a "front person" and many psychics use them at the fairs. A good front person can help you make money but a bad front person can actually cause you to lose revenue since they can scare people away and do more harm than good. Fortunately, Lisa had always been a good front person.

At one point the fair was a little quiet and I was standing gossiping to Lisa when the shaman appeared. She was black, beautiful and British. However, she was also bananas as I found out to my cost for years afterwards. I am going to call her Simone for the purpose of this narrative even though it is not her real name. It is very important that I protect her privacy.

But back to the psychic fair. This strange brilliant creature appeared in front of us and started to complain about the oddest things. She talked to us rather than us talking to her. She spoke and we listened. It was immediately apparent that she was a little different from the normal run of human beings. She addressed us with the utmost familiarity and as if she had known us both all her life rather than the ten strange minutes she stood talking to us. Her main complaint seemed to be with the Canadian immigration authorities who had held her at the airport on the no doubt grounds that she was a little on the eccentric side and probably had no luggage or money with her. I found out later that this was quite a normal way of existence for Simone.

I suppose one could say she was not just a homeless person but also an internationally homeless person. And yet she had some way of charming even the most difficult immigration officer. It seems she screamed and shouted at the poor official at the airport, which may not seem that charming I suppose. However, at some point he made a phone call to England to check on her and came back with tears in his eyes. Or at least this was her version of the story to us. We listened to the adventure with jaws dropping for two reasons; one the astonishment of the tale and two, the fact that she was telling this amazing story to two complete strangers she had just met at a psychic fair. The most astounding part of the tale is that the representative of Canada Immigration allowed this strange, black, British thirty-five year old homeless woman with no money to leave the airport to wander the great heartlands of Canada and to finally confront two strangers at a psychic fair with the whole wondrous story.

I was fascinated with this strange person especially her British accent since I was somewhat starved of hearing such accents much in Canada. Call it homesickness or nostalgia or whatever you wish. Her personality was bubbly and funny despite her obvious eccentricity and I think I fell in love with her immediately. Yet I felt obliged to make a cursory attempt at business matters and asked her if she wanted a reading whereupon she responded, "I have no money. I am down and out. I live on the street!" I replied, "You seem to be very articulate and intelligent for someone who lives on the street". She replied "I have great gifts and I am very psychic".

She then explained that she was a shaman and had studied these matters on a native reservation. She said that her name was Light Spirit. Despite the fact that I found it a little incongruous for a black British woman to possess such a name I was nevertheless quite fascinated by the matter. Years later, I said to her, "Simone, you are black and British but you are under the illusion that you are a North American Indian". She replied without missing a beat, "Yes, but it's a good illusion, isn't it?" I had no ready answer for that one so I agreed that it indeed was.

I asked her what a shaman actually was and she exclaimed that it meant she was a healer. In time to come I cried often over her and wished desperately that she could heal herself. She tried so hard to free herself from the demons that plagued her and I tried hard also to do what I could in my limited way to free her from her distress. And of course it distressed me too.

However, she was indeed a shaman and her knowledge of Native American/ Canadian culture was incredible, particularly the healing arts aspect of things. In fact as I grew to know her I discovered she was an absolute authority on all things metaphysical and in some ways I think it may have been partially responsible for her deterioration at times. You can have too much of a good thing and taking things to an extreme in the psychic realm can be detrimental. Of course her knowledge was a double edged sword and I am sure that on many occasions her belief and interest in these matters had a healing aspect as well since at times it must have been a great comfort to her—a placebo effect if you will. Or at least a placebo effect to my cynical mind anyway since I will readily admit there are many people who believe and indeed benefit from these things.

She further informed us that she had a teacher who was helping her develop her intuition and psychic gifts but that he abused and beat her up from time to time. I suggested that she might find it beneficial to find a less exacting tutor but she did not react to this astute observation. She explained that this teacher was also homeless and in addition a drunk, and she was trying to help him in return for the knowledge he was giving her. The blind leading the blind I suppose you might say.

She went on in this vein and I wished that I had more time to hear her explore these matters but business was pressing and I needed to make a living so I started to wonder how I could get rid of her politely so that I could resume my efforts to persuade those passing by to sign up for readings. I retired to the back of my booth and decided to let Lisa see what she could do to persuade our unusual visitor to move on. I let her talk to Lisa who was just as fascinated as I was and accordingly also found it difficult to shift the focus to attending to customers.

Then suddenly I had a brainwave. I made a spur of the moment decision that on reflection as I write may have been a rather fateful and emotionally draining one in the long run. On the other hand it has given me considerable material for this memoir so there is always a silver lining in the cloud, I suppose.

I uttered the fateful words, "Would you like a reading free of charge?" I reasoned that if I did this I could free Lisa so that she could continue with her job of trying to sign people up and further entice customers by the fact that I was already doing a reading. It is well known in the psychic fair business that if you are already reading someone it is far easier to sign people up than if you have nobody in front of you. I figured it would be worth giving a free reading just to gain this effect. Of course the real reason was that I felt strangely drawn to Simone and I was enjoying the company of this crazy woman.

Naturally, she agreed immediately to the offer and sat down with me. In the reading I advised her strongly to find a "teacher" that would not beat her up. I also told her that she was destined to do psychic work and that one day, she would no longer be homeless. I was also wondering how I could get to know her better but I have always been shy with women so had no idea how to go about it. I found out later that she was waiting for me to make a move on her but I never did and she was somewhat disappointed about it. Of course her intentions may well have had an ulterior motive that were more financial than romantic since her skills at charming men (until they found out how crazy she was) were part of her survival instinct.

In the end I gave up my romantic ambitions and brought the reading to a close. Now I had to figure out a way to reluctantly get rid of her so I could get some work done and earn some money. I suggested she should learn palmistry and I walked her to the booth of a psychic who was a specialist in that kind of divination. I suggested she have a look at his promotional material and left her there, wishing her the best of luck. I found out later she was not pleased at being taken away from my booth and dumped at some palmist's place of work.

Around an hour later Lisa remarked to me, "I thought that girl said she had no money—she is having a reading with another psychic!" And to my astonishment she indeed was! I was surprised certainly but not flabbergasted. The flabbergasting part of the experience came later in the day when I spied her having readings with two other psychics! I discovered later from the psychics themselves that Simone hadn't paid them any more than she had paid me! The fee she paid was zilch! I couldn't get over how she was able to scam so many free readings from both male and female psychics. This was a person with great gifts of communication and a certain eccentric charm that enabled her to do this. Her laugh alone would charm the birds off the trees. I assumed naturally that I would never see her again but she certainly stuck out in my mind. Two years went by and on the odd occasion I wondered what had become of her. Alas I was about to find out.

A couple of years after our meeting I decided to do the psychic fair in Vancouver again. After all, it was very profitable to attend even though I had to travel all the way from the other side of Canada to do so. The profit made was quite surprising when one considers that I had to pay a booth fee rental, plane fare, hotel, front person (sometimes even the air fare of the front person) not to mention fees for a reading table, taxis and meals. Yet in those days I could pay all this and still come out with a profit. I am not so sure it would work out that easily nowadays.

I was in the middle of a reading and suddenly my front person (not Lisa this time) handed me a note. Although I was irritated at the interruption, I read the note nevertheless. It said, "You gave me a reading two years ago and everything turned out to be correct". I couldn't figure out who had written the note since there was no signature but then I looked up towards my front table and there she was in all her wondrous glory. I didn't recognise her straight away. I just wondered who this beautiful black girl was who was grinning away at me. She was wearing the most beautiful gown that I later discovered she had made herself. And then it dawned upon me that this was the strange and wondrous person from two years ago. I broke away momentarily from my reading and quickly told her to hang around until I finished it up. I knew I had nobody else who had signed up for a reading and I would have a chance to talk to her.

When I finished I went over to her and said, "I remember you, how have you been?" She answered, "I was down and out, homeless and on the street when I met you but now I am on top because of your reading". I said, "I'm really glad to hear it" and I felt a thrill of accomplishment although I was eventually to find that I actually hadn't accomplished that much after all. I asked her how I had helped her and she astonished me by saying, "You told me I was going to do psychic work and I am. I have a booth in here". My jaw dropped when I heard she had somehow been able to afford a booth in the fair since I knew this was an expensive proposition for a regular person never mind a homeless one. I didn't realise at the time she had used her charm on the fair promoter to obtain it and her financial position was just as precarious as ever. She had shown great courage in approaching the fair organiser who always wanted some money up front and for a homeless and somewhat mentally erratic person to achieve such a thing is a feat quite unimaginable to those of us who live more normal lives. Up to this point she had done fortune telling on the street and for her to actually obtain a booth at the fair by using her charm and street savvy must have seemed like the big time to her. Realising the supreme courage that it must have taken her to do this brings tears to my eyes as I write.

I pieced together later from the fair promoter and from Simone herself that she approached the organisers in person and asked for a booth. She straight out told them that she was down and out and did readings on the street but wanted a booth and would pay when she made some money. In a similar manner to the way she charmed me and other psychics to give her a free reading two years before, she used her powers to pull off this negotiation. I was told the promoter had tears in his eyes when he allowed her to work whereas his assistant was somewhat more reluctant to get involved but gave in at the end. With incredible confidence in her ability she charged far more money for her services than the other psychics did including me and made a remarkable profit after paying for her booth, which she was indeed able to do. This must have been one of her major achievements in life and probably one of her happiest times. The success didn't last because of course with her state of mind and circumstances the odds were stacked too highly against her. However, it really boggles my mind even as I write to realise what a significant battle she won. She may have lost the war but the magnificence of this one victory in the battle of life is in its own way as incredible an achievement as mountaineers climbing Mount Everest or a scientist discovering a new vaccine that can cure a terrible illness.

I said, "Show me your booth" whereupon she took me over to view it. I was astonished to see that she had a sign up stating that her readings were $80 which at the time was a considerable sum for a regular psychic to charge at a fair let alone a homeless one. I myself was only charging $60 at this event. However, Simone had a couple of advantages that I didn't have. First, she had a great location and I speculate that the promoter gave it to her deliberately out of kindness and wanting her to do well. Second, she was very well known in Vancouver from doing readings on the street and I think this helped her achieve success at the fair.

The booth was quite attractively dressed and she actually had a front person. However, I was highly amused to find that instead of her paying the front person she had arranged matters so that the front person paid her! It seems that the front person had jewellery of her own to sell and Simone let her do so providing she acted as a front person for her and gave her 20% of all sales. Simone may have been homeless and nuts but she wasn't dumb! One of my favourite moments with her was the time she said to me, "I might be mad but I'm not stupid!"

The fact that she knew she was mad paradoxically proved that she wasn't in a strange kind of way. I have always thought that Simone was not mad despite appearances but she was certainly troubled of which more anon. However, one thing I can say is that she was definitely one of the most intelligent people I have ever met despite her demons. And demons she had in plenty. I find it painful to write about her since she was the only woman I ever truly loved and recalling her "episodes" of screaming distress and anger that I witnessed on many occasions is upsetting to me but I shall persevere with the tale nevertheless.

I admired her booth appropriately and resolved to get to know her better during the fair. This had been the opening day and there were two more days left. I bade her goodbye for the moment and wandered back to my own booth full of wonder at the resurgence of this unforgettable person. When I returned to my booth I looked at the comment book on my table. These books are very useful tools for marketing readings at psychic fairs and the idea is that satisfied clients write comments for others to view. And I saw that Simone had actually written a comment that I have in the book to this day. Here it is:

"I had a reading from you two years ago when I was down and out! Your predictions of astounding detail re: my career and actual earning figures had incredible accuracy!"

I was pretty busy that day and didn't get much chance to talk to Simone and of course she was busy too. Her booth was also a good way away from mine and was located in a part of the hall that I couldn't see from my location. Added to the mix was my natural shyness at going over to approach her. However, I decided to get in early the next day to talk to her when she set up. I was encouraged by a remark she made to me when she originally took me over to see her booth. She had said, "You'll have to take me to lunch".

Accordingly, the next morning I arrived at the fair bright and early but she hadn't yet arrived. To pass the time I spoke to the neighbouring psychic across from her who didn't seem to have a high opinion of Simone.

He remarked, "Oh, she does readings on the street" and seemed to know of her precarious situation. He really didn't approve of Simone and I got the same vibe from all her psychic neighbours as the fair progressed.

I went for my breakfast and then returned to her booth to find her in a grumpy mood. She gave me a filthy look and a very unimpressive welcome. She did not look very pleased to see me and I wondered what I had done wrong. I very hurriedly made my goodbye and wished her luck at the fair. I kept well away from her that day and resolved not to go near her booth. She quite scared me off. I had no idea at the time that I had just met Grumpy Spirit. As I got to know her I found out that there were four people I had to deal with rather than one. First, and best, was Light Spirit although sometimes I dubbed her Happy Spirit. This was the cheerful and funny person that I loved so much. Then there was Arty Spirit who was a wonderfully talented and creative individual. She was a gifted artist and in her better days had public exhibitions of her work. Next was Grumpy Spirit who was merely grumpy and irritable but at least not insane. That was Nasty Spirit who could just as easily be dubbed Angry Spirit or Scary Spirit. Nasty Spirit was the one who frightened people and was Simone's own worst enemy. Nasty Spirit was my nemesis as well as her own. It was the spirit who unleashed torrents of demonic rage and scared everyone who came into contact with her. It was probably the Spirit who made her homeless in the first place and the Spirit I tried to control with all my might. She did too but it was too strong for her. Who could know why this cruel spirit had been allowed to infest the mind of such a brilliant, talented and creative person? It ruined her life in so many ways and I just couldn't fight it although God knows I tried. And of course she tried too but it was asking too much for the Shaman who could cure so many others to cure herself.

Although I kept well away from her and she well away from me we were both aware of each other's presence at the fair. I bumped into her going to the washroom at one point and she seemed to be in a much better mood than before. She told me that she attempted to give a lecture at the fair like the other psychics did but it was a bit of a washout since she wasn't used to it and even worse she had to follow my hypnosis demonstration, which I did at the fairs. It certainly would have been hard for an experienced lecturer to follow that let alone a homeless beginner. Still, it indicated her resilience and courage to have even attempted such a thing.

All in all, my contact with Simone at the fair was pretty limited as a result of my own shyness and the fact that we were both very busy doing readings. On the last day, however, a curious thing happened. It was right at the end of the fair within minutes of closing time. I had by that point given up all hope of connecting with Simone. My front person was a magician named Don Parker who had worked for me many years before and who was an old friend remarked, "It will be good to talk magic with you after the fair". I replied, "It sure will," whereupon he responded casually, "Yes, and I got rid of that girl. She wanted to hang out with us afterwards". I said, "What girl?" but somehow knew the answer. He replied, "The black psychic girl". In a state of consternation I responded, "You mean you actually turned her away?" Don responded in surprise, "You mean that you actually want her to come with us?" I gasped out, "Of course I do. I had better go and tell her!"

I then shot over to her booth like greased lightning to tell her she was welcome after all. She looked quite pleased but told me she would be quite a while packing up her booth. I told her that would be fine even though I knew that Don would not be pleased at the delay since it only would take us a few minutes to pack up and we would have to wait for her. We started to have quite a pleasant conversation and I ended up sitting down getting a taped reading from her that I still have to this day.

I found the session to be very peaceful and relaxing after the three days of stress that is always present at a psychic fair. Doing reading after reading is a very draining experience and can really get to you. However, Simone was very soothing in her words and I supposed I liked being with her, which was very calming in itself.

It was arranged that she, her front person, Don and I would go somewhere to get a bite to eat. Accordingly the four of us walked through the streets of Vancouver to find a restaurant. Don was a little disappointed that I wouldn't be able to give him a private audience so that we could discuss magic and was also not happy that things were getting so late because of Simone's delay in closing down her booth. Suddenly, we passed a street corner and I was surprised to see Simone's front person drift away mysteriously from us without saying a word of goodbye. I suppose she had experienced quite enough of Simone at that point and was glad to get away from her. I do know that Simone treated her very roughly during the fair and screamed at her once or twice. Or at least Nasty Spirit did.

So now there were three of us. However, Don suddenly said, "You know, it is getting too late for me to come with you. I hope you don't mind if I pass on the restaurant. I would like to go home". I said, "Sure" and left it at that. After saying goodnight to Don I realised that it was now just Simone and me. I was quite thrilled at this turn of events since it meant that now I could have time alone with the woman who fascinated me so much. Simone herself seemed to be quite happy with this change of circumstances too.

She said she knew a good place to eat and led me through some darkened streets off the main pathway. For the first time I felt uneasy since I had no idea where she was taking me and I was visualising all sorts of muggers and homeless characters springing from the dark to attack me then run off with Simone to split the money. However, I was suffering solely from an over-active imagination and we did indeed arrive at the restaurant safely.

I really got to know her a little bit better and I bonded with her quite well during the meal. She told me all sorts of surprising things about herself, her work and her situation. Some questions she plain wouldn't answer and I know, that to this day, I am sure she kept back information about herself to me.

At dinner she pointed out the waitress and said, "That woman helped me to survive until the psychic fair came up. I wouldn't have been able to make it if she hadn't been around". I gathered from the remark that she either got free meals or financial handouts from the waitress and it was quite interesting to note that after the meal Simone left her a large tip. Now that she was finally in the money it must have given her great pleasure to make the gesture.

The moment during the meal that I really bonded with this strange and beautiful woman was when I asked her what work she had done in the past. She mentioned that she had been a social worker, which makes the mind boggle as to how she got the job in the first place. Of course, she could seem quite sane on occasions. In fact most of the time. I have always said that Simone was perfectly normal and delightful 70% of the time but perfectly abnormal 30% of the time. The trouble was that the pain of the 30% rather ruined the delight of the 70%.

However, the moment of bonding really came when I persisted in asking what was the last job she had before she ended up on the street. A mischievous smile came over her face and she said, "I was a prostitute!" I was in the middle of my soup and sputtered it all out with a great gasp on hearing this, whereupon she burst out laughing. Her laugh was one of the most delightful things about her and it must have charmed so many and got her out of a multitude of difficult situations. When I recovered my composure I said, "Are you serious?" She replied, "Yes, but I only had one client. He was about sixty years old and I lived with him for this purpose. It was my job and we got on very well". Her great delight at my consternation and her laughter at me spluttering my soup out was the moment we connected and I really took a liking to her.

After the meal I asked her to show me where my hotel was since I was out of my usual area. She was staying in some cheap seedy run down place herself and I now in hindsight think she wanted to stay the night with me in my more salubrious quarters but in my usual naivety in these matters I didn't pick up on it. When we arrived there I was about to say goodnight to her then I realised that I needed someone to accompany me on the elevator because of an abnormal fear I have of such vertical methods of transportation. I am just about okay in an elevator if someone is in there with me but I cannot travel alone in one. I suppose a charitable person would say that it proves I am human and an uncharitable person would say simply that I am not hooked up right. I explained that I needed her assistance to help me take the elevator and I explained to her why. She agreed to accompany me upstairs but thought I had an ulterior motive and remarked with a smile, "Oh yes! A likely story!" She must have known I liked her and she naturally assumed that I wanted to get her in my room for reasons of an amorous nature. I wasn't that devious (or at least not in that one area) but of course she didn't know that since we weren't acquainted long enough for her to figure me out yet.

Anyway, up in the elevator we went and she did indeed enter my room. Of course, when we got there all I did was talk about numerology and the psychic fair and she wondered when I would make a move on her. I never did and just chattered on to her consternation. I did tell her that if she was ever in Toronto to give me a call. However, in the light of future events I found out that she misinterpreted this simple remark to assume that I was inviting her to stay with me. I don't know what I said to make her think this but think it she did.

Finally I bade her farewell and she walked dejectedly out of the room and down the hallway. She remarked sadly as she left, "I suppose we are all played out now", and I finally realised what she wanted. I did not give it to her and let her leave thinking I would never see her again. I was sad too. I was beginning to love her and I thought of her on the plane back to Toronto the next day. Since she had no permanent address or phone number, I had no way of contacting her and assumed that would simply be that. I did leave her my phone number but didn't expect any contact. She would become a strange memory.

Nope. That wasn't what was to happen. I hadn't seen the end of Simone yet. It was only just beginning….

A few months later in Toronto my phone rang. It was the shaman herself. I was terribly excited that she had actually phoned and was in a dream when she told me she was coming to Toronto. I asked her when and was astonished when she said, "Tomorrow!" I said, "Why are you coming?" and was amazed when she said "You!" I couldn't believe my ears but in my usual negativity I assumed that she meant something else. I knew a major Toronto psychic fair was coming up in a few weeks and I assumed this was the reason she was there. I can be pretty dumb sometimes. However, in hindsight and from things she said later, I believe at the time she came to Toronto she was looking at me more as a career move than as a romantic one. She was still associated with the drunk who beat her up and had continued her relationship with him. In fact she made no secret that she was actually in love with him. I found out later that she had discussed her visit to Toronto with him and they had both decided that Mark Lewis was the key to Simone earning money. As I have already mentioned, she had stated that, "I may be mad but I am not stupid". I do believe that in time she developed some kind of affection for me but her initial reason for coming was more financial than romantic. She had reasoned that I would help her get back on her feet. I found out that she had told the drunk "teacher" that, "There is money around this man" showing him my psychic promotional leaflet. Little did she know!

I arranged to meet her at the airport and took note of her flight number. That evening I went out to the bus station to research some cheap hotels that I knew were posted on a notice board there. I knew she wouldn't be staying in anything expensive but would be looking for the cheapest and most basic rooms available. I had no idea that in her mind she intended to stay with me and that she had assumed that this was going to happen. She didn't tell me that she wanted to stay with me so I assumed she didn't. I didn't really have the space anyway and there was only one bed although I had a spare mattress in a closet somewhere.

She was scheduled to arrive early evening the next day. I waited for her at the luggage carousel, which was the standard place to wait for domestic flights within Canada. Everyone from that flight had to go there to pick up their luggage. Of course at that point I didn't know that Simone travelled without luggage and had no worldly possessions to speak of although I think she had a little bag with her that she carried on the plane. At first I panicked because I couldn't find her but then I saw a forlorn dejected figure wandering aimlessly around the airport with her head down. My heart went out to her and I just wanted to help her. I approached her saying "Simone?" whereupon she looked at me without expression and with great sadness in her eyes. She looked completely broken in spirit and very tired. This wasn't the funny, crazy person I had eaten with in Vancouver.

I found some place to sit down with her and told her that I had found a place for her to stay that was affordable and clean. She looked really sad when I said that and I couldn't figure out why. She said, "I don't want to go there. I will stay here". I told her she couldn't stay at the airport. She hinted strongly that she wanted to stay with me but I told her that I plain didn't have the space and only one bed. I didn't click that was of no concern to her since I have always been very innocent in these matters. She seemed reluctant for me to take her to a hotel and it didn't dawn on me that she had taken for granted that she would stay with me. Finally I said, "Look, you can stay with me one night to get your bearings and then tomorrow you can find somewhere else to stay". At that a slight smile came over her and she said almost to herself "He is weakening". Of course she was right—I couldn't leave her on the street in a strange city.

Accordingly, I took her into town to my apartment. I fished out the mattress from the closet and laid it out on the living room floor. All I then needed were sheets and blankets plus a pillow. I knew a huge discount store that was open quite late and that would be likely to stock those items. I decided that was where we should head so I dragged Simone out with me to buy what we needed. I found out later that she was very puzzled by my activity. She figured that if there was one bed that was the one we should both sleep in. She didn't reckon on my Victorian morality, and of course, I hardly knew her anyway. Still, she went along with my search and assisted me in the doing of it. In the meantime I had decided that she could stay for more than the one night. In about four days or so there was a psychic fair coming up in Pickering, a small town just outside Toronto and I figured she could be my front person there. It was a little way out of town and I would be staying in a hotel. I figured that she could stay with me in my apartment until the fair came up and then stay with me in the hotel room for the three days of the fair. After that she would be able to stand on her own two feet and could find her own room somewhere because I plain didn't have the space. And of course, she would earn some revenue from me as a front person.

She gradually warmed up from her dark mood at the airport and started to talk with me. She talked so deeply about spirituality and psychic stuff that I realised my values were completely different from hers and that we had little in common with regard to our respective belief systems. I began to think that perhaps this strange girl wasn't for me after all. And of course her odd lifestyle and behaviour was a little off putting too.

It was late and we were both tired so I bade her goodnight and let her sleep. However, she insisted on lighting a candle, which she put in a little glass on the floor beside her as she slept. This made me very nervous since I considered it a fire hazard but I let it go and retired to my own room hoping that we wouldn't be burned alive overnight.

The next morning she was still fast asleep when I went into the living room and thankfully the candle had burned out. I wanted to phone my friend Lisa who had met Simone two years before to tell her all about my strange visitor. Obviously I didn't want to phone from home in case Simone heard the conversation so I left the apartment to make the call from a payphone down the street. When I spoke to Lisa she expressed mild disapproval of the whole matter which I suppose was fairly understandable. I then returned to the apartment to await the wakening of the shaman. When that momentous event happened I enquired if she had slept well. She replied, "Your friend Lisa has been psychically attacking me in the middle of the night". I enquired as to what on earth she meant and she told me that Lisa had been kicking her while she tried to sleep. I enquired as to how that was possible since Lisa hadn't been in the house. Simone explained that it was a psychic attack and that Lisa didn't have to actually be there. It was a little weird and perhaps indicative of Simone's strong psychic ability since I had just called Lisa who expressed her disapproval of my visitor.

There was certainly some wariness between Lisa and Simone at first. Lisa explained to me that she liked Simone but as my friend she wanted to protect me from her since she obviously felt that I could be hurt by my relationship with this unusual woman. However, I am glad to say that they both warmed up to each other in time. Simone gradually began to develop a good feeling for Lisa who in her turn developed great sympathy for the plight of Simone.

Over the next few days I got on very well with Simone who had brightened considerably and was back to her amusing self. I introduced her to some of my friends who no doubt raised an eyebrow or two over her unusual ways but I think she charmed most of them nevertheless. It was a fairly happy time for her I think and her demons were kept to a minimum although I think that anyone who met her in that period probably sensed something wasn't quite right. Nevertheless, she was happy and bubbly most of the time.

We went to the psychic fair in Pickering and shared a hotel room with two beds. At the fair Simone fared relatively well except on one or two occasions when I saw her demons raging for brief moments. I had gone to a payphone to check my voice mail messages and for some reason this enraged her. She started to yell at me that she wanted me to attend to my booth and her anger was way out of proportion to the offence but I shrugged it off. There were a couple of other times she showed flashes of rage but most of the three days of the fair she was in a good mood and we had quite a bit of fun together. She was a pretty dreadful front person who broke all the rules of the game but it didn't seem to matter. We were having so many good laughs that the customers sensed it and seemed to sign up with us. The happy energy seemed to attract them. At one point when business was slow she commented, "We're not going to make it" as if to say that it was not going to be a profitable fair. I replied "I don't give a damn" and I really didn't. I enjoyed being with Simone so much that the profitability of the fair was really my secondary priority. It was in actual fact a slow fair and the other psychics were having a struggle to get clients. However, because of our happy energy and banter together people picked up on it and signed up with us rather than the competition.

Mind you, there was a glitch on the opening day. There seemed to be negativity towards us from the other psychics possibly because of Simone herself. Someone complained that she was standing out in the aisle and mentioned it to her, which wasn't a smart thing to do since her retort was somewhat on the aggressive side. Standing out in the aisle to attract business is a no-no in the psychic fair world but Simone was only there for a brief moment and it wasn't something she did on a regular basis. She sensed the negativity from the other psychics and hardly left my booth except for brief moments to take a break.

Because of this negativity coupled with the fact that foot traffic was slow on the opening day we didn't do that well. Simone remarked, "I am going to fix those other psychics so they do badly tomorrow and we will do well". I asked her how she would do that and she said she would conduct some sort of metaphysical ceremony in the hotel room. I decided to humour her and thought "Whatever". She had a little wooden model of a snake that I had given to her after she had taken a liking to it. I had used it as display material for demonstrating the magic worm novelty known as the "squirmle" which I often pitched along with the Svengali deck. Simone used this thing for her ceremony and indeed it was a big part of it. She arranged things on the hotel dresser very carefully putting the snake in the centre. She also put other stuff around it but at this stage I cannot remember the details. Perhaps it was leaves, rice, feathers or something or other—I just can't remember. I think it was some kind of native ceremony she had learned on the reservation.

I didn't pay much attention to the display and, of course, didn't take it seriously. Unfortunately, I didn't respect it as much as I should have done and moved it inadvertently a couple of times when I made phone calls. This set Simone off screaming and shouting in a demonic rage but thank the Lord the torrent didn't last long. However, the incident at the fair when she screamed at me when I made calls to check my voice mail coupled with the anger displayed when I moved the snake should have given me an early indication that this person had serious problems. However, love is blind and by this time I had developed a very strong affection for her that has lasted to this day. I haven't seen her for years but I still pray for her every day. I am the showman and she is the shaman and the showman still loves the shaman that he will probably never see again. But yet who knows...?

As for the results of the ceremony I don't believe in this stuff and yet all I can tell you is that it seemed to work. The remaining two days of the fair the other psychics starved and we were making loads of money. If I weren't such a sceptical cynic I would tend to say that Simone really did have strange powers. I saw them manifest themselves on many occasions. It was almost as if she could read minds. If there really is such a thing as a psychic Simone would be it. For example, at this particular fair Simone would relay all the gossip from the other psychics and yet she hardly left my booth and as previously indicated the other psychics wouldn't talk to her anyway.

She was very amusing as a front person and on one memorable occasion I said to a client, "I see you being married for many years". Front persons will often hear parts of a reading but they generally have their back to the reader and client giving a sense of semi-privacy. Furthermore, they are usually so busy talking to potential clients that they are not in a position to listen in very well to a reading in progress. Simone overheard my remark and without any sense of privacy for the client suddenly turned around and interjected herself into the reading (which is a no-no in itself) exclaiming to me, "I thought you never tell anything bad to people!" At least the client laughed! Simone had a wonderful sense of humour that must have been a salve for her pain on occasion.

We did well at the fair and developed a bond with each other. We found out that we had a fair bit in common and that we even liked the same food. The main thing we shared was a sense of humour. The primary difference between us was our outlook on psychic things. She regarded me almost as a fake because of my showmanship and this disappointed her greatly. She even told the psychic fair promoter that I was a fake whereupon he remarked in response, "Whatever he does, he does it very well!" Of course, there was nothing remotely fake in what I did but my showmanship and cynical attitude to the psychic world made it seem so to her.

The three days at the fair turned out to be very pleasant and apart from the odd angry moment Simone kept her demons at bay for the most part. At one point she watched my hypnosis lecture and observed, "My life is changing". When I asked her how my hypnosis lecture was changing her life she said, "I don't know people like you who do shows and make speeches. I am in a different league now. My life is changing". I am distressed, however, to admit with great sadness as I write, that her life didn't change. I cannot express fully my despair over her unhappy fate and this is why I find this narrative so painful to communicate. Her meeting with me gave her so much promise that her demons wouldn't let her fulfill. At least I think she experienced a somewhat happy time at the fair and I am grateful for that respite in her misery.

It was, however, time for her to find somewhere to stay since I just didn't have the space. She had decided to stay until the Toronto psychic fair and I helped her to pay for the booth by lending her some money, which to her credit she did eventually pay me back. She did not do well at this fair because she was feeling under par and she hadn't taken her vitamins. It was in the middle of the harsh Toronto winter and she had contracted a bad cold that affected her efforts. She did not lose money but did not come out with a lot of profit either.

She did find some cheap hotel to stay at and I don't think it was very comfortable. One morning I met her for breakfast and she was in a very bad mood because of this. She snapped at me and I got so irritated that I pretended to leave saying, "I've had enough of you, Simone!" and stormed off. Of course, I came back about a minute later but my brief departure scared her because she assumed I meant it and she would have been all alone in Toronto. Of course I could never abandon her and indeed I once promised her that I never would. And I never will. At the time of writing she seems to have abandoned me but if ever I hear she is in trouble I will run to her side. I promised I would never abandon her if she needs me and it is a vow that I will always keep.

She seemed very grateful that I returned and I found out that many people had walked out on her before and she had been rejected many times because of her flaring demons. Of course, at breakfast that morning I had only been dealing with Grumpy Spirit. Nasty Spirit was a much more terrifying spirit to handle and up to that point I had only seen brief glimpses of her. In time to come I would see her in full frightening fury.

The few weeks I spent with her in Toronto were overall quite positive and pleasant. I did eventually become intimate with her and I let her stay with me more and more until I eventually gave in and let her live with me even though there really wasn't room for both of us. She was quite funny and one of the craziest moments was when I was discussing serious business on the phone with someone and she wandered across the living room stark naked whereas she had been fully clothed at the time the conversation started. I could hardly concentrate on the business at hand and naturally I didn't tell the other party to the conversation the reason for my distraction. Simone certainly knew how to make me laugh and I believe I did the same for her. I used to answer Lisa's scepticism about the relationship by saying, "I make her happy and she makes me happy" and it was indeed very true.

I even found her a few psychic clients that she could do readings for. She was brilliant at handling the very difficult cases that I dreaded doing. I simply passed them on to my strange female visitor. Every psychic gets difficult and demanding clients that they would rather not read. Simone seemed to have a magic touch with them and calmed them considerably. One particular woman used to drive me crazy by phoning and talking about all sorts of weird things yet she would never actually make an appointment to have a paid reading. Of course, as I write this, I am retroactively thinking that it was just as well. It got so bad that I actually became quite curt with her and even hung up a couple of times. However, one day I passed the phone to Simone and was amazed at how well she handled the woman. She also insisted on being paid for her time and that the woman make a proper appointment. Eventually, even Simone had to hang up but the way she did it was a most mystical experience. She took the phone receiver in both hands and held it horizontally. Ever so slowly she moved it downwards towards the rest of the phone to end the call. I could still hear the woman yapping on the other end very loudly but Simone ignored it and seemed to be in some sort of metaphysical trance with her eyes semi closed. It was almost as if she was praying as she put the phone down very, very, gently. It was a most beautiful and mysterious thing to watch. I have certainly never seen since such a most peaceful way of hanging up on someone! I do know that I never heard from the woman again.

Eventually, Simone decided to go back to Vancouver. I can't remember at this stage whether I paid her fare or she managed herself although I must say that the former is much more likely than the latter. I do know that I was worried that she would not have enough money to get back into town when she arrived at the airport and I gave her $40 or so. After her return I often used to wire money to her in Vancouver when she needed it and I became a regular visitor to Money Mart in Yonge St, Toronto to carry out this function.

We took a bus to the airport and I hinted about my growing affection for her. She seemed to hint back but was too vague about it for my liking. I pressed her for a more specific answer and she stated that she loved me. However, I got a vibe that she was simply just saying it out of politeness and was a little half hearted about it. I said, "Are you sure? I don't think you really mean it". Her reply didn't make me feel any better. She responded, "How would you feel if I didn't mean it and was just saying it to get what I could out of you?" She had certainly got quite a bit of money out of me and I used to joke about it quite a bit to her and hear her laugh uproariously every time I used to complain. However, her response to my question about her true feelings made me a trifle despondent and I replied, "If you are just saying it so you can get money out of me I think that would be very cruel and unfair". She didn't respond to me and I felt uneasy about her true motivation. Mind you, I had seen written notations to herself in my Toronto apartment that I came across accidentally and these did show she really had some kind of affection for me. She had said in her notes that I was the male person she felt most close to at the present time. Still I felt a little saddened and uneasy by her unenthusiastic response to my probing.

At the airport I was unhappy to see her go and I believed she was sad to leave me too. I saw her go through the security section and felt a little troubled by her remarks on the bus but decided to think of something else. After she departed from sight I decided to get a coffee and wander round the airport. Perhaps half an hour later I decided to check my voice mail and found an airport pay phone. I was surprised to find a message from Simone herself that she had left within the preceding half hour. She must have gone to a pay phone and left a message on my voice mail not long after she had left me. The message was "Everything is as it seems. There is no illusion. I do love you and I really look forward to seeing you again".

After I heard that I was walking on air and felt a surge of happiness. I was as happy then as I am sad now to relate this story.

Several months passed and I kept in touch with her as much as I could. She had, of course, no fixed address and certainly no phone number. I had to rely on talking to her when she wanted to talk to me. She would phone me sometimes, naturally always calling collect. She had intended to take a booth at the upcoming Ottawa psychic fair that was run by the same promoter as the Vancouver and Toronto fair. I ended up paying the deposit for her booth as well as my own. I told her that she could pay me back once she had made a profit. She had arranged to stay with me again before we both headed to Ottawa by train. I am pretty sure I ended up paying her airfare from Vancouver to Toronto as well as the train fare from Toronto to Ottawa.

I had decided that she could stay with me despite the lack of space. I figured we had become much closer than before. However, a shock was in store for me. We had planned she would stay a couple of weeks with me in Toronto before we travelled to Ottawa. However, within hours of landing she told me that she was finishing with me. She had consulted a psychic in Vancouver who advised her that I wasn't for her after all. She had been told, "There are two men in your life. One you will marry and the other one you will merely travel with". She had interpreted this to mean that the drunk in Vancouver would be the one she would marry and I would be the one she would travel with. I was naturally upset with this revelation particularly since she had still decided that she would stay with me before we headed off to Ottawa. I brought this up with her only to be told it was for my own good. She reasoned that if she had arrived at the psychic fair and only told me then that the relationship was over I wouldn't have been able to concentrate on my work! Therefore, according to her logic, she had to stay with me for a couple of weeks so that I could get used to the bad news! It didn't seem to have occurred to her that she could have written or phoned me with this depressing news. It seems she still recognised that I might still be a good meal ticket.

She wanted to have her cake and eat it. She wanted to end the relationship yet still have free accommodation with me before the fair started. She said, "Don't worry. I know you have had a loss and I will conduct a ceremony to relieve you of the pain of the loss". She wanted me to be naked before her and she would dance around me sprinkling some leaves and feathers or something. I declined the offer and told her that I was upset after she had left a message at the airport that she really did love me and it was no illusion.

Furthermore, I thought it peculiar to end a relationship but still take advantage of free accommodation and other benefits. As I stated previously I am pretty sure that I paid her fare from Vancouver to Toronto. I also know that I paid for her train fare from Toronto to Ottawa. I felt pretty used.

I did try to adjust to it in the hope that she would change her mind and sometimes she gave the impression that she had. However, probably in her heart it really wasn't so. That is why at the very beginning of this saga I explained that this is a one sided love story. There were times she said she loved me but of course love can take many forms. Perhaps the form it took with her wasn't the form that it took with me.

The next couple of weeks were not easy ones. It was nowhere nearly as pleasant as the first visit. Nasty Spirit appeared more frequently as did Grumpy Spirit. It was a relief when we finally headed to Ottawa by train. I hoped that the change in scene would alter the unpleasant atmosphere between us. However, it actually got worse and in Ottawa all hell broke loose.

The train ride was reasonably stress free and in fact we went first class which she seemed to like. I designed a mail order leaflet for her that advertised her psychic services and she was happy with that. When we arrived we went to the hotel, which was rather a salubrious one. The fair organiser had arranged a special rate for the psychics there and it was within walking distance of the Ottawa Congress Center where the psychic fair was being held.

After settling into our room we decided to go for a walk around the downtown area where the hotel and exhibition centre were located. We went into the mall adjoining the Congress Centre and wandered around. She seemed fairly settled and I thought our stay in Ottawa would be more positive than the time we had spent in Toronto. I then made a fatal mistake. I decided to check my voice mail and went to a pay phone. For some odd reason I noticed that she would get very agitated when I went to make a phone call from a public pay phone. It had happened at the previous psychic fair on her first visit to Toronto and I have already related how angry it made her. I am not sure why this stirred her up so much and I have never quite figured it out. As I made the call I could see she was getting agitated so I finished very quickly indeed. However, she erupted to me, "Why did you make that call? Could you not see there was a black boy waiting to rob you?"

I wasn't sure what she was talking about and I asked her to explain. She informed me that a black youth had been eyeing me with intent to rob. He had been watching me with evil intent and only Simone's presence—according to her anyway—had scared him off. I am not sure there was any "black boy" there in the first place and if there was I am quite prepared to believe Simone had scared him off. Her fiendish persona would scare anyone off. I brushed her concern aside and there was the fatal mistake I spoke of earlier. She erupted as if the heavens had fallen in. Nasty Spirit appeared with a vengeance and she screamed and berated me for being so ungrateful for her protection from the "black boy". Frankly, I almost think I would rather have been robbed by the alleged youth than have had to go through the horrendous experience of being screamed at in a public place by a clearly disturbed young woman. People in the mall stared at the scene and I must have been as white as a sheet with the shock and sheer suprise at the ferocity of this verbal attack. I had seen her erupt before but for much shorter periods and with less intensity.

Suddenly she stopped and walked away leaving me distraught and I confess in tears. I was quite shaken by the experience but after a few minutes gathered my wits to go after her. By now she had left the mall and gone into the street. I caught up with her and found that she had calmed down. She turned to me and to my surprise said, "I am sorry. That was horrible wasn't it?" It was as if she had done this with many people many times before. She knew it was something she had no control over and she was well aware that this was something she shouldn't be doing. I hugged her and told her everything would be okay. I knew full well that this was a decent person who was simply unstable for whatever reason and needed help.

We proceeded along the street and she produced one of those solutions that kids make bubbles with. You put a plastic stick with a hole inside the liquid and blow bubbles into the air. I have no idea why she was carrying this but I remembered using the stuff myself when I was a kid. She proceeded to blow bubbles into the air and got some strange looks from passers by since she was being very ostentatious about it. I didn't mind—I preferred the bubble blowing behaviour to the screaming maniac behaviour. All the same it was apparent she wasn't acting in a normal manner.

Suddenly we bumped into some exhibitors from the fair. One of them noticed Simone's bubble blowing and remarked, "Oh, the bubble lady!" This produced no reaction from Simone and I just shrugged my shoulders with the embarrassment of it. I remember wiping tears from my eyes and hoping that nobody would notice. I was terribly distressed by all that was going on.

Eventually, we got back to the hotel. Simone found a headset in her luggage and started to listen to music. This seemed to calm her down and bring her somewhat back to normal. There is an old saying about music calming the heart of a savage beast and Nasty Spirit could certainly be a savage beast. Encouraged by this I prematurely asked if she wanted to go out and eat. She hissed at me so I left her alone. Later I did go out to eat with her and it was a very unpleasant meal not because of the food but because of the company. When we returned to the hotel she became aggressive again and so much so that she picked up an electric razor of mine and made as if she was going to throw it at me. I decided then and there that I had just about enough and I started to worry about my safety. I told her that I was going to book her into a different room that I would pay for. This would be for one night only and then she would be on her own. I then went down to the lobby and asked for the manager. With great embarrassment I explained the situation as best I could and told him that I would pay for one night's accommodation for Simone but she would have to be in a different room. I then said that from the next day I would not be responsible for any bills she ran up. I figured that since she would be making money from the next day at the fair I could let her go on her own from that point. When I got back to my room I told Simone that I had arranged another room for her a few floors above. She demanded that I move there, as she was quite happy with the room she was in! I told her no. I didn't like elevators otherwise I would probably have given in. She reluctantly moved and I settled in alone quite distressed and unhappy about everything that had transpired. I am sure Simone was just as distressed but I had to do what I had to do.

She moved out of the hotel the next morning and found some cheaper place to stay. However, she had left some of her underwear in the room I had evicted her from. The fair hadn't started yet and I went over to set up taking her clothing in a bag intending to give it to her there. On the way to the fair I walked over a bridge and who should be coming the other way but the shaman herself. She was bright and breezy and it was obvious that Happy Spirit was in charge of her this morning. She giggled at me when I gave her the underwear and joked about it. No mention was made of the previous evening's turmoil and it was if nothing had happened.

When I got to the fair I saw that she had been given what seemed to be a good location. Or at least it would have been a good location if I had been there. For Simone it was actually not a good place to be since she was surrounded by top psychics. Opposite her was a tough old lady with a heart of gold named Laura who had been in the business many years. Furthermore on each side of her were two other veteran psychics who knew how to get business. It was a good location but it would take an aggressive personality to fight for business against such formidable competitors. As the psychic fair promoter later remarked to me "I am afraid she is swimming among the sharks where she is". Simone certainly had an aggressive personality but not in the way required. In a business sense she was pretty passive and she made matters worse on the opening day by refusing to go after customers and spent her day "meditating" as she put it. Perhaps she needed the meditation to calm her down from all the stress and turmoil going on in her mind. However the odds were pretty stacked against her making money.

The odds were stacked against me making money too. I found I was in a pretty dreadful spot where nobody passed by. Pillars obstructed my booth and I knew I was done for. The ironic thing is that I found out later that I was supposed to be in the good spot where Simone was but they decided to give her the chance of a good location because the promoter wanted to help her.

I needed to find a reading table and so did Simone. I went to a psychic I knew who usually had tables to spare and asked if he had two. He only had one and I was about to let Simone have it but she was in one of her nasty moods so I thought, "The hell with it" and simply took the table to my own booth and let her fend for herself. When I introduced the guy who lent me the table to her I said, "This is Light Spirit," whereupon she snapped at him and he remarked "Her spirit doesn't seem very light to me". He skedaddled away very quickly and I can't say I blame him.

The other psychics didn't take to her at all. Laura said to me, "Mark. What is this I hear about you having a girl friend?" She had no idea it was the strange person working opposite her booth. When I informed her she looked displeased and exclaimed, "Oh, her!" with a scowl. I tried to explain that Simone had led a troubled life and she wasn't that bad a person underneath it all. Laura responded, "As a friend. Let me give you a word of advice, Mark Lewis. Dump her!"

Actually, Laura relented slightly during the fair and in fact, sent Simone a few customers out of the kindness of her heart. The shaman never knew.

During the fair there were one or two friendly moments with Simone but they were few and far between. There was a very unpleasant atmosphere between us and I decided that I had absolutely enough of her and that everything was ended between us. She still owed me a pile of money for the booth deposit but I didn't expect to see it again. The fair promoter came over to my booth and I made it plain to him that I was taking no responsibility for any further payment on Simone's booth and he would have to get the balance from her if he was able to. He asked me, "Have you finished your association with her?" I replied with a sigh, "I am afraid she has rather an excess of spirituality for me," as a polite explanation for our parting of the ways. However, he was pretty sharp and he said, "Mark, have you considered another possibility?" I responded, "How do you mean?" His reply was, "Have you considered that she might be mad?" I was startled at the question and he continued, "Many of our exhibitors are very sincere believers but a few of them are actually mad! Simone would be in the insane category!"

I have never considered Simone insane but as I have already indicated she was extremely troubled and life had dealt her a cruel blow that made her behave in such a bizarre manner. However, I laughingly had to agree with the promoter that "insane" might not be a bad adjective. He indicated to me that he expected to receive no money from her but his assistant had other ideas. She came over to me during the fair and asked if it was true that I would not be paying for Simone's booth. I confirmed it and remarked, "There is more chance of Simone paying you than me being struck by lightning!" However, I was to be proved wrong since an hour later the assistant came by with a triumphant smile saying, "I suppose you are going to be struck by lightning now. Simone has paid me".

It must have been tough for Simone to pay but I had to harden my heart to her predicament because there was no way I could help her anyway since I also made no money and had a dismal fair.

At the end of the fair I approached Simone to say goodbye and she was as unpleasant as ever. On a vindictive whim I remarked to her, "What about the money you owe me?" Of course I knew I wasn't going to get any but I was in a wicked mood. She glared at me as if she wanted to kill me and said, "I think you'd better leave!" Of course she was right. I did leave and travelled back to Toronto alone and left her to her own devices and that I thought would be that.

It wasn't. Three weeks later I got a phone call from her saying "I want to apologise for my behaviour". I didn't know how to take this. She had already upset my emotional applecart and I didn't want any more of it. But yet deep down I still loved her and I was therefore torn two ways. On one hand I never wanted to see her again and on the other I cared deeply and worried so much about her. I took her address and said I might write to her. She didn't seem to have a phone number or at any rate she didn't want to give it to me. She had somehow used her survival skills to charm a holistic healing centre to look after her for free.

I did write to her saying I didn't know if I loved her or hated her. I actually told her I was torn between my feelings for her and my inability to handle her aggressive behaviour. Of course love won out in the end and I continued to correspond with her and would receive phone calls (collect!) on occasion. She had managed somehow to get back to Vancouver no doubt with the help of one of the many benefactors she managed to charm.

One day I was astonished to get a postcard from England. Somehow she had managed to return to her original homeland. She seemed to be staying with friends and she gave me a phone number which I called, to hear her as bubbly as ever and it seemed that Happy Spirit was back in business. She had actually found a job in a factory and things were apparently looking up. However, the relief was only temporary and sadly she ended up back on the street again. She had given up the job in the factory which I think she found boring and somehow got a job as a social worker, I kid you not. Of course, she had past experience in this kind of work and probably charmed the interviewer who had no idea of her unfortunate history. Naturally, the inevitable happened and she blew up in one of her usual furies at some woman in a wheelchair that she was supposed to be looking after and that was the end of that.

She ended up in the streets of London no doubt because she was hard to live with and her friends probably threw her out. She had no money and no job—only her survival skills. When I heard all this I was terribly distressed and I probably sent money to her. I do know that I sent her some special balloons that magicians use for sculpturing balloon animals so that she could sell the balloon models to passers by in the street. She used to sleep with other homeless people outside a magic shop in Charing Cross Underground Station. At least this way she was indoors and not subject to the inclement British weather. It seems that she became quite talented at making the balloon animals and used to go into the magic shop to purchase more.

I do know that she managed to purchase a harp from a music shop. It seemed that the harp cost eighty pounds which Simone naturally couldn't afford. She laughed at the shop owner and said, "Look at me. I am down and out and completely homeless! I can't afford eighty pounds. You have had that harp on sale for months and months and nobody wants it except me. I'll give you twenty quid. It is all I have in the world". Believe it or not, the shop owner gave in and Simone had a new musical instrument. As she had previously remarked, "I might be mad but I'm not stupid!"

And she wasn't. She used the harp to earn money playing it in the street and asking for donations. She had survived once again. She phoned me and told me about the harp. I asked if she could really play it and she got irritated and replied, "Of course I can!" I was sceptical and demanded proof. She reluctantly fetched the harp and I listened to the most beautiful music. I was convinced she had put on a record or the radio and I asked her if it was really her that was playing the instrument. After a while it was obvious that it indeed was and Arty Spirit was in charge of her during the phone call. It pains me to think what cruel fate ruined her life and prevented her from using her great artistic and creative gifts to their full potential.

At one time a recording studio executive saw her playing in the subway and whisked her to the studio to make a recording of her music. I asked her if he had paid her any money and she replied, "Of course not". I said, "That is disgraceful. They should at least have given you something".

She got irritated with me stating, "You don't understand. It is a big honour for a homeless person to be taken to a studio and have their music recorded". It seems that the recognition and boost to her self-esteem was reward enough.

From time to time she would stay in homeless shelters but end up getting thrown out because of her screeching rages. One time I contacted a shelter and asked for her only to be told, "Simone isn't here any more. There has been an incident". Naturally I asked what kind of "incident" was referred to. It seems from the explanation that I was given that Simone had erupted at something or other and started to throw property around. The police were called and she was taken away.

This alarmed me so much that I managed to trace the police station where she would have been taken and made enquiries. I spoke to the officer in charge of looking after the prisoners and he did indeed remember Simone. He informed me that "She didn't seem a bad person" so after she had calmed down they let her go and she was given the names of other shelters who would take her in. I explained that she was ill and her sickness made her scream at people. The cop answered with a sigh, "Oh, we're quite used to people screaming in here. Simone isn't the only one. Listen to the noise in the background". I was amused to hear all sorts of screaming in the distance from various inmates who presumably were not happy with their situation and I realised what the cop meant.

I was eventually able to trace Simone to another shelter and spoke to her by phone. I mentioned that I had been in touch with the police and this made her extremely angry. She said, "Why do you have to embarrass me like that?" I responded that I cared about her and that I would never abandon her. I had also decided that I could do very little for her from three thousand miles away and that I had decided to come to London to see what I could do to assist her. She seemed to welcome the suggestion so I started to make travel arrangements.

The night before the flight I contacted her at the temporary shelter and gave her my flight number. However, during the conversation she began to scream at me for no apparent reason that I could fathom and I felt quite helpless and started to cry with the stress of it all. She responded by saying, "That's it. All you can do is cry! Go on! Cry! Cry away!" She then said that she didn't like me feeling sorry for her. I replied, "I don't feel sorry for you". She screamed "What is it then? What is it?" Again I repeated, "I don't feel sorry for you" and again she shouted, "Then what is it?" I finally responded, "It's love, Simone". Suddenly the torrent quietened and she made no response. There was silence on the phone for quite a while. When she eventually responded she had calmed down sufficiently for me to conclude the conversation is a more peaceful manner. However, when I hung up I started to wonder if going to London was a wise thing to do. However love is blind and I had already purchased the ticket so away I went wondering what the journey would bring.

I didn't have to wait long to find out.

CHAPTER THIRTEEN

The Showman and the Shaman—Part Two

IT WAS AN EARLY evening flight from Toronto scheduled to land early the next morning in Britain. By now Simone had left the shelter and stayed at the airport all night to greet me. I suppose she slept on chairs and suchlike and would not have been noticed as a homeless person especially since she had a small case with her. It would have looked to people that she was just a traveller like anyone else. When I arrived off the plane she was there to greet me and actually seemed pleased to see me. I was in great trepidation as to what mood she was in but it turned out to be not bad at all. I hugged her tight and didn't want to let her go. All I wanted to do was protect and look after her as best I could and as a matter of fact it is all I ever wanted to do from the very beginning. She had purchased some herbal soap for me which she thought would help me with a skin ailment I had. I was touched that she would buy me a gift considering her meagre financial situation.

As we went into London on the subway system known by the locals as "The Tube" I alluded to her shouting at me on the phone previous to the flight and was brave enough to say, "I am glad to see you but I hope you are not going to start screaming at me again". She replied by saying, "You must remember that I am very vulnerable". I remember thinking uncharitably that it was the person being screamed at, namely me, that was "vulnerable" but I let the remark go. Of course she was right and she was indeed vulnerable and in this calmer moment she explained it to me. I don't think I appreciated her vulnerability properly at the time. When you are being screamed at with relentless fury you tend to focus on your own vulnerability rather than the attacker's. However, in the cold light of day I do see how vulnerable she was and how her behaviour would be an even bigger burden because by its very nature it would not attract sympathy.

We got off at Earls Court station since I had booked accommodation in this area. However, to my surprise Simone didn't want to stay with me there straight away. She said she needed to go somewhere else for a few days but she said if I showed her where the hotel was, she would join me there later in the week. I had no idea where she wanted to go and I still don't know but I was happy to agree to this. I knew I would be paying for her so the fewer days the better I supposed.

And then she did a very interesting thing. She offered to buy me breakfast! I think it was a matter of pride for her to do this so I agreed readily since I wanted to help raise her self-esteem in any way I could. We spent a very pleasant breakfast together and she seemed to be back to a cheerful mood and Happy Spirit reigned once again. She revealed that she was seeing a psychiatrist who had prescribed some medication that calmed her down. I was of course glad to hear this. However, I wished she had taken said medicine a couple of nights before when she had screamed at me on the phone.

After breakfast we agreed to go our separate ways except for one brief excursion of which I shall tell more anon. I had shown her where the hotel was and assumed she would show up in a few days. I wasn't a hundred percent sure of this since life with Simone was always unpredictable to say the least. The hotel was full of grafters since a major exhibition was on. This was the Ideal Homes Exhibition sponsored by the Daily Mail newspaper and the exhibition hall at Earls Court was just a couple of blocks away. Terry, of whom I have spoken earlier, was there as well as other grafters some of whom I knew and some of whom I didn't. I had been out of Britain so long that new faces in the grafting business were beginning to emerge and I didn't know them all.

Just before Simone and I went our separate ways I suggested we visit the exhibition. I knew Terry was there and I hadn't seen him for a while and was anxious to meet up with him again. Simone had once spoken to him on the phone when she was staying with me in Toronto. I had handed the phone over to her to speak to Terry for the first time. She duly informed him that she spoke to trees on a regular basis. Terry, quick as a flash retorted, "That is because you are barking mad!" Simone burst out laughing but vowed she would get revenge on him one day!

Simone was in a merry and mischievous mood when we entered the exhibition. We discovered Terry's booth but he hadn't seen us yet. She knew he would have no idea what she looked like so she decided to surprise him. She made me hide for a moment and went up to him and stated "I have been sent to say that I am your new employee and I am starting today!" She burst into laughter, however, which rather gave the game away and Terry asked where I was. She giggled and told him that she wanted to get him back for the "barking mad" remark. I appeared and introduced Simone properly.

Terry had arranged exhibition passes for both me and Simone so we could go in and out without having to pay. We took possession of them and departed to let Terry get on with his work. We met some other grafters there some of whom gave Simone frosty looks because they could perhaps sense there was something not quite right about her but one grafter called Norman treated her with great respect and for that I was grateful. In fact at a later stage he said, "She is one of us". even when he knew about her problems. At the time I considered that to be a classy thing to say and in fact I still do.

After we left the exhibition, Simone went to wherever she was going to go and I awaited her arrival at the hotel, which she promised to be a few days later. True to her word she did show up perhaps two days later and I paid for her to have a room. Unfortunately, at the hotel she unhappily started to show her aggressive side once again and it became clear that she wasn't taking her medication with as much self-discipline as she needed to. I found it very difficult to calm her down and she started to become a little paranoic as she often did when she was unwell. For example, service at breakfast was a little slow as it always was in this particular hotel. She started to mutter threateningly that the waitresses were racist and were ignoring her because she was black. I explained to her that there were lots of white people in the room looking irritated because they hadn't had their breakfast either. She became increasingly difficult to handle during our time in this accommodation and she started to frequently swear at me when I wanted to speak to her.

One day, we went to the exhibition fairly late in the evening and the adventure turned out to be a trifle disastrous. I showed my pass to the security man on the door but Simone couldn't find hers. She had a little bag of stuff with her and rummaged through it to no avail and finally snapped viciously at the guy and demanded, "I can't find it. Let me in. You are going to be closed soon anyway". The security man said, "I am sorry, Madam. You must show your pass". I could see where this was going so I said, "Simone. Just calm down and find your pass". Then I spotted it among all her multitude of papers and possessions in the bag and said, "There it is!" She aggressively pulled it out of her bag and showed it to the security man with the worst of grace and stormed past him snarling, "You are a racist!" For some odd reason this somewhat accusatory remark did not put the chap in the best of humour and he looked like he was going to explode. By this time Simone had started up an escalator leaving me alone with this poor harassed guardian of the Ideal Homes Exhibition. I quietly said to him so Simone wouldn't hear, "I do apologise. I am afraid she hasn't taken her medication today" then I skedaddled towards the escalator too. As I travelled upwards I heard him call after me, "Sir. I suggest she does take her medication in the future otherwise I shall be obliged to lodge a complaint".

Simone heard that and realised even in her agitated state that this would get Terry into trouble for giving us passes in the first place and she quietly admitted that this would not be a good outcome. It was her only lucid statement of the evening. She started to act in a very strange manner at the exhibition and I realised I would have to get her out of there fast and back to the hotel and insist she took her medication which she had left behind in the room. I went to Terry's booth without Simone since she had stopped nearby to loiter at another exhibitor and I felt I needed to get away from her for at least a brief moment. I said to Terry "I am here but now I have to leave just as soon as I have arrived. There is a problem". Terry has always been very perceptive and replied, "This has something to do with a certain black female, isn't it?" I said weakly, "You could say that, I suppose," and skedaddled over to Simone before she started to raise too much havoc.

She had cheered up but was acting in a very strange manner. She went up to a booth and we saw an important looking middle-aged woman going into a back stockroom. I assumed that this was the manager of the company or perhaps even the owner. Simone told a young salesgirl that she wanted to speak to the lady who had disappeared into the back. The girl looked very hesitant to bring the lady who was probably her boss out to meet this strange black girl in front of her. I said, "Come on Simone, let's go. It doesn't matter. You don't really need to see that lady". However, Simone insisted strongly, with great persistence, that she needed to see the woman. I was cringing inwardly and wanted to walk away but I couldn't leave Simone unattended in case there were eruptions of volcanic proportions.

The salesgirl gave in with great reluctance and the older lady appeared with a very quizzical look. Simone said to her, "I have to see you to offer you this" and gave the woman a candy saying, "It will bring you good fortune because you are a soul who needs it".

To this day I can't remember if the woman took the candy or not. I think she did but that is not my most vivid vision of the encounter. No. The vision is of the woman's face and the sheer astonished bemusement on it. One can only imagine what her inner reaction was to being dragged out of her stockroom where she was no doubt engaged in more pressing business simply to be offered a candy and a blessing. The poor salesgirl who fetched her probably got reprimanded for it, I imagine.

I knew I had to get Simone out of the exhibition fast before we both got arrested or at best thrown out by security so I dragged her out and back to the hotel as fast as I could and insisted she take her medication.

It continued to be a stressful time in Earls Court with Simone but the last straw was when I went into her room where she was awake and lying up in bed. Suddenly, she shocked me by blowing her nose into the bed sheets. I knew the cleaning staff would discover this and I could take the embarrassment no longer. I decided to move with Simone to a different hotel.

Before we left Simone insisted that we exchange luggage. This puzzled me since my suitcase was tattered and torn to pieces and it looked as if I were the homeless one who owned it whereas Simone owned a spotlessly clean and in good condition suitcase which I assume someone gave to her as a present since it was in such good condition and obviously fairly new.

I refused to give her my tattered suitcase in exchange for her much nicer one and thought I was doing the right thing. She explained, however, that her mint condition suitcase made her a target for theft in the shelters she stayed at. This never occurred to me and in fact wouldn't occur to those of us who lead more normal lives but when she explained it the logic made perfect sense. I accepted the deal with a vague sense of guilt nevertheless.

I didn't have a new hotel booked but I had a bit of an idea where to find one. However, I got an impression that Simone resented the idea of moving and she acted more strangely than ever. She must have been under a terrific strain when we left the hotel to go down to the area where I thought we would find accommodation. Sudden change made her very unstable and I don't think I realised that at the time. Of course she was pretty unstable to start with.

We got on the tube to Victoria station where she insisted she wanted to go to first before finding a hotel. I wasn't sure why we had to go there but I could see the warning signs of her mood darkening so I didn't argue.

The luggage was getting heavy to carry around so I suggested that we deposit it in Victoria Station left luggage office so that we could continue our wandering unencumbered. However, she said nothing and ploughed on regardless and I was forced to follow her. I could sense a storm brewing so I kept silent. She was very silent too and I was very apprehensive.

Eventually, we wandered into a street a little way away from Victoria station. It was a side street and slightly removed from the hustle and bustle. Simone seemed to know exactly where we were going but I didn't. It transpired that she had found out where there was a shelter that would take her in but didn't impart this information to me. She must have figured that once I had left London she would have to find some place to stay. Or perhaps the fact that I had decided to change hotels precipitated a desire on her part to find somewhere on her own. I have no idea what strange thoughts were going on in her troubled mind.

She was headed for this shelter but wasn't quite sure where it was. We entered a building that seemed a likely place and it indeed was associated in some way with the shelter, which was actually a few doors away.

We entered a lobby area and there were big glass screens all around the reception area. Behind the screens was a nun with her back to us on the telephone. I assumed this was a Catholic charity organisation. Suddenly Simone started to bang on the glass in a very aggressive manner to attract the attention of the nun who turned around in a very irritated manner to scowl at the cause of the interruption to her phone call. She then turned away again but Simone would have none of it and started to bang on the glass once more in a somewhat demented fashion.

The nun couldn't ignore Simone any longer and slid back a window in the glass saying, "Couldn't you see I was on the phone?" That set off Simone in a screaming rage and I wanted the ground to swallow me up. I didn't know where to look as the poor nun was berated as a racist and God knows what else. I tried to interject and Simone screamed at me to be quiet. The nun looked at me and said, "Who are you? Are you trying to help her?" I replied, "Are you the shelter?" Whereupon the nun said, "No, that is a few doors away. You will have to leave". Simone showed no sign of any willingness to depart although I certainly did. Instead, she screamed and shouted as if possessed by Satan and perhaps she actually was. Nuns aren't too keen on Satan and the holy one was getting very angry and did a bit of shouting herself yelling, "Get out of here otherwise I shall call the police!"

I decided that leaving the premises was a rather meritorious suggestion and I took advantage of it rather speedily. Simone, however, did not and as I stood outside in the street I could hear screeching and screaming from inside and I was beginning to wonder if the end of the world was nigh.

Eventually, a rather distressed Simone exited the premises and I tried to calm her down to no avail. She screamed and screamed at me and I thought the torrent would never end. I could take it no more and I walked away from her as fast as I could with my suitcase trailing behind me. I had arranged earlier to meet her outside Hamley's department store in Regent St at 6.00 p.m. where I had to do some business later in the day and I yelled out to her, "I can't take any more. I'll see you outside Hamleys at six p.m". She screamed in return, "I won't be there!" And she wasn't.

I continued walking for a few minutes then turned around and Simone was no longer there. I went back to see if I could find her. I located the shelter proper and managed to find my way in. Suddenly I saw her seated with her back to me talking to a staff member. She had stopped screaming but was obviously in some distress with tears flowing so I decided to sneak out the way I came and leave her in the hands of people who were trained to handle her.

I was crying my eyes out myself. I loved her but I couldn't deal with her. I have never seen her again from that day to this. However, the story wasn't over by a long chalk. There were still a few years left of contact with her by letter and phone of which more anon.

As I write all this I am overcome with wonder as to why I tried for so hard and for so long to help her. The reader of this train wreck of a story must be wondering too. Why didn't I dump her? Why didn't I cut my losses when I had the chance? Why didn't I cut loose from her misery that in turn was bringing me misery? Why? Why? Why?

Love. No other reason. And I love her still.

I wish this description and story were over so I could leave it behind me. However, there is more to come. I never saw her again but there were still years of contact left. Not easy years either. Let me plough on with this saga albeit with a heavy heart.

Later in the day, I went over to Hamley's to do my business and see if she was there to meet me as previously arranged. She wasn't. I had moved hotel by this time and I had called the shelter but they would give me no information on the grounds of protecting the privacy of those who took who took refuge with them.

At this stage so many years later I cannot remember how I did it but I managed to locate a nun who did some voluntary work at the shelter and spoke to her about Simone. She hadn't met her but said she would keep an eye out for her. She gave me encouragement and told me I had done enough for her and should move on. "You have done more than your share," she said. I knew I couldn't move on but wished I could. She also made a remark that resonated with me. She said, "These people in their more lucid moments do realise that those trying to assist them are not their enemy even though they appear to show great resentment towards them and often resist and refuse their help".

I did find that scenario with Simone over the years. When she was in a calm and lucid frame of mind she would realise that I had only benevolent intentions. I am afraid, however, that her calmer moments were not something to be relied on.

The wise counsel of the nun encouraged me and I continued my stay in London without Simone. Eventually, I returned to Toronto and resolved to make contact with her somehow. I had no idea how, of course, and I did not hear a single word from her despite sending letters to her care of the shelter. Of course I had no idea if she was even at the shelter any more. At this point it seemed like it was over but actually it wasn't.

I returned to London a year later on business so I took the opportunity of trying to find Simone. I went to the shelter but there was no sign of her. I spoke to one of the senior staff who would give no indication whether Simone was there or not because of the usual privacy stuff. I got the impression, however, that she knew her and I had a feeling that Simone wasn't there any longer but that she used the place as a mailing address. The woman suggested that I leave a letter for her, adding that it may or may not get to her. She would not confirm or deny that Simone visited but I took it as a hint that she did. I did write out something, sealed it in an envelope that the woman supplied and gave it to her.

As I left the shelter I noticed a row of little boxes on the wall with names of people. There was mail in the boxes. I figured that this was the shelter's mailing address service for their clients. As I have indicated earlier her real name was not Simone and that is being used here solely for the purpose of this book. Her actual name is a much more uncommon one and I figured that if one of the boxes had her name it would be a fairly safe bet that she was indeed receiving mail at the shelter. And indeed her name was there in all its glory. I realised with relief that she would probably receive my communication. In the letter I had indicated where she could contact me in London but I heard nothing. I left London with a heavy heart burdened by the fact that I couldn't find her.

When I returned to Toronto I did some investigating to see if I could find her. At this late stage so many years later I just plain can't remember how I located her, but locate her I did. As I write, I am racking my brains to recall how I did it. The only possibility I can think of is that she wrote to me out of the blue with a few clues as to where I could find her. I do remember getting two very puzzling and contradictory responses from her at one point. Possibly they were replies to me since I kept writing to her via the shelter. One was a postcard and one was a letter. They were both posted around the same time and in fact possibly the same day. They were both addressed to me and were very contradictory. The postcard was a very aggressive and nasty one full of hate and venom and the other was much friendlier with a picture of a happy face on it. I suppose one was written by Light Spirit and the other was written by Nasty Spirit.

I wrote back and answered the friendly message and ignored the venomous one. From this I managed to continue an erratic correspondence with her. There was of course, no way of making phone contact unless she phoned me, which was rare. I then set up a phone line for her that I still have to this day. It is a service where people can call me from the UK to Toronto and it costs them nothing. It costs me money of course but not the calling party. I called it the Simone Hotline and told her that she should call it any time day or night if she needed me. Calls were a little more frequent from her when I did that but still very sporadic.

When she was well I would receive birthday and Christmas cards from her, when she was unwell I wouldn't. I was terribly sad for her but I was getting a feeling that she was receiving more assistance from the social welfare authorities in the UK than she would ever have received in Canada.

One day she phoned me with wonderful news. She had been found a flat in London by the social welfare authorities. Not only that, she now had a phone in the accommodation that I could actually made calls to. She seemed happy to give me the number. A member of the support staff of the housing association visited her once a week. I got the impression that this was support housing for people like Simone and was a government project of some kind.

Apparently some homeless people who were deemed to be capable of looking after themselves with a little assistance from support staff were given free accommodation subsidised by the taxpayer. Her only expense was her phone and of course she had to buy her own food. I don't think the place was of great luxurious standard but at least she wasn't on the street and I was grateful beyond measure that she now had a roof over her head.

However, the best part of her news was the fact that it had been deemed by the social welfare authorities that she was entitled to disability payments because of her problems, since it was obvious that she would not be employable. Not only that, but it had been decided that she was entitled to several years of retroactive back payments. It turned out that she now had more money than me!

Even more good news was that she had reunited with her estranged family once again. She said that her brother was riding through the streets of London on a motorbike and spotted her. I said to Simone, "That was a piece of luck, wasn't it?" She replied, "Not really. I have six brothers. It was bound to happen sooner or later. I was just waiting for one of them to find me and I knew he would".

It seemed that she reunited with her family once before but went out for a walk and couldn't find her way back to their address and so ended up on the street again. This time at least she had an address and phone number where they could find her if she ever got lost again.

Her sister took an interest in her welfare but I got a vibe that sometimes she got on with her sister and sometimes she didn't. One of the hardest parts of dealing with Simone was that if you offered her help she would often refuse it. She hated being treated like a charity case and had great pride. However, she was indeed a charity case whether she liked it or not. Having said all that, I imagine that it would have been quite difficult for her sister to always be able to help her as efficiently as she may have liked to. I know I bloody couldn't.

Overall her situation was vastly improved but Simone was still Simone. She had always been her own worst enemy and now was no exception. I don't think she was entirely happy with her accommodation because of its location that was quite a way from downtown London where she preferred to haunt. I know she felt quite lonely and would sometimes tell me she preferred to be on the street where all her homeless friends were. This of course saddened me and I advised her to stay put. I told her to contact me any time she wanted on the Simone Hotline that I previously mentioned. I also said I would phone her from time to time to make sure she was okay.

Once she told me a story that made me very sad. It appeared that she made friends in a park with a man from Glasgow. It seemed that she was sitting on a park bench and got into conversation with him. I think she met him previously a few times in the park. She had a mouse in her flat that she was terrified of and she invited him round to visit in order to protect her from the mouse. He declined the invitation and she felt rejected and in addition to this, scared of the mouse. I was three thousand miles away and couldn't help her with the mouse but I advised her to talk about it to the support officer who came to visit her once a week.

I believe the loneliness and isolation of where she lived was beginning to hamper her return to a normal state of mental health and I was getting quite concerned. I would get messages from her on my voice mail that she believed that she had a missing twin that was in the womb with her at birth. That was only one of her departures from reality; there were many more. For example she once phoned me and asked for three thousand pounds for some psychic procedure that would free her from her torment. I declined because first, I didn't have three grand to give away and second, I wasn't terribly excited about "psychic" cures anyway. Don't get me wrong. I would give any amount of money tomorrow if I could cure her and bring her back to good health but I felt this nonsense wasn't the way.

She was so lonely that she offered another homeless woman some shelter in her apartment. This lady was living in her car. However, the deal fell through rather quickly when Simone hit the lady in the head with her shoe in one of her usual fits of temper.

This is the person that I loved and still love. As I write this account I am beginning to wonder if I am just as crazy as Simone. How could a sane person love someone like this? I must take a deep breath, count to ten and attempt to continue this painful narrative.

Sorry. I can't. I must stop. I am going out to the park to meditate or something. When I return I shall continue….

I have returned and still cannot continue. Later. Later….

And now we continue. One day she phoned me with in great panic and distress saying she was going to be thrown out of her apartment by the housing association. Accordingly, I phoned up the housing association on her behalf and talked to a lady who knew Simone. The woman was most indignant and said they wouldn't dream of throwing anyone out on the street and it was purely a matter of some bureaucratic paperwork that Simone couldn't handle but that the housing support officer would help her with. She remarked that she thought originally that Simone was very nice but was taken aback once to find her in one of her screaming moods. It seemed that she had met both Light Spirit and Nasty Spirit on two different occasions.

She referred me to the lady who was her support officer and gave me her phone number. This particular lady was very open and friendly and I think probably the best support officer that Simone ever had. I was sad when she moved on. However, she spoke to me and told me she liked Simone very much and agreed with me that she wasn't as insane as people thought she was. She agreed to keep my calls to her secret since she knew that they would get a negative reaction from Simone. She told me that Simone was coming to Canada on a certain date and I was very surprised by this. However, I was assured that it was true and my contact informed me that she had helped Simone buy the ticket.

I mistakenly assumed she was coming to Toronto to see me and got all excited. However, on the appointed day of arrival I heard nothing. I thought for sure she was going to phone me. I found out later that she was headed for Vancouver and obviously hadn't given me a thought. As it happens her flight was cancelled because of bad weather conditions and I think a hurricane was involved somehow. She eventually got a refund from the airline with the help of the housing support officer.

When I never heard from her it dawned upon me that the immigration authorities might have detained her. I do know that she had previous problems with them in Vancouver and had been asked to leave the country. It seems that she was supposed to buy a ticket, go to the airport and after her luggage was checked in for the flight, go to the immigration authorities to hand in her departure papers and go through some bureaucratic rigmarole. She intended to leave but it went a little haywire. She did indeed buy a ticket. I am not sure how she got the money since she wasn't being deported but by the sound of it merely being given a "departure notice" which wasn't quite as serious but it did mean that she had to leave under her own steam.

However, as always she had no actual luggage so there was nothing for her to check in as baggage although she did check in and receive a boarding pass.

She then went over to the immigration department as she had been instructed to do but apparently the place was mobbed with people and very busy. It seems that an overtaxed immigration official told her to "just drop the paperwork in there" and then waved her through.

She was now in the airport with a boarding pass and no actual luggage on the plane. She therefore decided that she didn't want to leave Canada after all and headed back into town.

Eventually, of course, she left Canada as has been previously discussed in this narrative. However, she was coming back and it seemed to me that the immigration department would have had a record of her shenanigans and may have detained her at the airport. It seems that she had been designated as a special needs person by the airline that allowed her to travel. All this made me nervous that she wouldn't get past immigration so when I heard nothing from her I decided to investigate.

I called immigration at the airport but they seemed to have no record of her arriving. Eventually, I was put through to an immigration officer who asked some details about her. He ran her through his computer and it was evident there was something there which raised his eyebrows. He said, "We don't have her in detention but if she calls you, I suggest you contact the police". I asked why but he wouldn't tell me. He did give me her first name, which wasn't Simone as I thought. That was actually her second name. He also told me her date of birth and it was obvious that they had some record of her.

I assumed that she had somehow slipped through immigration into Canada but I was wrong. I had no idea she was headed for Vancouver and not Toronto and I was a little hurt by this. I also had no idea she didn't make it to Canada after all, but that the flight had been cancelled and she had to get a refund.

Then one day the isolation got too much for her. It was near Christmas when all hell broke loose. I once read that there are more suicides around the Christmas season than any other time and I quite believe it.

She phoned me in great distress one night saying that there were aliens from outer space entering her mind and possessing her. It must have been around 3.00 a.m. British time when she called. She had complained about aliens before but to a much more mild extent. She told me the aliens were making her do things she didn't want to do such as going into freezing bus shelters for no reason. She told me that the aliens were telling her to kill herself and I became greatly alarmed.

I made a three-way phone call to someone I knew who was an expert on UFOs to see if he could advise her on the matter and calm her down. This was to no avail and she continued to threaten suicide. I advised her to go to hospital but she would have none of it. I told her I was getting on a plane to come and see her. She said, "By the time you arrive I won't be here so there is no point coming".

I was frightened and quite distressed. I then made a three-way call to Lisa who by now had moved to Las Vegas. Simone had now grown to like Lisa and had grown away from her initial distrust. I figured also that Lisa would bring some calmness and objectivity to the situation because I was in such a state of fear and emotional distress myself that I couldn't think straight while talking to her. I was truly scared she was going to kill herself. Now it is possible that she was saying those things merely as a cry for help but I couldn't take a chance on that and was scared half to death by her threats of suicide.

Lisa spoke to her very quietly and soon calmed her down. Between both of us we managed to persuade Simone to check into a hospital. I truly believe that Lisa saved her life that night although I can't say it for certain. However, I do know that if I hadn't called Lisa, God alone knows what would have happened to poor Simone.

She was accepted into one of the wards of the hospital. I think it was a psychiatric hospital she had been a resident of on a previous occasion. I phoned her a few times to see if she was okay. I was alarmed to find that sometimes she wasn't there and had been allowed to roam the streets of London and come back to the hospital to sleep. Of course, my imagination was working overtime and I was still in fear of her harming myself. I was very panic stricken during this period and I demanded to speak to her doctor. The nurses told me that if I wasn't a relative I couldn't speak to her doctor. I retorted that I was the one that persuaded her to admit herself to the hospital in the first place and moreover, I was concerned that she had been allowed to leave the hospital where she could do harm to herself. Furthermore, I told them that I knew her better than anyone else and I could give the doctor some insight about her. I was assured that she was perfectly safe and in a perfectly decent state of mind to leave the hospital. Now, in retrospect, I am sure they were correct but at the time I was in a state of panic and stressed out over the whole thing. Consequently, I couldn't think straight.

I gave them the Simone hotline number and told them that it wouldn't cost the hospital anything to phone me in Canada and let me know what was going on. Again I demanded to speak to the doctor.

Lo and behold, a day or two later the doctor actually phoned me and I told him all that I knew about Simone. He said she was on medication and was fine. I asked what her illness was. He paused and said, "She suffers from some sort of personality disorder". I remember thinking that you didn't have to study at medical school for years to figure that one out.

Simone had for some time diagnosed herself as suffering from Asperger's Syndrome and kept telling me how autistic she was. I thought she didn't fit the description of autistic to me since she was very communicative indeed but she explained that she was mute as a child and had made great improvement. For quite a while she convinced me that she did indeed suffer from Asperger's Syndrome because a few of the symptoms seemed to match her when I made some uneducated research on the matter.

I asked the doctor about this and he laughed and said, "No, she doesn't have Asperger's Syndrome although she likes to think she has and it gives her some comfort to believe it!"

I told him I was surprised to hear she didn't have it and he told me that he knew her as an old patient and in the past she had been thoroughly checked by specialists because of her insistence that she had it. It seemed the specialists were adamant she didn't.

I told him about the "aliens" that were bothering her and he didn't really seem to know about them or appear particularly concerned. I do know that she had told me that she didn't want to tell doctors about the voices in her head in case she was "sectioned". This is the expression used in the UK for people who are detained under the Mental Health act for their own safety and the safety of others. He merely told me that he found my information about Simone very useful and that she was in good hands and I shouldn't worry about her.

Of course, worry about her I did and when I spoke to her at the hospital I told her that maybe I should come over and visit her. She said I could if I wanted to so I started to make plans to visit her as soon as possible. I tried to purchase an airline ticket to London. However, airfares over the Christmas season were inordinately expensive and I realised I couldn't afford to visit. Suddenly, however, a very cheap ticket became available and I snapped it up without thinking and purchased it on a friend's credit card since my own credit card had reached its limit.

Then to my horror as I calmed down from my panic I realised that I had wasted my money and I couldn't afford to come after all. This was because one of the conditions of the cheaper ticket was that I would have to stay at least three weeks and keep to the specified dates. I realised that I hadn't thought the matter through and that I couldn't possibly afford to stay three weeks in expensive London with no work or income coming in over there. I cancelled the flight with no refund and had to pay my friend back the money for the ticket I hadn't used.

All in all, my relationship with Simone was one disaster after another. But love is blind and I cared terribly about her. I phoned and told her that I couldn't come after all and she seemed to accept it too readily for my liking saying, "Perhaps it is just as well".

She eventually left hospital and went back to her flat. She seemed to make good progress and I was beginning to hope that the worst was over. She told me that she still heard the aliens talking to her but the voices weren't as strong. No doubt this was because of the medication she had been given. Once I got brave enough to hint to her that the aliens were in her imagination and she got very angry with me screaming in the usual manner over the phone.

However, overall there seemed to be great progress and my hopes were high that she was back on track. Alas there was more distress to come.

For quite a long time she seemed to be doing great and when I phoned her I experienced lucid and intelligent conversations and all was well. She still complained about the voices in her head but they seemed very muted. Then one day I phoned her and she hung up without a word. I thought perhaps I had dialed the wrong number so tried again with exactly the same result. She hung up.

I couldn't figure out why she would suddenly hang up when all previous calls over the preceding year or so had been perfectly amicable. Still, I knew she would get into strange moods so I decided to leave it for a few days before phoning her again. However, again she hung up. And again and again over the next few days. I couldn't figure out what was wrong.

I knew her mother lived in Jamaica and had invited her over to stay. Presumably the mother paid for her flight. She had told me her mother was a healer who would help her. I had my doubts but I could do nothing to influence the situation. I figured that since she would shortly be leaving for Jamaica I would wait until she returned before I tried to contact her again. When she was in Jamaica I left a message on her London answering machine wishing her a good trip and that I would contact her when she returned.

I also wrote her a letter before she departed. I figured it might make her angry as hell but I had to say what I had to say. I felt I couldn't go along with the aliens story any more. I knew that you weren't supposed to tell people who were under a delusion that the delusion wasn't true but I couldn't take it any more and let rip. This is what I said.

Dearest Simone,

I have been worried sick about you. I just want you to know that I still care about you and want to help you in any way I can. That is all I have ever wanted to do.

At the risk of making you angry I have to tell you that there are no "aliens"—THEY DO NOT EXIST. It is simply your mind playing tricks on you. When you realise this then your "cure" will come.

I don't believe you are mentally ill and never have. You are as sane as I am. However, I do believe that your nerves have been sensitized beyond measure by your difficult and stressful life and because of this your mind is playing tricks on you.

Your isolation isn't helping either. When you are alone moping it must make things worse.

I know that these "aliens" seem real to you. I know it is difficult to accept that they don't exist. Well, they don't and never did. I cannot humour you with this stuff any longer. I believe that a lot of this "psychic" and "new age" stuff is harmful to you. Don't forget I know quite a bit about it too.

Your trouble is that you are too much of an expert on this stuff and it is not good for you. A little can be helpful but too much is a mental toxic.

You can show this letter to your doctor or anybody you like. I can assure you that I am sincere and always have been. I only wish you well and care about you more than I should.

I don't think you realise how distressed I get when you are going through all these hard periods. However I KNOW you are going to prevail in the end. Don't give in. There are people who care about you.

All my love,

Mark

One day a few weeks later I got a phone message on my voice mail from Simone telling me to phone a number in Jamaica and ask for someone called "Broom". I had no idea who Broom was but I knew by now that Simone had returned to London. I called her but as soon as she heard my voice she hung up. I then phoned Broom, whoever the hell he was but was told I had the wrong number. I have often wondered whether the number she gave me was that of her mother and she had confused Broom's number with that.

I phoned her again and before she could hang up I said "I phoned Broom!" There was a pause and then she spoke. "What did he say?" I told her she had given me the wrong number and asked her the correct one. She gave me another number and then abruptly hung up on me. I had no idea what was going on.

I phoned the new number in Jamaica and asked for Broom. A woman said in a thick Jamaican accent that I could hardly understand, "Broom not here. Why you want Broom?" I told her that I had no idea why I wanted Broom but that I was told to call him by a lady in England. A difficult conversation followed since I could hardly understand a word the woman said and she sounded very guarded and reluctant to put me in touch with Broom. I smelled something very fishy going on and I didn't like it. The woman told me to call back.

I did many times and Broom never seemed to be available. Furthermore, I couldn't understand a word the woman was saying with her thick accent. I enlisted the help of my good friend Paul Pacific whom I had taught the psychic fair business to. Paul is a very fine mentalist stage performer. For those of you who do not know what a "mentalist" is I can only describe it as a magician who does magic tricks with a mindreading theme. Paul was the friend I mentioned previously whose credit card I used to purchase my aborted air ticket to London.

When I phoned Jamaica I sometimes passed the phone over to Paul to see if he could make out what the woman was saying. He didn't do much better than me.

Eventually, by some miracle I actually got through to Broom. It turned out that he was a very old man in his seventies or eighties and he was even more difficult to understand than the woman. I made a three-way call to Paul who was at that time standing on a station waiting for a commuter train. Paul had his cell phone with him and tried to assist me in understanding Broom. However, neither of us could make head nor tail of Broom's mumbling. I got the impression that Broom had never heard of Simone or certainly couldn't remember her. In the end neither Paul nor I could understand Broom and I am quite sure he couldn't understand us either so that as they say was that. I ended the call and wondered where all this was going. My phone bill was mounting up with all these useless calls to Jamaica and I was no wiser as to what Broom was supposed to tell me. I had an instinct, however, that he was some kind of psychic or healer.

I was about to give up on all this nonsense but I thought I would give it one last shot. I had resolved not to speak to Broom again but to talk to the woman instead since she seemed more articulate and I could understand her better than Broom. I phoned her and tried to explain the situation with Simone as best I could. I gleaned some information this time that made me feel very uncomfortable indeed.

She remembered Simone and told me that she had arrived for "healing" with her mother who presumably brought her. She said, "You must mean the very nice girl who brought her mother. She had voices in her head". I agreed that this was the person I was concerned about. It seemed that Broom was some sort of healer but I was getting a vibe from the guarded conversation that Simone had been scammed out of a lot of money and I was quite upset.

It seems that she had been given some liquid that was supposed to cure her before she left for the airport back to England. She was supposed to drink it before she got to the airport because if the authorities found it there would be big trouble. I have no idea what the drink was or why the authorities wouldn't like it. I smelled a rat and didn't like the whole thing which sounded like some kind of psychic scam of which there are a great many.

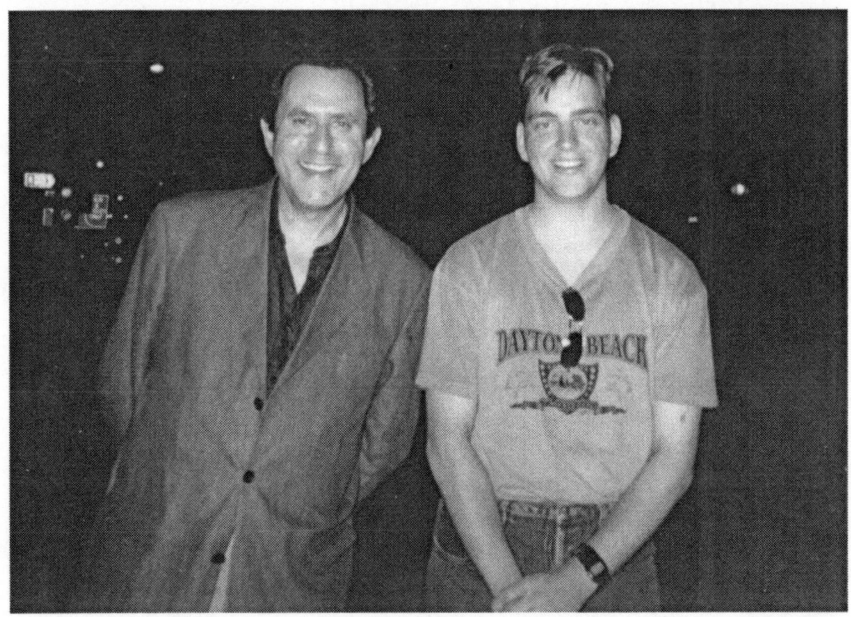

Paul Pacific and Michael Vine

I ended the call which at least gave me some clarification. I still had no idea why I was supposed to phone Broom but I am now speculating that perhaps he told her to have nothing to do with me and that she was to instruct me to phone him and he would tell me himself. Of course, he didn't and I am sure he never gave her a thought once he got rid of her and took her money.

I called Simone and before she could hang up informed her that I had finally spoken to Broom. Again she wanted to know what he said and I replied that he didn't say much at all and what he did say I couldn't understand. She abruptly hung up on me when she heard that.

At that point I had no idea what to do. I think in fact that I just gave up. I couldn't call Simone any more since she would simply hang up and it dawned on me that if I wrote she probably wouldn't read the letter or if she did, would throw it in the garbage in a great fury.

I decided at that point to just let God take care of her because I didn't know how to. I prayed for her but made no further attempt to contact her. I had figured that I could do no more and that it was all finished.

However, Simone doesn't go away that easily. Perhaps nine months later the phone rang in the middle of the night. I just knew that it was Simone. If she wanted to leave a message and she didn't want to speak to me personally she would phone when I was asleep. Of course the phone would always wake me up. I dragged myself over to the phone to see if a message had been left. It had. This is the message:

> *"This is Simone. Things are much better for me now. Especially since you have stopped contacting me. I don't know what else to say. I don't hate you. I don't have a problem with you. I just wanted my space and I'm glad that I've got it".*

I went back to bed but couldn't sleep. I didn't know what to do. I was tempted to phone her and perhaps I should have. However, I didn't want her to hang up on me again and when I analysed the message I got a bit discouraged. On one hand perhaps, she wanted to make contact with me after all but on the other hand I didn't like the fact that she said "I'm glad that I've got it", referring to her space. It was in the present tense and seemed to imply that she was happy with the lack of contact with me and that was the way she wanted it.

On the other hand why did she call? I speculated that she might have received a letter from me a year or so earlier that she had not opened because it was from me. Perhaps she may have belatedly decided to open it just before she made the nocturnal phone call and realised it was full of compassion for her and had no ill intent. In the letter I probably expressed worry about her and she felt that she at least owed me the knowledge that she was all right. In fact I had been praying that I would somehow find out that she was all right and perhaps this middle of the night phone call was the answer to the prayer.

The next day I ruminated as to what my best option was. Should I call her and invite rejection? Perhaps that was the course of action that I should have followed but I decided not to. I took the coward's way out and decided to write to her.

This is what I wrote:

Dearest Simone,

I got your message. I am glad things are going better for you. I have been praying for it. You know I will always support you. Just remember that I am vulnerable too.

You want your space. You have it. I will only contact you from now on if you contact me first.

I don't know what else to say. You know where to find me.

Love,
Mark

She did not respond. I have not heard a word from her from that day to this and I don't suppose I ever shall. It has been some time now. I don't know if she is alive or dead. I don't know where she is or how she is doing. I don't know if there is a roof over her head or if she is lying in a gutter somewhere. I pray for her even though I don't believe in God. Yet I pray for her anyway just in case.

I told my brother that she didn't seem to want to speak to me any more and he said, "You have to respect that".

And I do. The end is the end. If it is indeed the end. Sometimes with Simone things are not always what they seem.

I will always love her though.

CHAPTER FOURTEEN

The Final Word

THIS WILL BE THE shortest chapter in the book. Mainly because I don't have much else left to say. I am sixty-five years old now and I am not quite sure how I got this far. It reminds me of the time I once spoke to a gypsy fortune teller, whom I knew in Blackpool, that was glaring at all the people that were walking by outside her little parlour on the promenade. Normally, she would be hustling them to come in by various methods but at this particular moment she just scowled at everyone walking by. The promenade seemed to be filled with fairly elderly people for some reason. Perhaps it was one of those weeks when all the old people visited Blackpool.

I asked her why she wasn't hustling them in to see her and she snarled, "I tell the future. These are old people who have no future!"

Despite the above, I think I still have a little juice left in me. At the time of writing in addition to the magic and hypnotism shows I still do I am active in promoting a rather different type of grafting. Terribly well paid and vastly higher class. I am a trade show magician.

Now the question arises, "What is a trade show magician?" Briefly the idea is that a company will hire me to work all day on their trade show booth. I attract crowds to the booth in exactly the same way I attracted crowds when I sold Svengali decks. I perform various card tricks and other close quarter magic and put the audience into a good mood and in a receptive frame of mind to do business with the company. During the show I pre-qualify prospects by asking one or two questions and ask for a show of hands. This show of hands indicates to the watching salesmen who are the best potential prospects among the crowd. At the end of the ten-minute-show I inveigle the crowd on to the booth to have their badges scanned and collect a free gift that the salesmen present to them for filling out a lead form and enables the representatives on the booth to increase the leads they get at the show. Companies find this a fantastic way to garner leads from exhibitors and my presence increases their business at the show.

It is exactly like grafting and in fact is just another form of it. There are other magicians doing this kind of work but I can immodestly boast that I have drawn more crowds at exhibitions than all of them put together during my long career. I can outwork and outsell them all. I am truly in awe of my wondrous capability as a human being.

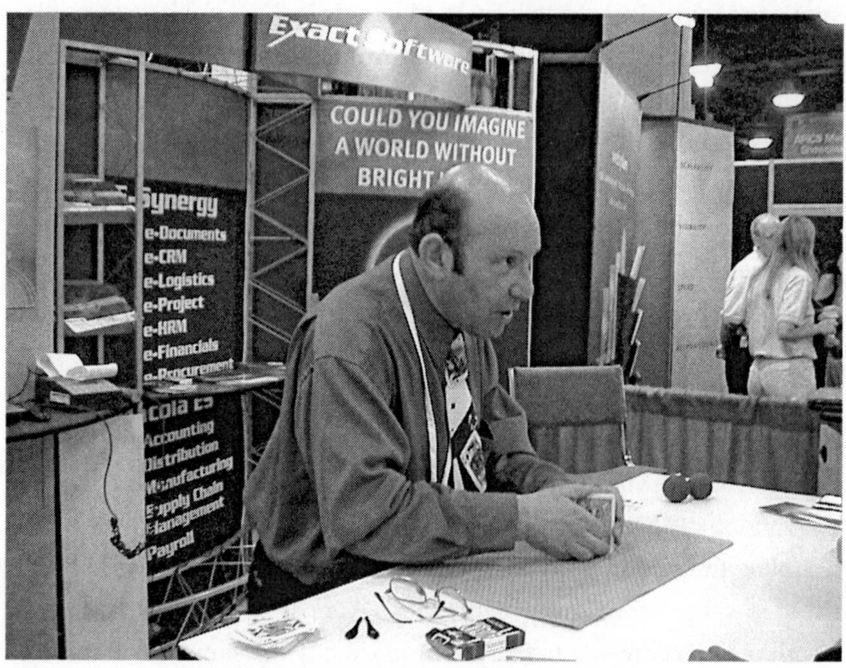

Working a trade show

I do hope my colleagues in this work emulate my modest disposition and I will be happy to act as a role model for them in this regard.

Seriously though, I have found that the only difference between being a trade show magician and a grafter is that I have to wear a suit and not insult the customers quite so much.

Trade show publicity card

Since I am a typical grafter I might as well get a commercial in. If any of my corporate readers want a trade show magician they can contact me through my website at www.marklewisentertainment.com. Here they will also find details of my corporate mindreading and hypnosis shows.

Now that my blatant advertising is over I must mention that an Atlanta magician named Joe Turner once referred to me thus, "I have met the devil and he is a Svengali pitchman turned corporate". I must say that this is my favourite description.

Now, a few years ago a young Vietnamese journalism student named Mai Nguyen was given an assignment to write an article about Toronto magicians. She phoned loads and loads of magicians in the city to see if she could come out and see one of their shows. She had no luck in this search until she came across me. I told her that there was indeed a place where she could come and watch me work. It was not at a corporate engagement, or a circus, or a night club, or a theatre. It was at a flea market. However, she could watch me for as long as she wanted and in fact she stayed for several hours.

Just before this book went to press I discovered that her professor was so pleased by the piece she wrote, that she submitted it in an application for the Jerry Gladman Memorial Scholarship and lo and behold she won!

She wrote such a charming little article that I wanted to include it in this book. Accordingly, I asked her permission to reproduce it here and she kindly allowed me to do so. I think it is a fitting conclusion to this memoir and describes me exactly. Read it and enjoy it. I shall now take my leave before I place you in her capable hands. Good health, good luck and goodbye.

> *The magician wriggles Jeremy the Magic Snake through his fingers, attracting a curious young boy who inches closer and closer.*
>
> *"Would you like to look at Jeremy?" he asks. "He likes children. He had one for breakfast this morning".*
>
> *The boy's mother approaches from behind and watches as the magic man slithers the furry, blue snake swiftly between his fingers, around a basket and through a book. Suddenly, the snake stops moving and falls asleep inside a glass jar. "Oh no! Can you do me a favour, young man? When I say three will you wake him up?" After the magic salesman counted to three, the boy loudly shouts, "Wake up, Jeremy".*
>
> *Magically, the blue snake swiftly slides up out of the jar and slithers back through the trickster's fingers. People, engrossed by the trick, stop to watch at a distance. "Come in closer everybody. Don't worry, I won't pick your pocket. I've got a brother out there that does that".*
>
> *Sporting a black tie adorned with stars, playing cards and white rabbits, magician Mark Lewis regularly performs magic tricks at a Flea Market in Toronto. He commutes on weekends to promote and sell his magic products. His booth attracts some of the largest crowds at the flea market.*

"Sometimes it's tough to get people's attention, but normally I can get a big crowd going".

As people begin to gather around the booth, the boy whispers to his mother, begging her to buy the snake. "You nag your mother until she buys it," says the magician. "Make her life miserable until she does. If that doesn't work, try your father". The mother ignores her son and walks him away from the booth.

At the booth, he revealed to his audience one of his most captivating tricks, the three-card trick. He lays out a three of diamonds, a four of clubs and a five of spades, all face up. Carefully, he flips each card over one by one, keeping them in order.

He singles out a young blonde woman. "Can you tell me which card is the four of clubs, please?"

She chooses the card in the middle with confidence. Before revealing it, he flips over the other cards, the three of diamonds and five of spades. He flips over the middle card. It's not the four of clubs. It's the queen of spades. The young woman is speechless. He picks up all three cards, fans them out and shows the audience. Now, the queen of spades had turned back into the four of clubs. The young woman's mouth is wide open.

"How did that happen?" says the young woman. "That is insane".

A young boy leans towards his sister and whispers, "How did he do that?"

Facing an open-jawed and wide-eyed audience, the magician continues with the performance. "Can anybody tell me where the queen is? Does anyone know where the queen is right now?" Everyone is silent. "I'll tell you where the queen is," he says. "She's in Buckingham Palace, that's where she is". The silence is replaced with laughter.

He continues with a new trick and whips out a deck of cards, showing the audience that each card is different. He fans the entire deck across the table, face down. He asks a man wearing a leather jacket to pick a card. The man pauses, contemplating which one to choose.

"You're quite slow," the magician comments. "Do you work for the post office?" The man finally chooses a card, keeping it hidden from the trickster. He reveals the card to the rest of the audience. The magician interrupts. "Just make sure you remember that nine of hearts, sir". The man smiles and returns the card. Indeed, it was a nine of hearts.

"Yes, we British are rather clever," says the UK magician. "That's how we won the Empire. I don't quite know why we lost it".

"Now, I know what you're thinking," he continues. "You're thinking that all the cards were nine of hearts. Well, you're wrong". He flips through the entire deck of cards, revealing each card to be different. "I told you. They're all different. If they were all nine of hearts, it would look like this". He quickly fans the same deck of cards across the table, revealing them now to be all nine of hearts. A bewildered woman grabs her partner's arm and hides her face in his sleeve. "Don't worry, though," says the magician. "They're not all nine of hearts because like I told you, they're all different". He collects the deck and flips through it once more, revealing all the cards to be different again.

Some audience members look at each other in astonishment. Some simply gaze at the cards. A teenager stares intently at the deck, rubbing his chin, trying to figure out how the trick was done. The bewildered woman and her partner are impressed. "How much is it for those cards?" asks the woman's partner.

The snake is $5. The magic cards with instructions are $10. A cup-and-ball trick is $5 and the three-card trick is $3.

"You can have the entire package, which comes with a book of 102 tricks, for just $20, but you can have my mother-in-law for free". The audience laughs. "This entire package comes with a money back guarantee," says the salesman/magician. "Providing you can find me".

Meanwhile, the young boy who wanted to buy Jeremy the Magic Snake pushes through the crowd and returns with his weary-looking mother. "He won't stop begging me," she says. "He has been nagging me to buy the snake this entire time. I give up". She lets out an exhausted giggle as she reaches into her purse to purchase the toy snake.

With the toy snake in his hands, the boy walks away with a smile on his face.

Lightning Source UK Ltd.
Milton Keynes UK
06 February 2011

167036UK00002B/3/P